Ageing, Lifestyles and Economic Crises

T0361986

No society can escape population ageing. This demographic phenomenon has profound social consequences on the lifestyles of individuals and societies. In the light of the accelerated ageing of the Mediterranean area, the analyses which inform this work aim to understand how the age-related policies of Nation-States are partly responsible for the behaviours of the generations. They also highlight how the lifestyle changes are the result of trends which are common to these societies. The Mediterranean area constructed here by the researchers offers an in-depth reflection on the national cases presented, in terms of their specificities or societal singularities, as well as of their dynamics of convergence.

Drawing on empirical research in sociology, demography, geography and economics; exploiting the most recent data available; and setting the present in historical perspective, *Ageing, Lifestyles and Economic Crises* studies Mediterranean societies in relation to three major challenges which they now confront. These are population ageing and its implications in terms of intergenerational family support relationships, increasingly insecure adult professional trajectories and their consequences for the evolution of social gender roles in an economic context commonly referred to as a 'crisis' and lastly the role of Nation-States' public policies in the social reproduction of these gender inequalities.

These three issues are the keystone to understanding the ongoing transformations in the lifestyles and life cycles of Mediterranean societies. This volume marshals a wealth of recent data that will be useful not only to many academics and scientists but also to local and national policymakers.

Thierry Blöss is a Full Professor at Aix-Marseille University, France, and researcher at the Institute of Labour Economics and Industrial Sociology (CNRS). He is also the academic leader of the international programme ANR SODEMO-MED, from which this book stems.

Routledge Studies in the European Economy

For a full list of titles in this series, please visit www.routledge.com/series/SE0431

Ageing, Lifestyles and Economic Crises

The New People of the Mediterranean

Edited by Thierry Blöss

**In collaboration with
Isabelle Blöss-Widmer, Elena Ambrosetti,
Michèle Pagès and Sébastien Oliveau**

Routledge
Taylor & Francis Group

LONDON AND NEW YORK

First published 2018 by Routledge
2 Park Square, Milton Park, Abingdon, Oxon OX14 4RN

52 Vanderbilt Avenue, New York, NY 10017

First issued in paperback 2020

Routledge is an imprint of the Taylor & Francis Group, an informa business

British Library Cataloguing-in-Publication Data
A catalogue record for this book is available from the British Library

Library of Congress Cataloging-in-Publication Data
Names: Blèoss, Thierry, editor.
Title: Ageing, lifestyles and economic crises : the new people of the
    Mediterranean / edited by Thierry Blèoss ; in Collaboration with
    Isabelle Blèoss-Widmer, Elena Ambrosetti, Micháele Pagáes and
    Sâebastien Oliveau.
Description: New York : Routledge, 2018. | Includes bibliographical
    references and index.
Identifiers: LCCN 2017023465 | ISBN 9781138040267 (hardback) |
    ISBN 9781315175218 (ebook)
Subjects: LCSH: Older people—Mediterranean Region—Social conditions. |
    Mediterranean Region—Social policy. | Sex role—Government policy—
    Mediterranean Region. | Women's rights—Mediterranean Region.
Classification: LCC HQ1064.M386 A54 2017 | DDC 305.2609182/2—dc23
LC record available at https://lccn.loc.gov/2017023465

ISBN 13: 978-0-367-66756-6 (pbk)
ISBN 13: 978-1-138-04026-7 (hbk)

Typeset in Times New Roman
by Apex CoVantage, LLC

Contents

Illustrations

Figures

Tables

Boxes

Appendices

Contributors

Mohammed Amar is professor at the National School of Agriculture of Meknès (Morocco). He holds a PhD in socio-economics (2002) from the University of Ghent (Belgium). He is a member of an international research group (France, Morocco, Senegal) funded by the National Center for Scientific Research (CNRS, France). His research deals with the analysis of public policies, the role of institutions in development and changes in familial solidarities, in particular towards the aged.

Elena Ambrosetti is assistant professor in demography at the Faculty of Economics and affiliated with the Department of Methods and Models for Economics, Territory and Finance – Sapienza University of Rome (Italy). She holds a PhD in demography and economics (2006) from the Paris Institute of Political Studies in Paris. Her main fields of interest are demography of the Mediterranean countries, population ageing, fertility transition, gender issues and migration in the Mediterranean area.

Serena Arima is assistant professor of statistics at the Department of Methods and Models for Economics, Territory and Finance, Sapienza University of Rome (Italy). Her research activity is focused on developing statistical methodologies in various fields such as economics, demography and biology, with particular attention to the issue of model choice issues in a Bayesian context.

Laura Barrios is a mathematician and head of the IT service of the Information Technology General Corps at the Spanish National Research Council (CSIC). She runs the Statistics Department of the Scientific IT Service, providing support for research and researcher training in applied statistics and IT. She is a member of the CSIC bioethics committee.

Thierry Blöss is full professor of sociology at Aix-Marseille University and researcher at the Institute of Labour Economics and Industrial Sociology (LEST-CNRS, Umr 7317). He is the scientific director of the ANR international project 'SODEMOMED', from which this book stems. He is the author of many books, chapters and peer-reviewed journal articles on changes in the ages of life and intergenerational relations, family relations and policies and social gender relations.

Isabelle Blöss-Widmer is senior lecturer at Aix-Marseille University (France) and researcher at the Mediterranean Laboratory of Sociology (LAMES-CNRS, Umr 7305). She holds a PhD in demography from University Paris I-Sorbonne. She is head of the Mediterranean demographic observatory (DemoMed, www. demomed.org). Her current research is mainly on the demography of the Mediterranean countries, in particular the causes and consequences of demographic ageing studied on the different administrative scales of the territories.

Giorgia Capacci is a graduate of economics at Sapienza University of Rome, with a PhD in Demography. Since 2002, she has worked for the Italian National Institute of Statistics, Department of Demographic Statistics. Her main fields of interest, regarding European countries, are ageing and counterageing, and the relationship between health status and ageing, social exclusion and living conditions.

Margarita Delgado holds a PhD in sociology from Complutense University of Madrid and has been a researcher at the Spanish National Research Council (CSIC) since 1990. Her main research areas are fertility, the family and reproductive health in the developed countries. She is the author of numerous publications on adolescent fertility, contraceptive behaviours and the incidence of abortion in Spanish society.

Pietro Demurtas is a sociologist and currently researcher at the Italian Institute for Research on Population and Social Policies (IRPPS), Italian National Research Council (CNR). He holds a PhD in methodology of social sciences. His main research fields are time-use studies, labour-market analysis in a gender perspective and international migration trends.

Alessandra De Rose is full professor of demography at Sapienza University of Rome and director of the Department of Methods and Models for Economics, Territory and Finance. She is a former president of the Italian Association for Population Studies and is dean of the European Doctoral School in Demography for the years 2015–17. Her main research areas are family demography, marriage and union dissolution, gender studies, and analysis of the relationship between population dynamics and environment.

Ilham Dkhissi is an assistant professor at the International University of Rabat. She holds a PhD in economics from the University of Caen Basse-Normandie (France) and University Mohammed V, Rabat Agdal (Morocco). She is a member of the international research group ESIRAMed, 'Social economy, responsible investment, insurance' (France, Tunisia, Algeria, Morocco). His specific research interests are social protection, living standards and poverty among old people in the countries of the Maghreb.

Yoann Doignon is researcher at the ESPACE research centre (CNRS, Umr 7300) and the Mediterranean Laboratory of Sociology (LAMES-CNRS, Umr 7305). He holds a PhD in geography at Aix-Marseille University. His research focuses on the convergences spatial of demographic ageing in the Mediterranean. He is currently working in the Mediterranean demographic observatory (DemoMed).

Marta Domínguez Folgueras is an associate professor at SciencesPo Paris (Paris Institute of Political Studies) and a doctoral member of the Juan March Institute in Madrid. She holds a PhD in sociology from Complutense University of Madrid and the Juan March Institute (Spain). Her research focuses on the sociology of the family and gender relations.

María José González is an associate professor in the Department of Political and Social Sciences at Pompeu Fabra University (UPF) in Barcelona (Spain). She holds a PhD in social and political sciences from the European University Institute in Florence (Italy). Her research focuses on the family sociology, gender inequality, child welfare, family policy, social inequality and comparative sociology.

Valeria Insarauto is a researcher at the School of Advanced Hispanic and Iberian Studies (EHEHI, Casa de Velázquez, Madrid). She holds a PhD in sociology from the School of Advanced Studies in the Social Sciences (EHESS, Paris, 2013). Her research interests lie at the crossroads of the sociology of work, social policies and gender studies, and, in particular, questions of atypical work, reduction and organization of working time and the articulation of social times, with a particular focus on the countries of southern Europe.

Noelia Cámara Izquierdo is an associate professor at the Public University of Navarre (Spain) She has a BA in sociology from the Public University of Navarre, a PhD in methods and techniques for the study of population (Centre for Demographic Studies, Autonomous University of Barcelona) and a postgraduate diploma in population and territory (Department of Sociology II, Complutense University of Madrid). Her current research is on ageing, longevity, dependence and quality of life in old age.

Irene Lapuerta is lecturer in the Department of Social Work at the Public University of Navarre in Pamplona (Spain). She holds a PhD in political and social sciences from UPF. Her research focuses on the study of family policies, the labour market and gender inequalities.

Maria Herica La Valle is a graduate research student in social statistics and demography at the University of Southampton (United Kingdom). In 2014, she was awarded a research grant for a project on 'caregivers and patients with disabilities and/or sensory deprivation' in the scientific area of geriatrics and gerontology, Department of Cardiovascular, Respiratory, Nephrologic and Geriatric Sciences, Sapienza University of Rome (Italy). Her research interests are demographic ageing, gender disparities and health.

Irene Lebrusan has a master's in sociology and is a pre-doctoral researcher of the Ministry of Economic Affairs at Complutense University of Madrid. Her doctoral thesis is on old people and housing. She is currently taking part in the national research project 'PROVISO: Transforming to Protect: Sustainable Restoration of Twentieth-Century Social Housing in the European Context'. Her main research themes are housing and old age, elderly households and residential inequalities.

Francisco Zamora López is full professor of sociology and political science and director of the Department of Human Ecology and Population at the Complutense University of Madrid. He has degrees in demography from the Universities of Bordeaux I (1982) and Paris V Sorbonne (1985), and a PhD in sociology and political science from Complutense University of Madrid (1993). His current research is focussed on demographic ageing, fertility and demographic perspectives in Spain.

Adele Menniti is senior researcher at IRPPS-Institute for Research on Population and Social Policies, CNR-Italian National Research Council and currently head of the Department 'Analysis of Social and Demographic Behaviour'. She is a demographer, and her main research fields relate to societal change and population behaviour, gender roles and use of time and gender equal opportunities in science.

Sébastien Oliveau is senior lecturer in geography at Aix-Marseille University and researcher at the ESPACE research centre (CNRS, Umr 7300). He holds a PhD in geography from University Paris I and a Habilitation from Aix-Marseille University (2011). His research focuses on the spatial analysis of populations. He is currently working in the Mediterranean demographic observatory (DemoMed).

Michèle Pagès is senior lecturer in sociology at Aix-Marseille University. She holds a PhD in sociology from the University of Toulouse Le Mirail (France). She is a researcher at the Mediterranean Laboratory of Sociology (LAMES-CNRS, Umr 7305). Her research is centred on social gender relations in the areas of marriage and the family and the social construction of relations to the body.

Alain Parant is a demographer and a researcher at the French Institute for Demographic Studies (INED, Paris). He is also a scientific advisor to the Futuribles International group (Paris). More specifically his research interest focuses on demographic ageing in European and Mediterranean basin countries with particular emphasis on the future.

Francesca Rinesi holds a PhD in Demography (Sapienza University of Rome) and works for the Italian National Institute for Statistics (ISTAT) in the Socio-demographic and Environmental Statistics Department. Her main research interests are family demography, fertility, fertility intentions, gender issues and population ageing.

Muriel Sajoux is senior lecturer in economics at François-Rabelais University, Tours (France). She holds a PhD in economics from the University of Pau (2001). She is a member of the CITERES research centre (CNRS, Umr 7324). Her research is on the ageing of the population in the countries of the South, especially in Africa, and the links between the transition in fertility and development in the Maghreb. In particular, she is a founder member of the International Research Network 'Ageing in Africa' set up in January 2015.

Maria Rita Sebastiani is senior lecturer in statistics in the Department of Methods and Models for Economics, Territory and Finance, Sapienza University of Rome (Italy), since 2000. She was previously a researcher at the ISTAT. She has researched a wide range of topics from applied statistics to the social sciences. She is currently working on statistical methods for measuring well-being and gender inequalities in the labour market.

Donatella Strangio is full professor of economic history at the Faculty of Economics and affiliated with the Department of Methods and Models for Economics, Territory and Finance, Sapienza University of Rome (Italy). She is the author of numerous books and articles on national and international journals. Her most cited works are on famine in the pre-industrial age, international migration, public finance, long-run economic growth and the history of tourism. She holds a PhD in economic history and has been a research fellow at the London School of Economics and the House of Human Sciences in Paris.

Acknowledgements

This work is the result of an international research programme and a collective reflection which has involved almost 30 researchers from several countries. I would like to thank them all for their contributions and in particular those who have always been on hand to ensure the readability and coherence of the analyses offered: Isabelle Blöss-Widmer, Elena Ambrosetti, Michèle Pagès and Sébastien Oliveau. This work has benefited from the support of Yoann Doignon, who devoted valuable time to putting the manuscript together. At his side, Marie-Laure Trémélo, an engineer at the National Centre for Scientific Research (France), has worked equally hard on the cartography and harmonization of the figures. I would like to thank Hélène Widmer for taking on the task of translating the original book proposal submitted to Routledge, and for doing so with great professionalism. I also wish to thank Jean-Claude Azoulay who, scrupulously and patiently, revised in English all the chapters of this book, so as to ensure a better understanding for the reader. Finally, I would like to thank our correspondents at Routledge, in particular Emily Kindleysides, senior editor, economics, for the confidence she showed to us and for her encouragements, but also Elanor Best, editorial assistant, economics, who was always available to assist us in the production of this work.

Thierry Blöss

Introduction: The Mediterranean area

A total social context

Thierry Blöss

Based on multidisciplinary empirical research (economics, sociology, demography, geography), using the most recent data available and placed in its historical perspective, this work[1] is distinctive in that it studies Mediterranean societies by the yardstick of three major cross-cutting issues whose challenges intermingle: the ageing of populations and its consequences in terms of mutual support relationships between generations in families, the increasing lack of security in adult career trajectories and its consequences as regards gender social roles in the context of a long-term economic crisis and, finally, the role of Nation-States' public policies in the social reproduction of these gender inequalities. These three issues under study are the keystone of this work for understanding the ongoing transformations in lifestyles and life cycles in Mediterranean societies.

The Mediterranean area: 'societal approach' and international comparison

What exactly is the Mediterranean? Until now, human sciences have answered this deliberately open question asked by Fernand Braudel (1977) in a sectoral manner in terms of their own discipline. However, anthropologists, geographers, historians, etc., have all led us to understand that 'if the Mediterranean exists, it is only a particular and fragile conjunction, a cultural invention or an exceptional social configuration' (Chastagnaret and Ilbert, 1991). The perimeter of the Mediterranean area fluctuates considerably depending on the analysis proposed, sometimes restricted to countries of the sea's southern shore (eastern side), sometimes to those of Southern Europe (western side), when it does not correspond to the comprehensive sum of all its geographical features – i.e., of all the countries which line its perimeter. As for its supposed unity, many analyses 'castigate the simplistic nature of stereotypes erecting the Mediterranean world as a concept' and argue that 'the Mediterranean world is a highly artificial category, especially since the populations of both shores do not recognise it' (Bromberger and Durand, 2001). Not to mention that this Mediterranean world, to call it so, is nowadays fundamentally defined by linguistic, religious, political, economic differences, etc.

In the face of so many arguments, the relevance of the Mediterranean setting as a field of study and comparison appears at first sight to present more theoretical and epistemological difficulties than research interest, unless one considers, as we will in this work, that 'what gives coherence to the project of a Mediterranean comparatism, is not so much the recognizable identities and similarities but the differences which create a system' (Bromberger and Durand, 2001).

Forty years ago, Braudel (1977) was the first to define as typically 'Mediterranean' a lifestyle which prominently featured outdoor living in a favourable sunny climate. In 2017, the social issues discussed in this work refer to quite different patterns of behaviour. They go far beyond this quaint, unambiguous definition of a 'Mediterranean lifestyle' (in the singular) and reflect the profound changes noted in recent decades. These changes are demographic, economic, sociological, but also political, if by this term we mean changes initiated by the development of Nation-States, whose impact on lifestyles probably contributed considerably to modifying the image of a common Mediterranean culture moulded for centuries by the intermingling of populations.

Consequently, if the Mediterranean area is neither a 'cultural area' (Pitt-Rivers, 1986) nor an all-inclusive entity, and is certainly not homogeneous, can it be considered a sociologically relevant space? This is definitely true if, as the certainly contrasted anthropological heritage indicates, it is part of a reflection advocating the 'relevance of the Mediterranean setting as a field of comparative studies' (Bromberger and Durand, 2001). From this perspective, scientific analysis in social sciences often seems to have a limited ability to objectify both the likeness or even the 'family resemblance' (Albera and Blok, 2001)[2] which may characterize the social behaviour of the various countries studied and their sometimes divergent public policy guidelines.

In this work, the sociological analysis of lifestyles is the main approach to both the differences and contradictions and to the convergences and similarities inherent in Mediterranean societies. A well-reasoned sample of key Mediterranean countries, consisting of Spain, France, Italy (Southern Europe) and Morocco (southern shore of the Mediterranean), will be examined to study the relevance of the Mediterranean social area. The international comparison approach followed will allow a deeper reflection on the national cases presented through their societal specificities or singularities and also their convergent dynamics. Thus the comparative research approach proposed in this work clearly differs from the often-extensive comparative norms[3] which systematically 'decontextualise their objects of analysis to make them comparable' (Guillemard, 2010). The comparative perspective used in this work is meant to be doubly cautious: cautiousness linked to the limited number of national settings studied. Cautiousness also in the implementation of this rational perspective, the foremost characteristic of which is not to supplant local and national regionalized analyses but rather to demonstrate their resilience. The selection of these key countries will allow an understanding not only of the great asymmetry between the Mediterranean area's northern and southern shores but also of how, against a background of economic globalization, neighbouring countries on the northern shore produce differentiated behaviours, time frames and institutions to adjust to this globalization process (Laïdi, 2008).

The ageing of the population: a 'dynamic' process

Resulting principally from increasing life expectancy, the ageing of societies has consequences on the age structure and more fundamentally on the balance and dynamics of exchanges between the generations involved. In return, ageing is informed by the dynamics of social relations, in particular between men and women, both in the public sphere – especially professional – and the private sphere, mainly in the form of the family. In other words, the significant changes to professional and family status and trajectories observed in recent years as consequences of job insecurity and increasingly unstable family relationships constitute a new socio-economic and socio-demographic order for the ageing process. What living conditions can be hoped for when upheavals in the life cycle (of entry into adult life as well as more widely throughout adulthood) make the transition into retirement and the beginning of old age even more vulnerable? What is generally referred to as a 'crisis' in reference to macroeconomic imbalances and to the globalization of trade and of competitions between workforce systems results in deregulation of life courses whose consequences for ageing are still widely unrecognized. It is indeed extremely difficult to understand the evolutions over the course of human life and to unravel the direct and indirect effects of economic contexts on ageing of the sociocultural tendencies and characteristics inherent to a society. In the context of a long-term macroeconomic slowdown, the main problems ageing presents for most societies are those concerning the increased financial pressure on pensions and at the same time on health and broader social welfare. However, these issues manifest differently depending on the national political systems in place (as regards pensions, health care and, more broadly, social assistance for the elderly) and depending on traditional family responsibilities which vary in accordance with culture and history (Bloom et al., 2015). Each country has thus to find the most appropriate response to the major challenges posed by the phenomenon of ageing, taking into account the specificities of its social and political organization.

Socio-demographic disparities and convergences in the Mediterranean

This work is divided into three parts. The first is dedicated to studying transformations in the life cycle in the light of the ageing of Mediterranean populations. It underlines the importance of taking demographic factors into account in the study of social issues affecting Mediterranean populations through the comparative study of ageing in these key countries. By studying ageing as a differentiated social process, this line of research aims to understand how life stages are defined differently according to social group membership, in particular according to gender categories. The increasing number of elderly in the population, resulting from factors due to human progress (lower mortality rates, trend improvement in living conditions and lifestyles, etc.) has over the years become a key issue in the organization of contemporary societies, in matters of retirement as much as in those of health, for instance. All societies are affected to different degrees and according to different historical timetables. However, this same demographic reality varies in significance according to the society and the manner in which its institutions, especially social welfare, 'construct the social definition of age and set, for example, working and retirement ages' (Guillemard, 2010).

Whether it is approached in terms of public policy or experiences, an important aspect of ageing is undoubtedly its territorial dimension. Whilst mentioned in a number of works, it often remains in the background. The aim of the first part is precisely that of exploring the socially differentiated 'territories' of ageing in the Mediterranean. As it manifests itself in different ways in the area, this process, as a result, modifies the demographic balance between ages and generations, as well as between genders.

Multigenerational societies and the evolution of family solidarities

The second part deals in-depth with the evolution of intergenerational dynamics within kinships in ageing societies, the lifestyles of which are largely shaped by the public policies of the Nation-States. In the Mediterranean, as elsewhere, many countries are becoming 'multi-generational societies'[4] as a consequence of the increasing life expectancy. This raises the issue of the role or usefulness of each person (especially the pivot generations) on the board, particularly during crises (of employment, of housing, etc.). In individual and collective representations, especially in Mediterranean societies, the family is usually associated with positive values, and the coexistence of generations is interpreted as a guarantee of mutual support, particularly 'in times of crisis'. Most recent surveys have assessed the extent of these family ties between generations. Their strength, previously underestimated or even unrecognized, allows us at the same time to understand their specificities and limitations compared to the panoply of social policy interventions (or institutional support systems) when these exist and to considerably modify the prevailing ideology of individualized family ties. In the societies of Southern Europe and the Mediterranean region, which are geographically close and culturally blended but possess historically distinct political systems, one of the fundamental issues of ageing is the relationship between the macroeconomic social welfare policies established by Nation-States in recent years and the capacities of the mutual support established by the kinship systems.

The presence 'on paper' of several generations, all the more so ageing ones, is not necessarily an indication of support if each person's daily reality is focusing on his or her own problems. The acuteness of these difficulties prevails more often than is realized on a daily basis over the capacity for mutual support, suggesting that these practices are not applied, automatically or unconditionally, in all circumstances, contrary to the widespread representation of them as being natural and universal acts. Families mainly feel solidarity with their descendants. Family mutual support is directed most clearly towards younger generations. Aid towards the ascending line does exist but often comes from 'mature subjects'. The reality of this intermediary generation has been described extensively in recent years.

It consists of adults who must face a double dependency of both their parents' and their children's generation. This intermediary generation is called upon most frequently in family exchanges as a result of the seniors' longer life expectancy and the younger generations' difficulties in entering the labour market. It reflects the gender division of domestic roles, which ultimately manifests itself throughout the family life cycle. In the practice of material solidarities between generations, women are indeed more involved than men. For example, assistance for the elderly is 'women's business' every day: the special mother/daughter as well as stepmother/stepdaughter or even grandmother/granddaughter bonds are the most visible examples of the asymmetries in the flow of assistance within the kinship network. They reflect the highly gendered nature of relationships between generations in the south and in the north of the Mediterranean. Indeed, an examination of mutual support relationships within kinships demonstrates that women are overwhelmingly assigned these responsibilities. The persistence of a social model which makes men the principal breadwinners and women the referents for domestic help is embodied in the gender division of intergenerational assistance in which men are largely characterized by the financial support they provide, whilst women are primarily defined by the domestic assistance they can offer.

Kinship is a biographical institution characterized by the relative permanence of unequal domestic relationships between men and women regardless of their marital status as well as by exchanges which are, to say the least, asymmetrical between generations. These exchanges effectively create different obligations and duties of mutual support based on the individual's gender and stage of life. They benefit those concerned unequally according to their age, and their effectiveness varies according to the family's socio-economic background. In other words, 'supposed family solidarities are unequal' (Déchaux, 1994). This is the concept which must be borne in mind, as a scientific approach, in order to go beyond the usual view: the misleading evidence of a multigenerational, supportive society. We should also remember that family, like any institution, has its limits.

Gender relationships in the Mediterranean: socio-demographic behaviours and methods of political regulation

The third part of the work is devoted to the evolution of women's roles in Mediterranean societies in the light of new forms of male domination, in an attempt to answer the questions raised over the course of life by interactions between transformations in employment and the family. The significance of these transformations undoubtedly lies in the daily dialectic between gender relationships in the labour market and in domestic life as well as in the methods used by public policies to reconcile professional and private life. Although the behaviours and trajectories of men and women have become relatively similar in recent years, they have not fundamentally challenged the social division of gender roles.

Indeed, at the beginning of the third millennium, the road to gender equality still remains uncertain. The evolution in behaviours in the private and public domains suggests the persistence of a structural principle of male domination. Studying this involves focusing on the content and the real effects of the changes which have taken place and examining their impact. The reproduction of social relationships between genders is indeed contrasted and contradictory. It requires sorting out the relevant elements for installing fairer relationships between men and women from those which are likely to reproduce the current gender inequalities. In reality, by way of a hypothesis, one could refer to a double uncertainty in the evolution of relationships between men and women: on the one hand, democratic progress (at school, in the job market, etc.) exists alongside conservative institutions and mentalities. On the other hand, the changes taking place, which cannot be reduced to a simple democratization of social relationships between genders, can themselves generate contradictory effects. One example is the public policies (notably family-related) of Nation-States torn between an official egalitarian logic of reducing gender inequality and a subtler differentialist (or positive discrimination) logic which aims to more or less preserve the social identities of gender.

An analysis of socio-demographic behaviours (birth rate, fertility rate, marriage rate, divorce, etc.) is enlightening as it is a way of questioning the uncertain process of democratising gender relations. Indeed, the social differences observed even within the female population demonstrate that a link exists between women's level of emancipation and their behaviours in these domains. In other words, it is as if the increasing education of women and their access to the labour market correlated with the evolution of the demographic timetables of human reproduction. Unlike men, women's socio-professional trajectories thus seem more dependent on their demographic timetables. This link is a priori two-directional. On the one hand, women's place in the family acts as a brake on their social and professional emancipation, this brake being embodied by the notion of reconciling family and professional life. On the other hand, the construction of women's careers seems to require them to move away from their traditional assignments: the rise of female celibacy and the rising age of motherhood are, from this perspective, manifestations of 'female choices' made in pursuit of their professional integration. This marked contradiction or competition between private/public lives seems a particularly feminine manner of articulating the various components of their individual trajectories.

In the light of the accelerated ageing experienced by the Mediterranean area, the analyses informing this work seek to understand both how the behaviours of generations vary according to the age-related policies established by the Nation-States and how these behaviours and lifestyles are influenced by common trends in these societies. The Mediterranean area constructed here by the researchers will serve as a *total social context*. By this expression we mean the collective wish of the researchers involved in this perspective to give the Mediterranean setting a reasoned and dynamic comparative dimension which allows us to consider the actions of institutions in this area's social reproduction.

Notes

1 This work is the result of an interdisciplinary research programme which has received funding from the Anr Transmed (The French National Research Agency), entitled SoDeMoMed (acronym). Transformations in lifestyles in the Mediterranean – a sociological and demographic study: www.agence-nationale-recherche.fr/en/anr-funded-project/?tx_lwmsuivibilan_pi2%5BCODE%5D=ANR-12-TMED-0005.

2 In the words which these two authors borrow from Ludwig Wittgenstein, in *Philosophical Investigations*, Oxford: Blackwell, 1958.

3 Within this comparative approach, the comprehensive study of the Mediterranean area, for example, corresponds to the sum of these geographical elements or countries.

4 The number of the elderly is increasing sharply in Southern and Eastern Mediterranean countries; the proportion of those 65 and over in Southern Mediterranean countries will increase by around 80% by 2025, from about 6% today to 11%. During the same period, the proportion of those 65 and over in Northern Mediterranean countries will also increase at a certainly high but rather slower pace (37% in 25 years).

References

Albera, D. and Blok, A. (2001). The Mediterranean as a field of ethnological study: a retrospective, in: Blok, A., Albera, D. and Bromberger, C. (Eds.), *L'anthropologie de la Méditerranée* (pp. 15–37). L'atelier méditerranéen. Paris: Maisonneuve et Larose: Maison Méditerranéenne des Sciences de l'Homme.

Bloom, D. E., Chatterji, S., Kowal, P., Lloyd-Sherlock, P., McKee, M., Rechel, B., et al. (2015). Macroeconomic implications of population ageing and selected policy responses. *The Lancet*, 385(9968), 649–657.

Braudel, F. (1977). *La Méditerranée, Tome 1: l'espace et l'histoire*. Paris: Arts et métiers graphiques.

Bromberger, C. and Durand, J.-Y. (2001). Faut-il jeter la Méditerranée avec l'eau du bain ? in: Blok, A., Albera, D. and Bromberger, C. (Eds.), *L'anthropologie de la Méditerranée* (pp. 733–756). L'atelier méditerranéen. Paris: Maisonneuve et Larose: Maison Méditerranéenne des Sciences de l'Homme.

Chastagnaret, G. and Ilbert, R. (1991). Quelle Méditerranée ? *Vingtième Siècle, revue d'histoire*, 32(1), 3–6.

Déchaux, J.-H. (1994). Les échanges dans la parenté accentuent-ils les inégalités ? *Sociétés contemporaines*, 17(1), 75–90.

Guillemard, A.-M. (2010). Les défis du vieillissement: âge, emploi, retraite, perspectives internationales. Paris: Armand Colin.

Laïdi, Z. (2008). Un temps universel, des vies différentes, in: Fabre, T. (Ed.), *La Méditerranée au temps du monde* (pp. 57–76). Rencontres d'Averroès. Marseille: Parenthèses.

Part I

Mediterranean disparities and convergences

The demographic order in question

Introduction

Population ageing: convergences and uncertainties in the Mediterranean

Isabelle Blöss-Widmer, Elena Ambrosetti and Sébastien Oliveau

In the last 20 years, increasing numbers of analyses have emphasized the soaring number of centenarians and the appearance of supercentenarians (110 years of age or more). Records in human longevity are being made increasingly frequently, and a growing number of people are dying at an older age. Debates on whether there is a limit for human life are more relevant than ever. It is this lengthening of the human lifespan which can be considered the principal engine of population ageing in countries at the end of demographic transition. Ageing has become inevitable in the face of rising life expectancy. During the twentieth century, there was a spectacular increase in life expectancy, particularly after age 60, meaning there was a substantial rise in the average number of years remaining after that age.[1] Over the same period, the average number of years remaining above 80 will soon have doubled. These developments, particularly brisk in developed countries, are equally notable in countries whose demographic transitions began later but were nonetheless rapid.[2]

The lengthening of the lifespan largely explains the growing number of the elderly, but it is not the only explanatory factor. Indeed, a population's age structure, studied over generations, indicates varying numbers of individuals of advanced age. Thus ageing is contained when generations with low numbers reach retirement age whilst it is accentuated by the arrival of abundant age groups. In the latter case, the phenomenon relates to the 'baby boomers'[3] but also to the input of the immigrant populations who, reaching retirement age, grow old in their adopted countries. The fertility rate is a final explanatory factor (ageing from the bottom of the age pyramid). Indeed, a fertility rate below the generation replacement level (two children) causes a progressive reduction in younger age groups, which contributes to the increase in the proportion of the elderly in the overall population.

The ageing of the population has implications on the number of people of working age and on dependency relationships[4] between generations – i.e., the growing burden of nonworking individuals (young and old) on the working population. Thus, in developed countries, the transition to retirement of baby boomer generations, who made generous contributions for their elders, means that the generations which follow are much less numerous, to the extent that labour shortages are henceforth expected. These will not be without a direct effect on 'Pay As You Go' public pension systems. In its report, the European Commission (2012) pointed out that the ageing of the population will make its effect felt on the very composition of the working-age population: the proportion of the oldest workers in the working population – i.e., those aged 55–64 – should increase substantially from 15% in 2010 to 23% by 2060. The working population itself is ageing. Three key factors, of uncertain developments, must be considered in order to understand the alterations in participation rates in the labour market. The first factor is that of the presence of women aged 25–54, whose level has continuously increased over the course of the past 25 years. The second concerns the young (15–24) whose numbers have reduced, mainly because of a lengthening of the time spent in education. The third factor is finally the participation of older workers, in particular men, whose levels have increased since the beginning of the twenty-first century, primarily because of the rise in the legal retirement age initiated by pension system reforms. Although all these developments remain uncertain for developed countries, they are even more so for countries which have experienced a recent and rapid demographic transition.

The scale of the ageing process

These broad trends conceal, indeed, evolutions that are more or less in line with the pattern indicated by the theory of demographic transition – i.e., that of the convergence of all societies towards very low fertility rates, heralding an undifferentiated population ageing and a single trajectory. There are nuances in the 'universal' demographic transition, the pace and extent of which are occasionally unexpected.

> There is no single demographic transition, caused by forces common to all places and all times. Rather, there are many demographic transitions, each driven by a combination of forces that are, to some unknown extent, institutionally, culturally, and temporally specific.
>
> (Greenhalgh, 1990)

Our purpose is not to divert the reader from the incontrovertible fact of an ongoing global ageing process (the global proportion of those aged 65 and over increased from around 5% in the 1950s to over 8% today), but to emphasize 'the common factors which make this ageing difficult to reverse [. . .] and the nevertheless significant differences in the extent of the process' (Blanchet, 2001). The pace and intensity of ageing may therefore vary, since its factors are particularly sensitive to economic conditions and political decisions as well as to societies' ideological aspirations which occasionally contradict the developments expected from the theory of demographic transition. In the Mediterranean, the wide variety of ongoing ageing realities displays an underlying convergence amongst all the area's countries but, simultaneously, it allows the nuances and complexities of the phenomenon to be analysed.

A more specific study of the phenomena of fertility rates and migration, in a time perspective which takes the political and economic context into account, allows for an understanding of the differences observed in the evolutions of ageing.

An analysis of this process, in particular at a fine geographical level, empha-sizes the importance of these factors and reveals local variations in the contexts of ageing. The increasing number of the elderly is in fact experienced and felt differently by the populations. Gerontogrowth is thus not an abstract concept. Subjectively, it translates in concrete terms into the internal perception each individual may have of his or her increased life expectancy and of its conse-quences in terms of his or her own capacity for residential mobility at the time of retirement. Objectively, it also translates into the increasingly large presence of the elderly or even the very elderly within the family circle and in munici-palities. The conditions of ageing change constantly, as do the ways ageing is experienced. This ageing process is also a reality for national and local decision makers who are responsible for its management but may postpone or ignore the situation in favour of more pressing problems (such as unemployment amongst the young) in specific geographical and socio-economic contexts. They may, on the other hand, try to mitigate the consequences by promoting specific facilities or by encouraging immigration or birth rates through proactive policy actions.

In this perspective, this first part of this work aims to study transformations in the life cycle in terms of the ageing of populations in the Mediterranean. It mainly employs demographic analysis tools to measure the development of the ageing of the population together with the lengthening of lifespans and the continuing decline in the fertility rate. The growing increase in the elderly amongst the popu-lation, resulting from factors synonymous with human progress (lower mortality rates, the trend for improvement in living conditions and lifestyles, etc.) has over the years become a major issue in the organization of contemporary societies in areas such as retirement and health, for example. All countries are affected to dif-ferent extents and according to different historical timetables. This part's chapters demonstrate that the ageing of the population, whilst an inevitable process, has not been manifested in the same way in the four key countries (Morocco, Spain, Italy and France) and has specific implications for each society studied. A careful examination of the situation in each country challenges the demographic theo-ries and models usually used. Placing the various situations of ageing and their explanatory factors in perspective allow us to consider demographic evolutions which are unexpected rather than heralded or foreseen.

Demographic theories at issue in the Mediterranean

The points of view developed in this first part of the work have in common an analysis of natural and migration dynamics in order to understand and predict ageing. They all implicitly question the theory of the first – and in particular the second – demographic transitions, emphasizing the paradoxical evolutions in fac-tors which disrupt expected evolutions in fertility rates and ageing. Chapter 3, for example, emphasizes how the Moroccan transition questions the classical first demographic transition model, whilst the developments devoted to Spanish and Italian demographic changes (see Chapters 1 and 2) ponder the consequences of the unexpected and long-term low fertility rates observed, mainly in Europe, over the last 40 years. This phenomenon, known as the 'second demographic transition', characterized by few descendants – i.e., by fertility rates constantly below generation replacement levels of around 2.1 children per woman (Lesthaeghe & Surkyn, 1988; Van de Kaa, 1987) – is not present in all the expected countries (i.e. those with the most significant transformations in family values and what some describe as the rise in individualism). Thus Northern European countries, often considered advanced from the perspective of the 'flourishing of post-materialist values' (Monnier, 2006), are also those where the average number of children is still relatively high (1.8 to 2.1 children per woman on average). As for births outside marriage (the rise of which is regarded as one of the characteristic indicators of this second demographic transition), these are not the prevailing norm in all post-transitional societies: Germany, Italy, Greece and Portugal are still countries in which births to married couples remain the majority. France, on the other hand, notable for its sustained fertility rate, registers a high number of births outside marriage. The direct consequence of this relatively high fertility rate for France is that the phenomenon of ageing has not yet been as great as in Italy or Spain. Hence, whilst theoretical generalizations are useful for an overall analysis, they cannot replace an analysis of the specific context of each country. The four countries analysed in this first part, although geographically close and also possessing a shared history, have not experienced the same demographic transition. Early in France, late and rapid in Morocco and close to theoretical models in Italy, the demographic transition has been slower in Spain. Nevertheless, unexpected convergences are emerging between these countries. France and Morocco now have a similar fertility rate which is close to the generation replacement level, whereas it is far below this figure in Italy and Spain. However, despite these apparent alignments, sharp differences are still emerging. Whilst Spain has undergone a long secularization process, resulting in a significant increase in births outside marriage, this process appears more incomplete in Italy, as most births still take place within the framework of this institution.

In the face of this complexity, certain major surveys provide valuable insight. The results of studies conducted since the early 1980s on European values (European Values Survey) and those of surveys carried out worldwide (World Values Survey) demonstrate a continued commitment to the family and the solidarities theoretically associated with it, including in countries with a very low fertility rate. Notwithstanding considerable nuances depending on the society[5] and the social status of the respondents, over 80% to 90% of respondents declare that the family is very important in their lives. Individuals' attachment to children and family values persists beyond contexts and more or less sustained reports of low fertility levels. The situations in Morocco and France, as well as those observed in Northern Europe (United Kingdom, Norway and Sweden), suggest that the rising number of the elderly could be contained by a long-term, robust recovery in fertility rates, if acceptable living, employment and security conditions are combined against a background in which public policies help to reconcile family and professional life. In addition, in societies such as those of the Southern and Eastern shores of the Mediterranean, where the gender division of roles within couples endures despite the increasing empowerment of women, the model of less than two children per woman is probably not the one that all countries will ultimately adopt at the end of demographic transition, as this model is not always culturally acceptable (Lesthaeghe and Vanderhoeft, 2001). Thus the unexpected upturn in the fertility rate in the Maghreb[6] has slightly modified the idea that it would drop below the threshold of 2.1 children per woman (Ouadah-Bedidi and Vallin, 2000) and helped to further highlight the role of societal transformations and their unexpected consequences on the behaviours of couples as regards fertility (Ouadah-Bedidi et al., 2012). To date, fertility rates in the Maghreb have never fallen below the threshold of two children per woman and are even climbing higher. Moreover, Muriel Sajoux insists that in Morocco, the steadily rising age of entry into first union stalled and even decreased for the first time in 2014 (see Chapter 3): 'The decline in women's average age at first marriage is unprecedented and could indicate that a maximum threshold has been reached, both in terms of postponement of the first marriage and the decrease in fertility'. She goes further by emphasizing that the convergence of Moroccan and French fertility rates can be explained by the 'particularly close ties between France and Morocco, from a migratory and economic perspective. The human exchanges deriving from these links can contribute to an increasingly shared vision and behaviour in matters of reproduction and family size'.

The countries analysed in this first part thus have significant similarities, from the point of view of demographic variables and simultaneously substantial differences which demonstrate that an uneven demographic transition process is taking place. This process has significant consequences on fertility rates and on the levels of ageing reached by these countries. The past demographic evolution is thus fundamental in order to understand the current situation, as well as future trends. Obviously, this demographic evolution has been influenced by many other factors, such as the specific economic, social, cultural and political context of each country or region. The socio-historical context of the country in question is therefore crucial for the analysis. On this point, the chapters on the situations in Italy and Spain (see Chapters 1 and 2) concentrate, each in its own way, on both the not insignificant role played by immigration in slowing ageing and also on its transient, sometimes very short-term, beneficial effect. In Spain, for instance, population ageing has been temporarily stabilized as a result of the high immigration observed since the 1990s. This mainly involved young adults with a higher-than-average fertility rate. However, the 2008 economic crisis, characterized by both a mass return of foreigners to their native countries and a departure of working Spanish people, led to a consequent upturn in indicators of ageing. Just like Spain, Italy experienced a rise in fertility rates in the 1990s, coming from both older women and from more fertile immigrant women (see Capacci and Rinesi, Chapter 1). However, since 2010, the fertility rate resumed its downward trend due to the combined effects of the economic crisis, the ageing of foreign resident populations, the decline in marriage and the postponement of having children. From a historical perspective, the periods of attracting migrants and a jump in fertility rates appear to be exceptions to long-term trends.

The territorial conditions of ageing

Whether it is approached in terms of public policy or lifestyle, another important factor of ageing is undoubtedly its territorial dimension. One of the objectives of this first part is therefore to explore the socially differentiated territories of age-ing in the Mediterranean, emphasizing how the conditions of ageing are marked by urban/rural divisions. Indeed, by spreading unevenly in the Mediterranean, ageing, as a consequence, has disrupted the demographic balance between ages and generations, but also between genders (inequality in life expectancy, access to care, risk of poverty or social exclusion, etc.). Within each country, regional differences are expressed by the degree of ageing reached: in Morocco, they are partly attributable to lower fertility rates in some areas but also to the emigration of those of working age (see Chapter 3). In France, they reveal the specificities of the Mediterranean coastline (see Chapter 4). Once again, internal migrations appear to play a fundamental role: since the urban environment is much more attractive than the rural environment to young adults who move within French territory for professional purposes, the pace of ageing is faster in the country-side than in the towns. In Italy, the authors also emphasize a north/south regional division in the process of ageing: the north, with its traditionally lower fertility rate, is now registering a swifter increase in the proportion of the elderly in the total population than is the south (see Chapter 1). The influx of foreign migrants, particularly high from the 1990s in Italy's northern regions, has somewhat dimin-ished or contained this process, without managing to reverse it. In Italy, the prov-inces with the most foreign nationals are actually those which are ageing the least, thanks to their favourable age structure and higher-than-average fertility rates. In Morocco, the emigration of young Moroccans abroad and their redeployment within the country have had a significant impact on ageing and are, with other factors, contributing to transformations in household lifestyles, particularly in the case of intergenerational cohabitation (see Chapter 3). In Spain, it is the double negative effect of the 2008 economic crisis on fertility rates and on the emigration of the young and working people which deserves emphasis. These two factors have undoubtedly accentuated the society's ongoing ageing (see Chapter 2).

'Reaching an agreement' on ageing: statistical reality and social process

More generally, the different results and questions which inform the first part of this work emphasize the importance attached to the very notion of ageing as a statistical reality but also as a social process which questions each individual's place in society. Population ageing has long had a negative connotation on the basis that the entire economy of the country would be fatally disrupted if there were too many old people burdening the community (Sauvy, 1929). To demon-strate that it is not, in reality, a tragedy (Héran, 2010), new indicators have been invented to take into account the gradual arrival of disability with age (Calot and Sardon, 2000; Bourdelais, 1993). In so doing, a new perception has been intro-duced whereby 'the rising importance of the old is not a mere incident in our evo-lution, or a historical accident, but a true revolution and a change in civilisation' (Loriaux, 2000). To be understood, this transformation requires joint, pertinent reflection from the disciplinary perspectives about issues relating to balancing life stages and the resulting social relationships, going beyond simplistic causal explanations. Thus though the drop in fertility rates is expressed mathematically by a smaller number of offspring on whom older generations can rely when their abilities decline, this in no way prejudices the nature and intensity of the family solidarities which may be expressed. Furthermore, the reduction in the number of descendants does not necessarily signify the abandonment, isolation or greater solitude of the elderly. Work in human sciences has shown that having fewer children allows parents to take better care of them and to care more for them. In return, can one expect these children to be objectively more grateful, available and supportive towards their elders? One of the challenges of the empirical studies included in this part of the work, but also in those which follow, is, therefore, to inform us about the state of current forms of altruism *versus* individualism in social relationships between family generations.

Notes

1 In developed countries, life expectancy at 60 years old has soared since 1950, rising nearly 10 years from 17 to 27 years.
2 In Morocco, for example, life expectancy at 60 has increased by 6 years since 1950.
3 'The list of baby-boom countries consists mainly of the northwest quarter of Europe: Scandinavia, Germany, Austria, Belgium, France, Luxemburg, the United Kingdom and Switzerland as well as, somewhat less clearly, Finland and the Netherlands' (Monnier, 2007). In France, 'the first generations of baby boomers, born just after 1945, are now reaching retirement age. They will enter old age in around 2025, and will pass away in the 2040s. The generations born in the middle of the baby boom, in the mid-1960s, will experience the same progression but according to a timetable displaced by twenty years: ceasing to work around 2025, entering old age in around 2045 and dying in the 2060s' (Monnier, 2007).
4 One of the most relevant indicators of the ageing of the population is the dependency ratio. Since the inactive population is composed of the youngest members (aged 0–14 years) and the oldest (65 years and over), two types of dependency ratios can be identified: green pressure and grey pressure. These estimate, respectively, the burden of the young and the elderly on the working population (Cagiano De Azevedo and Castagnaro, 2010).
5 Seventy-eight percent of respondents in Germany state that family is an important value in life, against 91% of Spanish respondents (WVS 2013 for Germany and WVS 2011 for Spain).
6 Particularly in Algeria.

References

Blanchet, D. (2001). L'impact des changements démographiques sur la croissance et le marché du travail: faits, théories et incertitudes. *Revue d'économie politique*, 111(4), 511–564.

Bourdelais, P. (1993). *Le nouvel âge de la vieillesse: histoire du vieillissement de la population*. Paris: Odile Jacob.

Cagiano De Azevedo, R. and Castagnaro, C. (2010). Il popolo dell'autunno: le sfide del cambiamento demografico. *La Medicina Estetica*, 34(4). Retrieved from www.lamedicinaestetica.it/categorie-articoli-xxxv-congresso-sime/item/788-il-popolo-dell%E2%80%99autunno-le-sfide-del-cambiamento-demografico.html

Calot, G. and Sardon, J.-P. (2000). La mesure du vieillissement démographique. *Espace Populations Sociétés*, 18(3), 475–481.

European Commission. (2012). *The 2012 ageing report: economic and budgetary projections for the 27 EU member states (2010–2060)*. European Union. Retrieved from http://ec.europa.eu/economy_finance/publications/european_economy/2012/pdf/ee-2012-2_en.pdf

Greenhalgh, S. (1990). Toward a political economy of fertility: anthropological contributions. *Population and Development Review*, 16(1), 85–106.

Héran, F. (2010). L'inexorable privilège du vieillissement. *Alternatives Economiques*, (85). Retrieved from www.alternatives-economiques.fr/linexorable-privilege-vieillissement/00059104

Lesthaeghe, R. & Surkyn, J. (1988). Cultural dynamics and economic theories of fertility change. Population and Development Review, 14(1), 1–45.

Lesthaeghe, R. J. and Vanderhoeft, C. (2001). Ready, willing and able: a conceptualization of transitions to new behavioral forms, in: Casterline, J. B. (Ed.), *Diffusion processes and fertility transition: selected perspectives* (pp. 204–264). Washington, DC: National Academy Press.

Loriaux, M. (2000). La 'géritude' est-elle un concept bidon ? *Espace Populations Sociétés*, 18(3), 461–474.

Monnier, A. (2006). *Démographie contemporaine de l'Europe: évolutions, tendances, défis*. Paris: Colin.

Monnier, A. (2007). Le Baby-Boom: suite et fin. *Population et Sociétés*, (431), 4.

Ouadah-Bedidi, Z. and Vallin, J. (2000). Maghreb: la chute irrésistible de la fécondité. *Population et Sociétés*, (359), 4.

Ouadah-Bedidi, Z., Vallin, J. and Bouchoucha, I. (2012). La fécondité au Maghreb: nouvelles surprises. *Population et Sociétés*, (486), 4.

Sauvy, A. (1929). La population française jusqu'en 1956: essai de prévision démographique. *Journal de la société de statistique de Paris*, 70(12), 8–13.

Van de Kaa, D.J. (1987). Europe's second demographic transition. *Population Bulletin*, 42(1), 1–59.

1 An overview of demographic ageing in Italy

Past, present, and expected evolution

Giorgia Capacci and Francesca Rinesi

Europe is not alone in having faced a progressive ageing trend which has had a significant impact on its economic and social organization. This important demographic phenomenon has been caused by the ability of man to control two important features of human life: early death and unintended births (Golini et al., 2003). However, this process has not affected European countries equally; it varies both in speed and in extent. Italy has been at the forefront of this ageing trend, having seen both a dramatic drop in fertility rates and a significant increase in life expectancy over the course of a few decades. In spite of constant migration, especially over the last few decades, the age structure of the Italian population has changed rapidly over time. This has resulted in an increase in both the absolute number of the elderly (i.e. persons over 65 years of age) and their relative proportion in the total population. The working-age population and those aged 14 and under have decreased rapidly, and the latest population forecasts show that the ageing phenomenon will continue in future decades. Italy is characterized by the rate of this population ageing and also for the fact that this phenomenon is not uniformly spread across the country; most of all, it is characterized by how quickly this intensity has been reached. In 1900, life expectancy at birth was approximately 45 years for both sexes: the latest estimates available for 2014 indicated a life expectancy at birth of 80.3 years for men and 85.0 years for women (ISTAT, 2015a).

The aim of this chapter is to present an overview of population ageing in Italy. We will focus our attention on the following themes, which are particularly relevant to Italian ageing: geographical heterogeneity, with the contrast between the North, where the population is older but the speed of ageing is tending to slow down, and the South, where the population remains younger but is ageing at a much faster rate; gender differences and their development; the impact of ageing in terms of health needs, given that there is a direct, proportional relationship between the lengthening of life expectancy and increased levels of non-self-sufficiency; analysis of the social conditions of the elderly, above all in terms of well-being and social exclusion; and, lastly, population forecast data. Will Italy also be one of the most elderly countries in the future? Will Italy also be characterized by the geographical and gender differences in the future? These are just some of the questions for which we will try to provide the answers.

Numerous data sources have been considered in analysing all these aspects of Italian population ageing. Drawing from resident population registers, a set of widely used demographic measures can be calculated (such as the ageing index, the proportion of elderly in the population, the dependency index, the old-age dependency index, mean age, median age). Data for analysing the development of future population structures come from the regional demographic projections for 2065 published by ISTAT in 2011. Data on mortality and life expectancy at varying ages come from life tables, which are the main source for evaluating the state of health of the resident population.

The impact of ageing on health conditions is analysed using data from a specific ISTAT survey about health: 'Health conditions and use of health services'. This allows objective indicators (such as healthy life expectancy or life expectancy without limitations) and subjective indicators (based on the population's own perception of their condition of health) to be studied; a complete picture of the state of health of the Italian population can thus be obtained. Data on well-being and social exclusion come from the EU-SILC survey (European Union Statistics on Income and Living Conditions), which collects timely and comparable cross-sectional and longitudinal data on income, poverty, social exclusion and living conditions at a national and a regional level for a number of European countries.

The dramatic increase in life expectancy during the twentieth century

As shown in Figure 1.1, population ageing in Italy is the consequence of both a rapid decline in the total fertility rate[1] and an increase in longevity. Migration flows – although constant over the last few decades – did not counteract this negative natural dynamic. The increase in life expectancy which occurred over the last century has been extraordinary: a man born in 1900 could be expected to live approximately 42 years (women 43). The corresponding estimated values for those born in 2014 are almost double, reaching 80.3 and 85.0 years, respectively.

The significant increase in longevity may be regarded as a consequence of the health transition (Frenk et al., 1991) within this framework; advances in life expectancy are, on the one hand, the result of better living conditions/lifestyles and, on the other hand, the result of advances in medical care. As effectively summarized by Vallin and Meslé (2004), the health transition encompasses two distinct stages: firstly, the defeat of infectious diseases and secondly, the cardio-vascular revolution. By analysing the most recent trends in life expectancy for industrialized countries, the authors hypothesize that a new stage is beginning: the fight against ageing and degenerative diseases. Although life expectancy at birth has increased significantly for both men and women, the gap between the two sexes has widened over time. At the beginning of the twentieth century, the lifespans of men and women were substantially the same. The gender gap started to grow after World War One and reached its maximum in 1979, when women were expected to live an average of 6.9 years longer than men. The life expectancy gap between men and women started to narrow in subsequent years, and this process is still ongoing: in 2014, women lived an average of 4.7 years longer than men. The excess in female over male life expectancy is the consequence of the

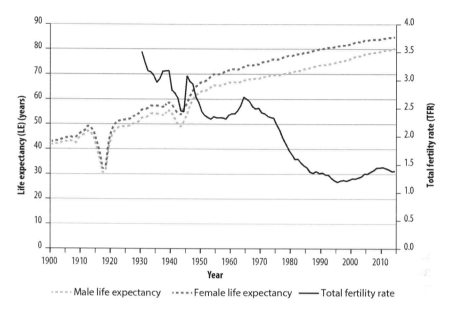

Figure 1.1 Life expectancy (LE) by gender and period and total fertility rate (TFR) in Italy. Years 1900–2014 and 1930–2014

Source: Istat, http://seriestoriche.istat.it

differential change in mortality patterns according to age and sex which occurred over the course of the twentieth century. As well illustrated by Caselli and Egidi (2011), during the first half of the century, Italy saw a constant decline in infectious mortality, which led to a rapid increase in infant and child survival. Over the same period, women's mortality at younger ages declined, greatly benefiting from the drop in maternal deaths, which had been a constant factor at the beginning of 1900. During the second half of the same century, first female and then male life expectancy benefited from the cardiovascular revolution and the consequent decline in mortality in adult life. As a result, the ratio of male-to-female mortality rates by age has changed over time. Male mortality currently exceeds female mortality at all ages with deaths concentrated at older ages (Figure 1.2). The sex differentials reflect a combination of biological, social and economic factors (i.e. participation in the labour market and quality of work, prevention, lifestyles), and they reach their peak in two periods of life. As shown in Figure 1.2, the excess of male over female mortality is higher in young adults and the younger elderly. In Italy, the greatest disparity between male and female mortality occurs at age 23, when the probability of death for men is about 2.7 times that of women.

The decline in the total fertility rate

As already mentioned, the ageing population is the result of both an increase in life expectancy and of a decline in the total fertility rate (TFR). Compared to past

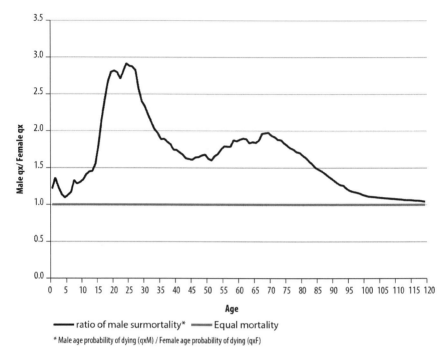

Figure 1.2 Ratio of male-to-female probability of dying (q_x) in Italy. Year 2013

Source: Istat, Life tables, http://demo.istat.it

decades, women in Italy are not only having fewer children but also becoming mothers at a later age than previously. Prolonged postponement of childbearing is a characteristic feature of reproductive behaviour in Italy. Women become mothers at a later age, so the mean age of childbearing has risen sharply, going from 27.5 in 1980 to 31.5 in 2014. Fertility postponement may be attributed to multiple factors including the increase in women's educational attainment, ideational change, a weak welfare state, unequal gender roles and a late transition to adulthood, to mention only a few (for further discussion see Billari et al. (2006) and De Rose et al. (2008)).

From the mid-'60s onwards, the number of children per woman decreased in many European countries, not just in Italy. This phenomenon gave rise to so much concern amongst scholars (given its direct implications for population dynamics) that a few of them (Kohler et al., 2002) introduced the concept of 'lowest-low fertility' for describing countries where the TFR was at or below 1.3. Their study showed that by the end of the 1990s, 14 countries in Southern, Central and Eastern Europe shared that characteristic. In Italy, the TFR reached its minimum in 1995 when there were less than 1.2 children per woman (Figure 1.3). A slight recovery in this conjunctural indicator was observed in subsequent years, and it levelled out during the late 2000s, but in recent years, it has begun to decline again. Note that in 2014, the average number of children per woman was 1.37, compared to 1.46 in 2010.

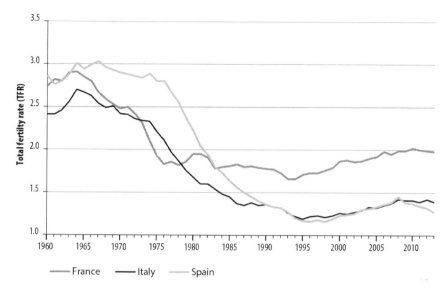

Figure 1.3 TFR by country, 1960–2013

Source: OECD database

The rise in total fertility rates from the late 1990s onward can be mainly attributed to the upturn in fertility in women of higher reproductive age and to the significant rise in births to women of foreign citizenship. In 2014, nearly 8% of all live births were to mothers aged 40 and over (ISTAT, 2014). The same figure for 2001 was 3.2%. During the same period, the number of foreign nationals living in Italy rose consistently, as did their impact on the country's fertility rates. Foreign nationals accounted for only 1.1% of the total resident population in 1994 and for 8.1% 20 years later. Foreign women have a higher fertility rate than that of Italian women (2.10 vs 1.29 in 2014) and a lower mean age at childbirth (28.6 and 32.1, respectively). Births to foreign mothers rose from 3.6 of all births in 1994 to 19.6 in 2014. It is thus clear that the above average fertility rate of female foreign citizens and the increase of foreign nationals living in Italy helped to boost the average number of children per women as well as the number of live births.

The greying of the population in Italy: towards major changes in population structure

The extraordinary improvement in life expectancy and the decline in fertility rates are the main drivers of the rapid population ageing which most developed countries – and Italy in particular – are currently facing. The important changes which have occurred in the structure of the population can easily be appreciated by looking at Figure 1.4, which compares the age and sex distributions of the resident populations in 1951 and in 2014. The population pyramid consists of a back-to-back bar graph: each bar represents the proportion of the population of a certain age and sex in the total population. By convention, males are plotted

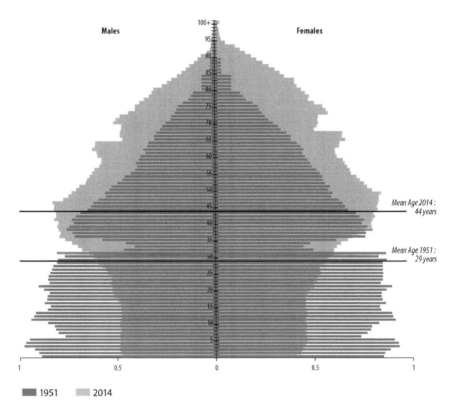

Figure 1.4 Population pyramid: Italy. 1951–2014

Sources: Istat, Census data (1951) and population register (2014) http://demo.istat.it

on the left side of the x-axis and women on the right. The changes in population structure over time are evident. The age pyramid for 2014 has an obviously narrower base (due to low fertility) and wider top (due to growth in the relative proportion of the elderly) than that of 1951. The life expectancy gender gap makes the relative weight of females aged 65 years or more considerably higher than that calculated for males. Moreover, it should be noted that the mean age of the resident population has increased considerably over the past 60 years: it was 29 in 1951 and 44 in 2014.

Numerous measures for population structure by age can be calculated. Here we present the figures for the ageing index, calculated as the number of persons aged 65 or over (conventionally considered to be the elderly population) per hundred persons under the age of 15 (the young population). Figure 1.5 shows the trend in the ageing calculated for the period 1951–2014. In 1951, the young population definitely outnumbered the elderly in Italy: the ageing index in that year was 31, meaning that for every 100 young people there were 31 aged 65 or more. A small gender gap can be seen: the higher female life expectancy resulted in a higher ageing index for resident women (35.1) than for men (27.7). As a result of

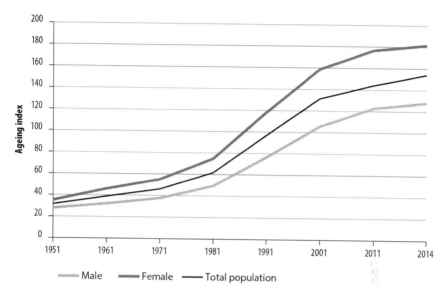

Figure 1.5 Ageing index. Years 1951–2014

Sources: Istat, Census data (from 1951 to 2011) and population register (2014), http://demo.istat.it

the sustained increase in longevity for both genders, and of the dramatic drop in fertility which occurred during the twentieth century, the ageing index has risen significantly over time, particularly since 1981. It should be noted that in 1991, the resident population aged 15 or under approximately equalled the number of people aged 65 or more. From that year onwards, the elderly population outnumbered the young. In 2014, the ageing index reached 154, which is five times higher than the value calculated for the beginning of the period under consideration. Not only has the ageing index increased over time but also the gender gap has widened over the same period, following the same trend observed for longevity. In 2014, the ageing index for women was 181.6 and 128.1 for men.

An important and unpredictable aspect of population ageing is the rapid acceleration in the number of centenarians. The centenarian rate has been increasing steadily since 2002, where there was one person aged 100 or more for every 10,000 of the resident population. In 2014, this rate equalled 2.9. Note that in the last calendar year alone – considering both men and women – the number of centenarians increased by up to 1,494, with an annual increase of 11%. Of particular relevance is the disproportionate male-to-female ratio in the number of people aged 100 or more: in fact, women represent 83.3% of the total number of centenarians. To be specific, on January 1, 2015, there were approximately 900 elderly people aged 105 or over in Italy (traditionally known as semi-supercentenarians). Women account for 85% of all semi-supercentenarians. There are 15 people who are 110 years old or more (called supercentenarians), all female. At the time of writing, the oldest resident in Italy is a woman aged 117 who lives in the North of the country and is the oldest woman in the world!

Population ageing and geographical heterogeneity

Population ageing is a complex process which is not equally distributed, not only amongst European countries but also within Italy itself. In fact, population structure by age differs significantly between the five main geographical areas which make up the country. In 2014, the mean age of the resident population ranged from 42.5 years in the South to 45.1 in the North-West. In the Centre of Italy, the ageing index was 166.9, while in the South, it was 131.1. Data clearly show the existence of a North-South divide in the ageing phenomenon: in fact, the composition of the population in the North is more 'elderly' than that in the South, as is highlighted in Figure 1.6, which shows the compositions of the resident populations in the five main geographical areas of Italy by age and sex. In the age pyramids drawn up for the North-West, North-East and Centre, the base of the pyramid is narrow (due to the low number of children and young people living in those areas), indicating a low birth rate. It should be noted that in the last few decades, the proportion of the young population has risen due to the significant contribution of foreign nationals (the interior, darker part of the pyramid), above all in terms of fertility. In fact, migrants are concentrated in the North of the country, and they have both a younger age composition and a higher fertility rate than Italians. Conversely, the South and the Islands are characterized by a smaller number of foreign nationals, as is shown by the age pyramid (the darker area) and by a higher number of young people (between 15 and 40 years) thanks to the higher total fertility rate which characterized those areas in the past.

As might be expected, women show higher life expectancy than men in all geographical areas of Italy, but there are significant geographical differences. If we consider the male population, in 2014, life expectancy was higher in the North of the country (80.6 years) and lower in the South (79.5). The same figures for women were 85.4 and 84.2, respectively. However, it should be noted that the decreasing life expectancy gender gap observed in Italy over the last few years can also be seen geographically (Figure 1.7). In recent years, men have obtained a greater reduction in mortality than women with geographical differences which have led to a reduction in territorial gender variability. In 1994, differences in life expectancy between males and females showed higher values in Northern areas (+7.1 in the North-East and +7.0 in the North-West between females and males) and lower in the South and the Islands (+5.6 in the South and +5.4 in the Islands). In the last available year (2014), these differences are greatly reduced: the gap is between 4.7 and 4.9 in all geographical areas.

The period TFR has traditionally been higher in the South and the Islands than in the rest of the country. Nationally, after the baby-boom peak, which was particularly notable in the North and Centre of the country during the first half of the '60s, the period fertility declined steadily in all the geographical areas under consideration over the next few decades. It reached its minimum in 1995, when it equalled 1.19 children per woman. An upturn in period fertility rates was observed over the next few years, mainly due to conjunctural aspects and exogenous factors, such as the aforementioned increase in foreign nationals. In 2010, the TFR reached its new maximum of 1.46 children per woman and subsequently started to decrease once more. This decline is due to a range of factors including the ageing

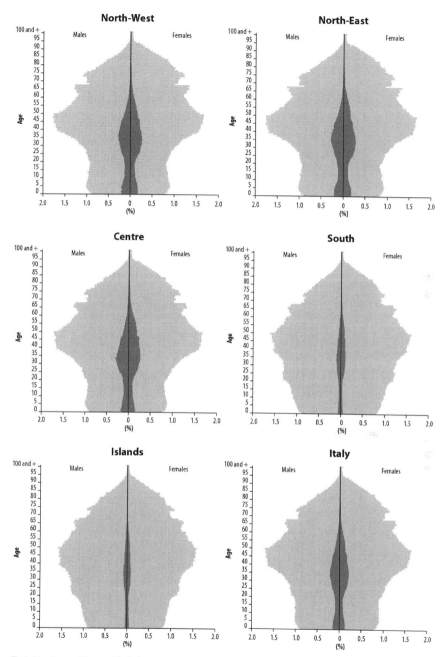

The dark interior part of the pyramid is the foreign nationals segment of the resident population, while the grey bars represent the Italian segment of the resident population.

Figure 1.6 Population pyramid by geographical areas and citizenship, January 1, 2014

Source: Istat, Population register, http://demo.istat.it

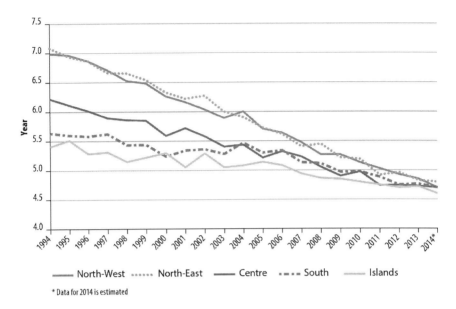

Figure 1.7 Gender differences in life expectancy by geographical area, 1994–2014

Source: Istat, Life tables, http://demo.istat.it

of resident foreign nationals, parenthood postponement, the decline in nuptiality and the persistent economic crisis.

The fertility dynamics described earlier are the result of important differential changes in reproductive behaviour in the geographical areas (Figure 1.8). The period TFR began to accelerate in the North and Centre of the country from 2005 onwards, though this increase was not observed in the South and in the Islands. As a result, when comparing the period fertility rates in 1999 and in 2013, we see a geographical reversal: in fact, in 1999, the mean number of children per woman was 1.18 in the North-West and 1.37 in the South. Fourteen years later, TFRs were 1.45 and 1.31, respectively. As already mentioned, one of the main drivers contributing to fertility growth in the North of Italy over the past decade has been the extremely significant increase in migration: in 2013, the period TFR of Italian women living in this geographical area equalled 1.3, while the same figure for foreign nationals was 2.2 (ISTAT, 2014).

Ageing: health and living conditions

The state of health of the elderly

Demographic changes are closely linked to social, health and also economic changes, and this relationship also emerges in the fields of health and survival. Having good health in old age is an essential component of a person's autonomy and well-being, as it allows the individual to maintain an active role within the

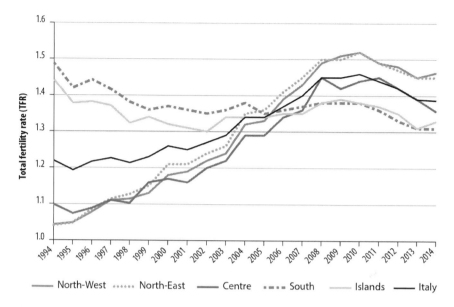

Figure 1.8 TFR by geographical area, 1994–2014

Source: Istat, Life births recorded in the population register, http://demo.istat.it

family and society. In order to have a more complete picture of population ageing, standard demographic indicators can be combined with those for the elderly's
state of health. It is particularly important to assess whether or not the increase
in life expectancy is associated with a good level of health. A useful indicator for
this type of evaluation is healthy life expectancy, which is the number of years a
person can expect to live without disabling diseases (OECD, 2014). This indicator is one of the main European structural indicators, and its importance has been
recognized in the Lisbon Strategy (European Commission, 2009); it combines
survival elements with the self-rated state of health.

Indeed, whilst Italy is found at the top of world lists for both the ageing index
and life expectancy, this is not the case as regards healthy ageing. Although
women live longer than men, they spend more years in bad health. Women are,
therefore, more often affected by less lethal, but more disabling, diseases then
men (e.g. diabetes, hypertension, arthritis/osteoarthritis, etc.). As we can see from
the next figure (Figure 1.9), women show higher life expectancy rates than men,
but the latter spend a greater number of years in a good state of health (59.8 male
against 57.3 female). Geographically, the highest values for both genders and age
classes considered are found in almost all the Centre-North's regions. The South is
doubly penalized because in addition to having a shorter life expectancy, its quality of survival is poorer; the worse condition in Southern Italy in terms of health is
probably due to the lower access to health facilities for the diagnosis and treatment
of disease; this has an important role in the state of a population's health.

Another important indicator of the quality of ageing is the life expectancy
at 65 years without limitations in usual activities, which expresses the average

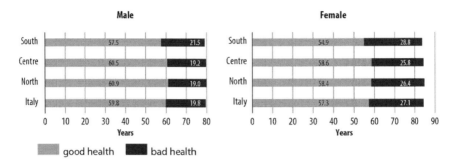

Figure 1.9 Healthy life expectancy by gender in Italy, 2012

Source: Istat, Health condition survey, http://noi-italia.istat.it

number of years expected to be lived without activity limitation. Men also have an advantage over women as regards this indicator: in 2012, a man aged 65 could expect to live 9.0 out of 18.3 years without limitations, whilst for women the same value equalled 9.1 out of a total of 21.9. Gender differences may be noted as regards the presence of chronic disease as well: to be precise, the higher the age, the higher the state of health gender gap. Up to about 75 years of age, men report the presence of one or more chronic diseases more often than women, whilst the opposite can be said as regards those over 75.

Regional differences in the state of health have increased over the last few years, with the South's disadvantages in terms of life expectancy, quality of life and infant mortality widening because of the recent economic crisis. Geographic differences in physical and psychological health remain, always to the benefit of the Centre-North, as well as the spread of behaviours leading to better lifestyles. In the South, the situation is critical because of increases in unhealthy behaviour such as sedentary lifestyles, excess weight and poor dietary habits, with the exception of alcohol consumption, which is more frequent in the North (ISTAT, 2015b). These negative behaviours will inevitably have a consequence in defining the state of health in old age. The effect of the current economic crisis, which is particularly strong in the South, is likely to have a similar impact.

As already pointed out, health conditions can be analysed by reference to both objective indicators (such as life expectancy) and subjective indicators; in Italy, these come from the ISTAT survey on health conditions. The self-evaluation that an individual makes about his/her own state of health can be interpreted as a synthesis of the different dimensions involved (physical, psychological, social relationships, family networks, etc.). Analysing time series data, it was noted that in Italy, the general increase in survival rates over the last few decades had also been followed by improvements in self-perceived health conditions, although a decline is expected over the next few years because of the global economic crisis, which has also affected Italy. Healthier lifestyles, greater awareness of the importance of preventive medicine, nutrition and more treatment are some of the factors which have had an impact, creating the best conditions for both the objective and subjective health of today's elderly. In general, by analysing Italian health data, we can point out that, although there is an increase in life expectancy, the general state of health amongst the elderly shows that their psychological well-being has worsened (ISTAT, 2015b). The latest available data confirm the increase in mortality in the elderly from dementia and diseases of the nervous system, especially amongst the oldest members; physical inactivity, excess weight and an inadequate consumption of fruit and vegetables are elements which characterized elderly Italians and which will inevitably have more consequences in terms of their state of health, particularly over the next few years.

Poverty and social exclusion of the elderly

The state of health is undoubtedly one of the factors (although not the only one) with a major impact on defining the elderly's social conditions, and it is closely linked to their living conditions: good health can be considered one of the most fundamental resources for social and economic prosperity. EU-SILC (European Union Statistics on Income and Living Conditions) is an important survey which aims to study – among other issues – the risk of poverty and social exclusion of European populations by analysing their social and living conditions. A person is considered as 'at risk of poverty or social exclusion' if at least one of the three following conditions is present:

- at risk of poverty after social transfers (income poverty);
- severely materially deprived;
- living in households with very low work intensity.

Reducing the number of persons in EU countries considered being at risk of poverty or social exclusion is one of the key targets of the Europe 2020 strategy (European Commission and Eurostat, 2015). Compared with other countries, the elderly in Italy show a higher risk of poverty than the overall population, surpassed only by Eastern European countries such as Bulgaria, Romania and Croatia. Amongst Western countries, only Greece has a higher value than Italy. In 2013, one out of five residents in the European Union (24.5%) was at risk of poverty or social exclusion, while for the elderly, this risk was lower (18.2%). Italy has a high risk of poverty or social exclusion both as regards the total population and the elderly. The relative figures are 28.4% and 22.6%, respectively.[2] In 2013, the same percentage for the elderly was 10.8 in France and 14.5 in Spain, lower than in Italy.

In 2006, the elderly had the same risk of poverty and social exclusion as the population as a whole. In subsequent years, a gap between the two rates has appeared, especially during the economic crisis (Figure 1.10). In 2010, the population aged 65 years or more had a risk of poverty or social exclusion 4.2 percentage points lower than that calculated for the total population. Note that the economic crisis led to an overall worsening of living conditions for the Italian population in general. However, the effect of the crisis had a lower impact on the elderly. It is probable that in a situation where unemployment

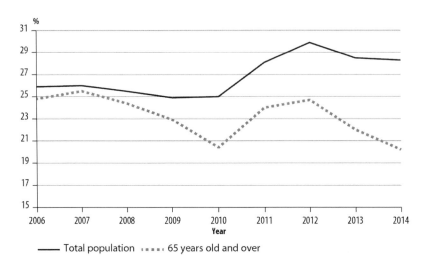

Figure 1.10 People at risk of poverty or social exclusion by age in Italy. Years 2005–2014

Source: Eurostat database

rates are increasing – in Italy, the youth unemployment rate is one of the highest in Europe – retired people have a lower risk of living in deprivation or poverty thanks to pension stability.

Nevertheless, in Italy, amongst the elderly, those aged from 75–84 have a higher risk of poverty and social exclusion (Table 1.1). Women are more at risk than men both in the elderly and in the total population, although the gender difference is higher for the former. As regards the geographical distribution, it should be noted that the situation in the South of Italy is always worse than in other areas. The elderly in the South have a higher risk of suffering from poverty and social exclusion.

One aspect of a person's well-being which is relevant, especially when considering the elderly, is his/her housing conditions. In fact, another important indicator provided by the EU-SILC survey is the severe housing deprivation rate.[3] In 2013, elderly people had a significantly higher rate than those living in France and in Spain: for Italy, this was 3.4, whilst for France, it was 0.3 and for Spain 0.2. The value has remained stable nationally for the period between 2005–2013; it was 3.7 in 2005.

Cirelli et al. (2015) demonstrated that in families where there is at least one elderly person, the indicator for severe material deprivation[4] has decreased in recent years, going from 16.2 in 2012 to 12.3 in 2013. The authors suggested that this pattern could be due to the role that the elderly have in families: in some cases, 'grandparents' may undertake a 'social assistance' role, helping other family members, especially with childcare. This underlines the importance of retirees in a system in which family structures are still relevant for supporting the younger generation. In general, it can be said that, as regards the

Table 1.1 The elderly and the total population at risk of poverty or social exclusion by age, gender, geographical area and household type, 2012

	At risk poverty rate or social exclusion	
	65 and over	Total population
Age		
65–74	14.2	–
75–84	18.7	–
85 and over	15.2	–
Sex		
Male	13.0	18.1
Female	18.6	20.7
Geographical area		
North	11.1	10.7
Centre	14.6	15.5
South and Islands	24.7	33.3

Source: Cirelli et al. (2015)

national situation, the condition of the elderly is better than the condition of the population as a whole, whilst at a European level, the condition of the Italian elderly is worse than that of other Europeans.

A quick look at the future of the ageing phenomenon in Italy

As regards population projections, Figure 1.11 shows the expected changes in the proportion of the population aged 65 years or more at the regional level up to 2030. In order to draw the map for 2015, data were sorted in ascending order and divided into quintiles: as a result, four class breaks were produced. All the subsequent maps were drawn using the same class breaks as the map calculated for 2015 in order to highlight the changes in regional ageing with respect to 2015, which was then used as a common-year basis for comparison. The maps clearly show that the population ageing process will involve the entire country. Obviously, it is a gradual process, and regions that are currently experiencing lower ageing index rates are those which will reach higher values of the indicators considered more slowly.

In 2030, 26.1% of the resident population in Italy will be aged 65 or over (+ 4.6% compared to 2015). The Italian Riviera – where it is expected that the proportion of the population over 65 will reach 30.4% of the total – will be confirmed as the most elderly region of Italy in 2030, whilst in Trentino-Alto Adige and Campania this proportion will equal values slightly under 24.5%. The latter areas will have the distinction of being the least elderly regions in Italy.

In terms of age structure, in 2030, the mean age is expected to be 47, the ageing index will be more than 207 and the total age dependency ratio will equal 63.2. In the same year, male life expectancy at birth will be 82.8 years and life expectancy at age 65 will be 20.7 years. The same figures for women will be 87.7 and 24.5 years.

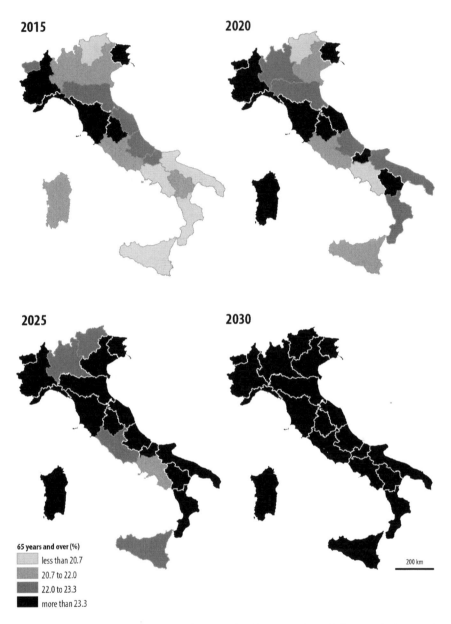

Figure 1.11 Regional population projections for the proportion of the population aged 65 years and over, Italy. Years 2015, 2020, 2025 and 2030

Source: Istat, http://demo.istat.it

Conclusion

The ongoing ageing phenomenon has profound consequences for social and economic organization both individually and nationally. As well-illustrated by a United Nations publication (2002), population ageing is

> unprecedented, (without parallel in human history) [. . .], pervasive (a global phenomenon affecting every man, woman and child – but countries are at very different stages of the process, and the pace of change differs greatly) [. . .] and enduring (we will not return to the young populations that our ancestors knew).

The decline in TFR has had – and will have – an important impact on population ageing. Migration flows could help to slow down this demographic phenomenon, but it should not be forgotten that those foreign nationals who began arriving in Italy from the second half of the 1990s are ageing and, inevitably, will contribute to the ageing phenomenon of the resident population in the near future. One of the causes of population ageing has been the great increase in life expectancy, which is still ongoing. This increase could have an impact not only on social organization and on pension system sustainability but also on future developments in public expenditure on health. The key point is to what extent will longevity translate into growing needs for health services? Some scholars have emphasized the importance of considering not only life expectancy but also healthy life expectancy (i.e. life expectancy in good health) since – as mentioned in the foregoing pages – the increase in life expectancy does not correlate exactly with the increase in years lived in poor conditions of health. It is important not to evaluate the growth of the population over a certain age threshold in absolute and relative terms but rather to evaluate what the future health conditions of such a population and their health needs will be. A considerable increase in the elderly population is not necessarily accompanied by a proportional increase in the absolute number of people with disabilities or ill health (Lutz and Scherbov, 2005). In the context of a general increase in longevity, understanding whether or not the increase in life expectancy is accompanied by a parallel increase in years lived in good health (or equally by an accelerating number of years) is indeed crucial for planning effective health services. In fact, this has an impact on other areas of life, such as on elderly's social and economic participation.

These considerations emphasize that population ageing is a multidimensional phenomenon which has consequences in many fields. Many social policies have been developed to enhance elderly participation in social and economic life both at national and European levels. Nevertheless, it must be highlighted that most of the measures used to study the evolution of population structures are based on static indicators as they referred to a fixed age threshold which divided the total population into 'old' and 'not old'. To date, we have traditionally considered a person aged 65 or more as old, mainly for economic reasons and to aid in comparisons between countries, but ageing is not simply a matter of biological age. Thus it will be useful to consider a dynamic age threshold – especially given the great heterogeneity of the 'elderly group' – and to evaluate the consequences in terms of ageing or 'counterageing'. Studies about dynamic thresholds have been done by Ryder (1975), Egidi (1994, 2013), Livi Bacci (1987) and others.

Notes

1 The total fertility rate (TFR) for a specific year is defined as the total number of children that would be born to each woman if she were to live to the end of her child-bearing years and give birth to children in alignment with the prevailing age-specific fertility rates. It is calculated assuming no net migration and unchanged mortality patterns (OECD, Fertility rates (indicator). doi:10.1787/8272fb01-en. Accessed on 10 June 2015).
2 Source: Eurostat, People at risk of poverty or social exclusion by age and sex, [last update 18.05.2015] http://ec.europa.eu/eurostat/data/database.
3 The severe housing deprivation rate is defined as the percentage of the population living in dwellings which are considered overcrowded whilst also exhibiting at least one of the housing deprivation measures. Housing deprivation is a measure of poor amenities and is calculated by reference to those households with a leaking roof, no bath/shower and no indoor toilet, or a dwelling considered too dark.
4 Severe material deprivation: persons living in households which cannot afford at least four of the following nine: i) to pay unexpected expenses; ii) a week's holiday away from home; iii) to pay loan, rent or utility bills; iv) to eat meat, fish or a protein equivalent every second day; v) to keep their home adequately warm; vi) a washing machine vii) a colour TV; viii) a telephone; ix) a car. (c) People living in households where members aged 18–59 worked less than 20 % of their potential during the past year. (d) People in at least one of conditions (a), (b) and (c).

References

Billari, F. C., Liefbroer, A. C. and Philipov, D. (2006). The postponement of childbearing in Europe: driving forces and implications. *Vienna Yearbook of Population Research*, 4, 1–17.
Caselli, G. and Egidi, V. (2011). Una vita più lunga e più sana, in: Golini, A. and Rosina, A. (Eds.), *Il secolo degli anziani: come cambierà l'Italia*. Prismi. Bologna: Il mulino.
Cirelli, M., Delle Fratte, C. and Lariccia, F. (2015). Redditi e condizioni di vita dei pensionati over 65 residenti in Italia. *Rivista Italiana di Economia Demografia e Statistica*, LXIX(1), 119–126.
De Rose, A., Racioppi, F. and Zanatta, A. L. (2008). Italy: delayed adaptation of social institutions to changes in family behaviour. *Demographic Research*, S7(19), 665–704.
Egidi, V. (1994). Strutture di popolazione, in: Livi-Bacci, M., Blangiardo, G. C. and Golini, A. (Eds.), *Demografia*. Torino: Fondazione Giovanni Agnelli.
Egidi, V. (2013). Invecchiamento, longevità, salute: nuovi bisogni, nuove opportunità, in: Egidi, V. (ED.), *Salute, sopravvivenza e sostenibilità dei sistemi sanitari: la sfida dell'invecchiamento demografico* (pp. 13–32). Fondazione CESIFIN – Instituto Niels Stensen.
European Commission. (2009). *Healthy life years in the European Union: facts and figures 2005*. European Commission. Retrieved from https://ec.europa.eu/health/archive/ph_information/reporting/docs/hly_en.pdf
European Commission & Eurostat. (2015). *Smarter, greener, more inclusive? Indicators to support the Europe 2020 strategy*. Luxembourg: Publications Office of the European Union.
Frenk, J., Bobadilla, J. L., Stern, C., Frejka, T. and Lozano, R. (1991). Elements for a theory of the health transition. *Health Transition Review*, 1(1), 21–38.

Golini, A., Basso, S. and Reynaud, C. (2003). L'invecchiamento della popolazione in Italia: una sfida per il paese e un laboratorio per il mondo. *Giornale di Gerontologia*, 6, 528–544.

ISTAT. (2014). *Natalità e fecondità della popolazione eesidente (Anno 2012)*. Retrieved from www.istat.it/it/archivio/140132

ISTAT. (2015a). *Indicatori demografici: stime per l'anno 2014*. Retrieved from www.istat.it/it/archivio/149003

ISTAT. (2015b). BES 2015: il benessere equo e sostenibile in Italia. Roma: Istat.

Kohler, H.-P., Billari, F. C. and Ortega, J. A. (2002). The emergence of lowest-low fertility in Europe during the 1990s. *Population and Development Review*, 28(4), 641–680.

Livi-Bacci, M. (1987). Invecchiamento biologico e invecchiamento sociale, in: CNR-IRP (Ed.), *L'invecchiamento della popolazione in Italia e nelle società occidentali*. Working Paper. Roma: Atti, Convegni, e Seminari.

Lutz, W. and Scherbov, S. (2005). Will population ageing necessarily lead to an increase in the number of persons with disabilities? Alternative scenarios for the European Union. *Vienna Yearbook of Population Research*, 3, 219–234.

OECD. (2014). *Health at a glance: Europe 2014*. OECD Publishing. Retrieved from www.oecd-ilibrary.org/social-issues-migration-health/health-at-a-glance-europe-2014_health_glance_eur-2014-en

Ryder, N. B. (1975). Notes on stationary populations. *Population Index*, 41(1), 3–28.

United Nations (Ed.). (2002). *World Population Ageing, 1950–2050*. New York: United Nations.

Vallin, J. and Meslé, F. (2004). Convergences and divergences in mortality: a new approach to health transition. *Demographic Research*, 2(2), 10–43.

2 Demographic transitions, ageing and 'the great recession' in Spain[1]

Francisco Zamora López, Noelia Cámara,
Laura Barrios, Alain Parant and
Margarita Delgado

Population ageing is one of the main challenges that any society undergoing a demographic transition faces, sooner or later. As a result of alterations in the level of economic development, lifespans tend to lengthen, the fertility rate declines and the population ages. Population ageing is the inevitable result of two trends that are commonly regarded as positive: longer life and fertility by choice. It is intense and sudden, and has serious and complex socio-economic and political effects. In the most developed countries, the rapid increase in the elderly population compared with that of working age is forcing Welfare States, mainly designed after the Second World War, to make fairly significant adjustments that limit social well-being. In Spain, between 1900 and 2014[2], the proportion of the population aged 65 or over increased from 5.2% to 18.1%. According to the 2014 projections by the Spanish National Statistics Institute (INE), by 2052, this could rise to 36.6%, which would place Spain amongst the most aged populations on the planet.

This chapter provides an analysis of the ageing process in Spain, from 1900, the first year for which there are relatively reliable data, until 2014, the last year of observation. It also analyses how this might develop, under certain conditions, from 2015 to 2052, according to the INE projections. Two past sub-periods have been defined, 1900–1981 and 1981–2014. These coincide with the first and second demographic transitions, respectively. Particular attention was paid to the period beginning in 1998, when the Spanish fertility rate reached its lowest level, and that since 2008, a period marked by one of the most severe financial and economic crises that the world has ever experienced. Although we are still struggling to assess all the consequences of this crisis, it cannot be ignored.[3] Numerous international bodies, such as the International Monetary Fund and the Organisation for Economic Cooperation and Development (OECD), have called it *The Great Recession* (Grusky et al., 2011) to distinguish it from *The Great Depression*, which began on October 29, 1929. The first subject of this chapter is thus an analysis of demographic transitions and their consequences on the Spanish population's age structure, combined with those of *The Great Recession*. The projection into the future that closes the analysis, a modest attempt at a prediction for 2050, merely aims to highlight the inexorable nature of population ageing and the scale of the challenge that the latter poses for Spanish society.

From one transition to the next: Spain's major demographic transformations

The demographic processes referred to as demographic transitions are the substantial changes that successively affect the schedule of mortality and the fertility rate level, and subsequently affect the structure by age of the populations. These fundamental movements, which reflect the profound social transformations occurring, are the reference framework to analyse a population's development and condition.

The first demographic transition

The first demographic transition (FDT) marks the passage from an original demographic regime, characterised by high mortality and birth rates that more or less balance each other out, to a contemporary demographic regime in which mortality and birth rates still reach a balance, but at greatly reduced levels. In comparison with other European countries, Spain's passage through these stages has been rather unusual, both for its chronology and duration. 'Although definitely part of old Europe, Spain has somehow undergone its demographic transition and done so in a different timescale to most of its neighbouring countries' (Nadal, 1984, p. 15). This delay is explained by Spain's late economic development compared to countries in central and northern Europe (Reques Velasco, 2006). Whilst in many European countries the transition process began in the nineteenth century, in Spain, it only began in the early twentieth century. Though late, the decline in mortality and birth rates have, nevertheless, until very recently, been clear and irreversible, other than exceptional rebounds during the 1918 influenza epidemic (Puyol Antolín, 1988) and the Civil War of 1936–1939 (Díez Nicolás, 1985) (Figure 2.1).

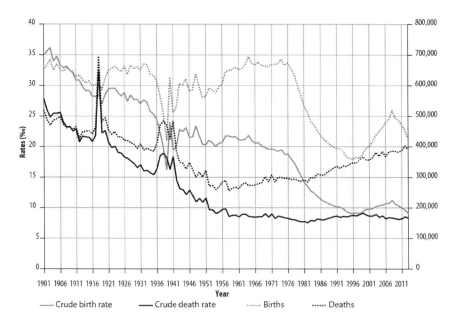

Figure 2.1 Crude death and birth rates, births and deaths. Spain, 1901–2013

Source: INE

From 27.9% in 1900, the crude mortality rate fell below 10% in 1952 and reached its lowest level (7.6%) in 1982. From 1983, it rose slightly – not due to an increase in mortality by age, but to an enhanced distribution of the population at advanced ages – and reached 8.32% in 2013. Several factors explain the continuous decline in the rate during the first decades of the twentieth century: the agricultural revolution, the industrial and scientific development, the introduction of hygienic practices, the discovery of penicillin and vaccines, etc. In particular, all these elements allowed Spain to better fight against infectious diseases (Kirk, 1996). Although infectious diseases were one of the leading causes of mortality until 1945, they were gradually replaced by non-infectious diseases (Arbelo Curbelo, 1962; Pascua, 1934). These advances caused infant mortality to fall from about 186% in 1900 to less than 3% in 2013 and, over the same period, life expectancy at birth rose by 46.1 years for men and 49.9 years for women (Table 2.1 and Figure 2.2).

As for the birth rate, it fell from 32.7% in 1900 to 9.1% in 2013. Although the decline was continuous throughout the twentieth century – with the exception of 1956 to 1965, the years of the Spanish *baby boom* – it increased sharply from 1977 onwards. The fall in the birth and fertility rates has more complex reasons than that for the decline in mortality. Landry (1934) interpreted the fall in birth rate neither as families' response to a previous drop in mortality, particularly that of children, nor by an increase in the cost of living or by a degeneration in morals, but rather as the consequence of a different view of life. 'The fundamental principle is, so to speak, a rationalisation of life'. This rationalisation – which means a de facto limitation of life – can result from altruistic feelings (children's interests) or from less disinterested feelings (individuals' attachment to their belongings),

Figure 2.2 Life expectancy at birth by gender and total fertility rate (TFR). Spain, 1900–2013

Source: INE

Table 2.1 Demographic transition indicators. Spain, 1900–1981–2013

	Population	Deaths	Births	P65+/ Ptotale (%)	P85+/P65+ (%)	MR (%)	IMR (%)	e0 M	e0 F	e65 M	e65 F	CBR (%)	TFR
1900	18,618,086	536,716	627,848	5.20	3.20	27.86	185.91	33.85	35.70	9.00	9.23	32.74	4.75
1981	37,683,363	291,790	530,622	11.24	6.21	7.76	12.45	72.52	78.61	14.77	17.93	13.24	2.04
2013	47,129,783	390,419	425,715	17.69	14.34	8.32	2.71	79.97	85.60	18.96	22.90	9.07	1.27

Source: INE

or even from selfish ones (children are a source of expense, grief, problems). He called this a 'demographic revolution': the advent of a demographic regime characterised by the widespread practice of birth control to meet the essential concern of raising the living standards of parents and their living children. This is a demographic regime in which the population is no longer in balance and where 'the population may even decline, despite the remarkable advances in both production techniques and medicine and sanitation'. The 'demographic transition', presented by Frank Notestein (1944, 1945) and Kingsley Davis (1945), which was highly regarded and later elevated to the rank of theory, quickly replaced Landry's 'demographic revolution'. It makes the onset of the fall in the fertility rate subordinate to the emergence of modern methods of economic development, to the expansion of education and to improvement in women's status. It implicitly sets out the idea of a post-transitional balance or near-balance.

The second demographic transition

According to Van de Kaa, 1965 saw the start of the second demographic transition (SDT) in the Old Continent. This was the year in which the fertility rate fell below the estimated replacement level of 2.1 children per woman under the mortality conditions of the most advanced countries. Unlike the FDT, based on an 'altruistic' idea of reproduction, the SDT may have an 'individualistic' basis, thus it is spoken of as a 'profound change in norms and behaviours' (Van de Kaa, 1987, p. 7). Amongst the most significant changes are the decreasing prevalence of marriage in favour of cohabitation, the refocusing of the family from children to the couple, the widespread use of contraception as a means to prevent unwanted births and choose the time of conception, the increasing complexity and diversification of the matrimonial journey and the types of households. In addition to the variables directly influencing the fertility rate, the second demographic transition also involves a wide range of other factors (marriage, divorce, cohabitation, contraceptive use and voluntary termination of pregnancy[4]), which are involved in family formation and its transformations. To a greater or lesser degree, these factors indirectly influence the fertility rate. Its evolution and level is in some ways a combination of changes in these various factors. An increase in the average age at the first marriage, combined with a growth in divorce and wider, more intensive use of modern contraceptives, is leading to a reduction in the fertility rate.

Without going into detail, it is worth remarking that the idea of the SDT has been criticised by many authors (Coleman, 2004; Lesthaeghe and Surkyn, 2004; Livi-Bacci, 2001; Cliquet, 1991) and by Van de Kaa himself (2002, 2004) because it may only be a continuation of the first. Although the analytical framework for the SDT displays a few shortcomings that limit its interpretative potential, it nevertheless has the merit of high operability (Caldwell, 2008; Sobotka, 2008; Van De Kaa, 2008) since it is only based on a single reference threshold: the passing of the fertility rate below replacement level. In Spain, this threshold was reached in 1981, bringing the first transition to an end and initiating the second demographic transition. That year, the total fertility rate (TFR) was 2.03 children per woman; it reached its lowest level (1.15) in 1998. The SDT in Spain is, by definition, the passing of the fertility rate below replacement level, but it also reflects a modification in behaviours as regards family formation. Figure 2.3 traces the evolution in five indicators selected to depict these transformations; the scale on the right concerns the TFR and that on the left women's average age at first marriage, the average age at first birth, the proportion of children born outside marriage and the proportion of voluntary terminations of pregnancy (VTP) per 100 pregnancies. All these indicators are considered to illustrate the SDT process.

Although the total fertility rate's evolution displays some deviations linked to the economic crisis (rising from 2.21 children per woman in 1980 to 1.15 in 1998, rising back to 1.44 in 2008 before a new, still ongoing decline in the TFR: 1.27 children per woman in 2013), the other indicators show a continuous upward trend. Whilst they were closely interlinked until the late 1990s, evolutions in women's average age at first marriage and their average age at first birth have manifestly diverged since 2005, the timing of the first birth now being earlier than that of marriage in general. This established fact may partly reflect the increased weighting of second or subsequent marriages; nonetheless, one cannot ignore the effect of the growing dissociation between motherhood and marriage, as is evident from the proportion of children born outside marriage. This proportion, which increased rather slowly at first (from 3.9% in 1980 to 11.7% in 1996), experienced a sudden acceleration from the second half of the 1990s; it was 39% in 2012, with its upward trend showing no deviation.

There may be various reasons for this dissociation between procreation and marriage. One is the intense secularisation movement among Spanish society. This movement resulted in a significant fall in the proportion of women declaring

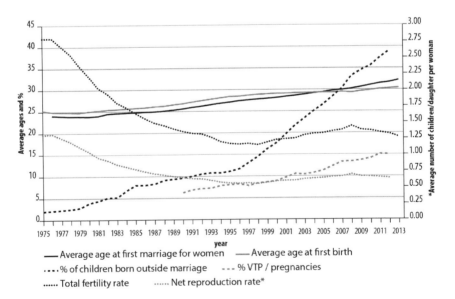

Figure 2.3 Evolution in certain indicators during the second demographic transition. Spain, 1975–2013

Source: INE

themselves practising Catholics and a rapid increase in the proportion of those stating that they had no religion (Delgado et al., 2009; Pérez-Agote, 2008). This coincided with the change in the value system indicated by Van de Kaa in his description of the SDT process. The average age at first birth is a factor that significantly affects the fertility rate (Delgado Pérez et al., 2006). The continued deferment of first birth – from 24.8 years of age in 1979 to 30.4 in 2013 – has generally been accompanied by a significant drop in the fertility rate (from an average of 2.37 children per woman to 1.27). In the period 1981–2013, there was a high inverse correlation between the average age at first birth and fertility rate (coefficient of −0.655) (Figure 2.4). Three quite distinct phases can be defined:

- 1981–1995: a phase of very rapid increase in the average age at first birth (from 25.2 to 28.4 years of age) alongside a marked decline in the TFR.
- 1996–2008: a phase of slower increase in the average age at first birth (from 28.5 to 29.3 years of age) and a simultaneous rise in the TFR.
- since 2009: a phase of accelerated growth in the average age at first birth (reaching 30.4 years of age in 2013, though this was not a ceiling) and a further fall in the TFR.

These three phases are very different, economically and socially. The first saw the consolidation of democracy after 36 years of dictatorship (1939–1975), accompanied by a liberalisation of behaviours. Having children was no longer Spanish women's only goal, and it was no longer imperative that they be married in order to procreate. At the same time, they benefited from mass access to higher education and effective contraception, which helped not only to separate

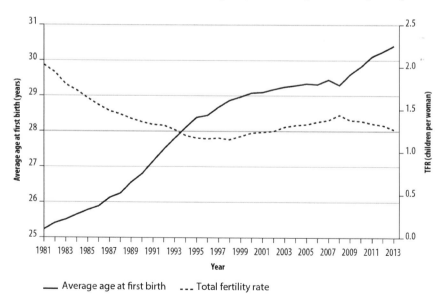

Figure 2.4 Total fertility rate (TFR) and average age at first birth. Spain, 1981–2013

Source: INE

sexual relationships from procreation but also to decide when to have children. All these factors led to a rise in the average age at first birth. The second phase was characterised by sustained economic growth and significant immigration of foreign populations attracted by the prospects of the Spanish labour market. The third phase was marked by the economic crisis which began in 2008 and resulted in a large number of redundancies, and reduced the job security of those working people who kept their jobs. Economic insecurity and its various consequences (increased difficulties in coping with mortgage payments, rent payments and loss of housing) caused a drop in setting up as a couple, a deferment of conception and a rise in the average age at first birth. During this period, women experiencing relative employment stability or who were economically solvent or those who, because of their age, felt that they could no longer delay the arrival of a child, constituted the majority of those who procreated. We will return to this particular period later. In addition, the correlation between the proportion of children born outside marriage and the fertility rate was lower than before 2009 (correlation coefficient of -0.365) (Figure 2.5), as there were compensations between fertility rates inside and outside of marriage, thus confirming the growing dissociation between the marriage and fertility rates mentioned earlier.

The proportion of VTP per 100 pregnancies is also continuously increasing (Figure 2.6). Despite decriminalisation, the use of contraceptives and their widespread availability in 1978, and recourse to abortion, decriminalised in 1985, is still similarly increasing. Clearly, pregnancy is no longer seen as an inevitable outcome; it can be terminated if it proves to be unwanted. However, the rise in the proportion of VTP can also be explained by the presence of a larger foreign population and their wider use of this method that the Spanish population.

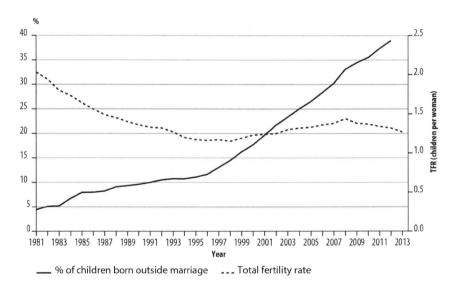

Figure 2.5 Total fertility rate (TFR) and proportion of children born outside marriage. Spain, 1981–2013

Source: INE

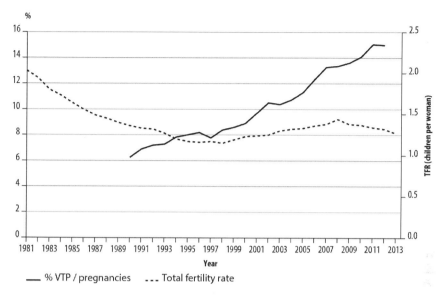

Figure 2.6 Total fertility rate (TFR) and the proportion of voluntary terminations of pregnancy (VTP) per 100 pregnancies. Spain, 1981–2013

Source: INE

There is no doubt that the Spanish population's most intimate behaviours have been profoundly transformed over the past 100 years: getting married, having children, terminating pregnancies, using contraceptives, etc. These demographic changes are both the result and an obvious sign of the profound transformations in Spanish society, which lived under dictatorship and then the return to democracy. These transformations, combined with a rapid reduction in mortality and a great volatility in migratory exchanges with the rest of the world, have had direct repercussions on the Spanish population's age structure, leading to accelerated population ageing.

Spain: an example of accelerated ageing

As demonstrated by Figure 2.7, the Spanish population has aged considerably since the beginning of the last century. In 1900, the Spanish population, affected by epidemics and recurrent famines, had a very low life expectancy at birth. It had a very young age structure, typical of older demographic regimes: persons under 20 years of age accounted for 41.9% of the total, those 65 or over only 5.2%.

The pyramid of 2011 displays the age structure of an aged population, resulting from low rates of infant mortality, high life expectancy and a reduced fertility rate. The numerically largest group is that of those of working age (20–64 years of age), partly belonging to the *baby-boom* generations. Those under 20 only account for 19.8% of the total; those 65 or over now represent 17.3%. The pyramid also shows a greater number of women of older ages: 57.2% of those 65 or

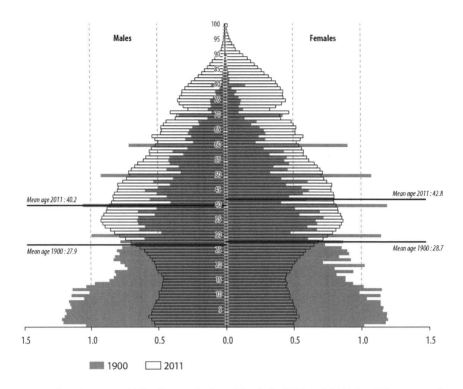

Figure 2.7 Age pyramid for the population of Spain in 1900 and 2011 for 100 persons of
each population's total

Sources: INE, Population Census of 1900 and 2011

over; 68.1% of those 85 or over; 77.1% of those 95 or over. Abnormally high male
mortality, which concerns Spain as other countries, explains the general over-
representation of women in old age and its increase with age.

Population ageing in Spain since 1981: the impact of the second demographic transition

In 2010, Spain ranked fourteenth in the list of the oldest countries in the world,
with 17.1% of its population aged 65 or over – that is, a proportion about six percentage points lower than that of Japan (23.0%), which occupied the top position.
By comparison, in 1950, Spain ranked forty-second and Japan seventy-fourth
(with 7.2% and 4.9% of the population aged 65 or over, respectively), far behind
the Channel Islands, which held first place (12.2%), followed by France (11.4%).
In 50 years, Spain and even more noticeably, Japan, have made an undeniable
demographic jump. A closer study of the ageing of the Spanish population since
1981 highlights a sharp inflection in the curves in the early 2000s (Figure 2.8).
After years of decreasing, the proportion of persons under 20 stabilised at a level
slightly above the proportion of those 65 or over, which also almost stabilised

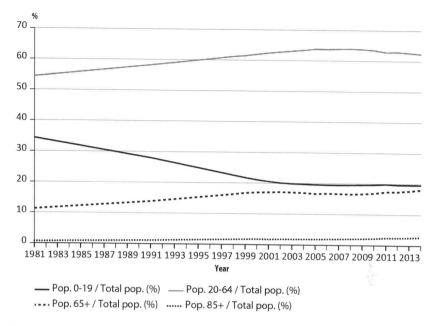

Figure 2.8 Population distribution by major age group. Spain, 1981–2014

Source: INE

after a period of uninterrupted rise, just as the proportion of those of working age (20–64) was dropping slightly at the end of the period. Described in such broad terms, the demographic ageing process in Spain appears to have temporarily stabilised. Note, however, that since 1981, the proportion of persons aged 85 or over has not stopped increasing: from 0.70 to 2.67% between 1981 and 2014.

Deeper analysis of the ageing process in Spain between 1981 and 2014 can be conducted using various indicators. Figure 2.9 traces their development: the proportion of persons aged 65 or over in the total population (EI),[5] the ageing index in relation to the young (AI)[6] and the super-ageing index (SI).[7] The scale on the right depicts the EI and that on the left the other two. A fourth indicator (mTFR) is also included. This is the inverse of the total fertility rate multiplied by 100, known as the modified TFR, which allows us to visualise a possible direct relationship between changes in the fertility rate and those of the other three indicators.

The EI and AI indicators, therefore, differ in their reference population: the total population in the first case, the young population in the second. Their evolution is quite similar: growth until the late 1990s – logically more rapid for the AI, as the older population increases faster than the younger population – then stabilisation (AI) or slight decline (EI) before a new rise from the late 2000s. The mTFR indicator shows a relatively similar evolution to that of the first two, although its changes in trend always precede those of the EI and AI indicators and are more clear-cut. There is an inverse relationship between the fertility rate level and the level of ageing. The relationship between the mTFR and the AI, the

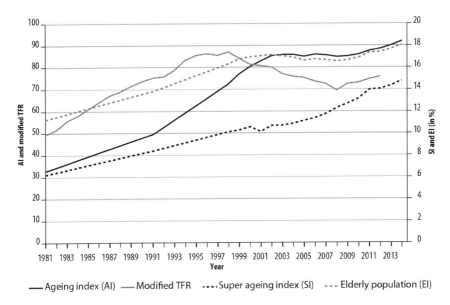

Figure 2.9 Indicators of ageing and the modified TFR. Spain, 1981–2014
Source: INE

denominator of which is directly affected by variations in the fertility rate, seems obvious. This is also the case of the mTFR and EI, also influenced, although more indirectly, by the fertility rate. The high immigration observed in Spain from the 1990s, which was mainly by young adults with higher-than-average fertility rates, resulted indeed in additional births (Delgado et al., 2008; Delgado and López, 2006; Delgado and Zamora-López, 2004). If we require proof that the ageing population of Spain is a formidable fundamental trend, it is the very limited effect of the incorporation of a substantial migration flow[8] of a young population with high reproductive capacity as regards the evolution of the process. Asymmetrically, the fall in the fertility rate after the 2008 crisis, the return of many foreign citizens to their native country and the emigration of Spaniards appear, on the contrary, to have exercised a more considerable effect. The SI indicator increased steadily over the period: amongst the population aged 65 or over, whose numbers are rising, the number of those 85 or over has grown even faster, showing a sustainable trend toward longer life expectancy in Spain. In the light of these observations, the impact of the second demographic transition on the ageing population is clear. But what were the consequences of the 2008 crisis on ageing and its repercussions on the two key elements, fertility rate and migrations?

The 2008 crisis and population ageing in Spain

There are several ways of defining 'crisis'. The first is the definition provided by economists. Thus, according to Uxó González (2015), 'an economic crisis is a situation during which significant adverse changes occur in key economic variables and, especially, in GDP and employment'. Various degrees of severity of an economic crisis can be distinguished: slowdown; recession, which involves the economy recording negative growth for at least two consecutive quarters (compared with the same quarters of the previous year); and depression. Under this definition, the economic crisis that began with a slowdown in 2008 turned into a recession in early 2009: Spain indeed recorded negative growth rates in the fourth quarter of 2008 (−0.7%) and the first quarter of 2009 (−3%).[9] According to the National Bureau of Economic Research's Business Cycle Dating Committee, recession is defined as

> a significant decline in economic activity spread across the economy, lasting more than a few months, normally visible in production, employment, real income and other indicators. A recession begins when the economy reaches a peak of activity and ends when the economy reaches its trough.[10]

However, we can also highlight the existence of an economic crisis by objectifying it through the development of different variables before and after the crisis. For Spain, from 2007 to 2013, it appears that the following observations can be made:

- The male unemployment rate (the persons most affected by this crisis) increased from 6.4% to 25.8%, according to the Labour Force Survey (EPA).
- The unemployment rate for those under 25 increased from 18.2% to 55.7%.
- The gross domestic product (GDP) decreased from 1,080,807 million euros to 1,049,181.
- The debt increased from 35.5% of GDP to 92.1%.
- The number of jobs fell from 20.4 million to 16.8.
- The number of foreign entries dwindled from 920,534 to 307,036.
- The number of Spanish emigrants increased from 28,091 to 72,749.
- The proportion of the Spanish population living below the poverty line increased from 23.3% to 28% (Europe 2020 Strategy).

Another possibility is to assess the population's level of perception of a sudden, intense deterioration of a situation that was previously considered favourable, using, for example, the consumer confidence index (CCI) of the CIS.[11] Whilst the CCI for the period was 79.7% in 2007, in 2013, it was only 42.9% – that is, a deficit of more than 35 points in only 6 years. The 2008 crisis arose at a time when Spain was fully integrated into the European economic and social system, when the population was enjoying a standard of living never experienced before and was considering the future under excellent conditions, despite some experts' doubts. This scenario was broken in 2008, with consequences made harsher by the persistence of the crisis. As Castells et al. report (2012): 'The crisis of global capitalism that has unfolded since 2008 is not merely economic. It is structural and multidimensional'.

As there is a strong interaction between economic and demographic variables, the crisis experienced by Spanish society had immediate repercussions on ageing indexes. The downward trend of the latter was interrupted by a crisis whose total effects have still not been perceived.

Fertility, migrations and ageing: before and during the crisis

To accurately investigate the significant changes in the indicators of ageing in Spain during the years 1998–2012, the period was divided into three main five-year sub-periods:

- That from 1998 to 2002, thereafter referred to as the 'early' period, because of its remoteness from the crisis that began in 2008. This was a period in which the indicators recovered after the Spanish economic depression of the early 1990s.
- That from 2003 to 2007, thereafter called the 'pre-crisis' period. For Spain, this was a period of social and economic euphoria.
- Finally, that from 2008 to 2012, thereafter mentioned as the 'critical' period. This was the period of crisis in which Spain is still submerged in 2017.

The impact of the 2008 crisis on the development of the Spanish population's age structure was measured using the following set of variables:

- The economic situation is illustrated by the GDP at market prices, GDP per capita, final household consumption expenditure and male and female unemployment rates.
- Fertility rate and migrations, whose close link with ageing was identified previously, were assessed using the TFR and the total number of foreign immigrants, respectively.
- Ageing was assessed from the proportion of those aged 65 or over $(EI) = (P_{65+}/P_{total})* 100$ and from the ageing index $(AI) = (P_{65+}/P_{0-19})* 100$.

The temporal evolution of these two indexes during the study period is illustrated by Figure 2.10. The data have been standardised in order to compare them graphically.

These indexes, which quantify ageing, underwent two major changes in Spain during the period studied, in 2002 and 2008. Their growth was rapid until 2002, from which date the proportion of persons aged 65 and over (EI) began to decline, and in 2008 almost reached the level before the increase. The growth in the AI also changed direction between 2002 and 2008, but without an actual decline. From 2008 onwards, both indexes increased again, but in a more pronounced and immediate way for the EI. The two indexes use different reference populations: only persons between 0 and 19 years of age are relevant for the ageing index, whereas the total population is used for the EI. Herein lies the explanation for their different evolutions. The two reference populations are closely related to the fertility rate and, very immediately, to the arrival of foreign immigrants, mostly young persons. This arrival directly adds numbers to the reference population (especially in the case of the EI) and much less to the numerator, because of the

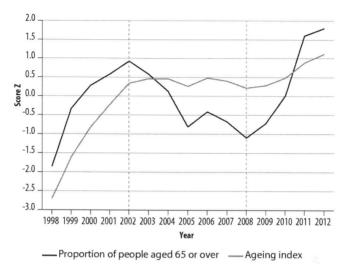

Figure 2.10 Proportions of elderly persons and ageing index. Spain, 1998–2012

Source: Author's calculations based on INE data

low number of seniors. Any change in these parameters is immediately reflected by changes in the values of the ageing indexes. For this reason, it is interesting to observe how the AI and EI indicators correlate with the fertility rate and migrations. Figure 2.11 illustrates the evolutions in the AIs, the TFR and the total number of foreign immigrants from 1998 to 2012. The data have been standardised in order to compare them graphically.

From 1998 to 2002, the four variables rose collectively. Ageing accelerated because Spain had recorded the lowest fertility rates ever during the previous years. From 2002 to 2008, there was an improvement in the fertility rate and migration – these two rates seemingly highly connected – which caused a decrease in the indicators of ageing, with an immediate change in trend for the EI, and the AI becoming stable. The 2008 crisis marked a turning point in the fertility rate and migrations. Although 2007 was the period in which the arrival of foreign immigrants was at its highest, 2008 marked the beginning of a downward slide. Fertility rates followed the same scenario a year later. There then began a period of demographic depression with sustained growth in the AIs, a return to the corresponding 'pre-crisis' trend.

Relationship between various economic indicators and population ageing

Fluctuations in the fertility rate and migrations influenced the evolution in the Spanish population's age structure from 1998 to 2013. It is then necessary to determine which of the economic indicators have the closest link with the fertility rate and migrations, and thus indirectly with the process of ageing. The following figures describe the relationships established between, on the one hand, GDP

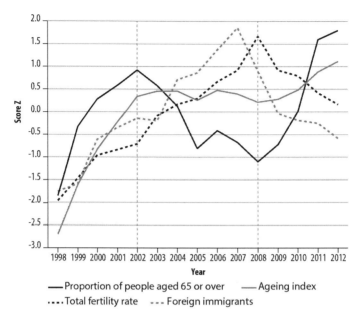

Figure 2.11 Ageing, fertility and migrations. Spain, 1998–2012

Source: Author's calculations based on INE data

at market prices, GDP per capita, household consumption spending, the female and male unemployment rates and, on the other hand, the total number of foreign immigrants (Figure 2.12) and TFR (Figure 2.13). The data have been standardised in order to compare them graphically.

From 1998 to 2007, all economic and employment indicators developed positively (rise in GDP, reduction in unemployment, etc.). This was accompanied by a rise in the TFR (Figure 2.13) and a sustained arrival of foreign immigrants (Figure 2.12). In 2008, a sudden change occurred: as noted previously, foreign immigrant inflows dropped significantly and, simultaneously, the GDP per capita fell and unemployment rates increased. A year later, these indicators were continuing to fall, and total fertility began a decline that coincided with a reduction in GDP at market prices and household consumption spending. Table 2.2 shows the variations in trends observed in Figures 2.9 to 2.12. The period 1998–2012 has been divided into three five-year periods to show the rates of variation of the various indicators and their average values in each of the three periods.

To be read as follows: the rate of change in the proportion of the elderly between 1998 and 2002 is 0.177, which means that this index has increased by 17.7% since 1998, with its average value over the period being 79.6%.

From economic parameters to ageing indexes. Relationship models

Is there, therefore, a relationship between the fertility rate and/or migration on the one hand, and ageing on the other during the 15 years analysed? To answer this

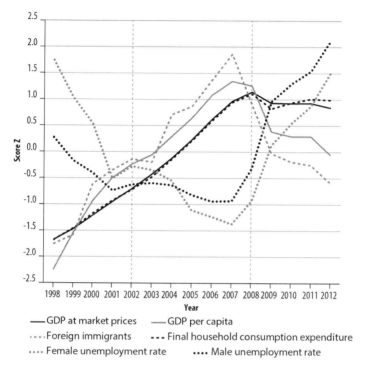

Figure 2.12 Growth, unemployment and migrations. Spain, 1998–2012

Source: Author's calculations based on INE data

last question, we used the technique of multiple linear regression in two stages. More information on the statistical breakdown can be found in Box 2.1. The relationship models used (see Box 2.2) allowed us to establish various relationships between the variables considered. Model 1 confirms that the growth in the TFR was mainly explained by the growth in GDP per capita with a delay of one year, with this index being also closely linked to the other economic variables. The variation in the TFR was a consequence of variations in the production of wealth and in the labour market of the previous year. Model 2 shows that the entry of foreign immigrants was very closely linked to the evolution in economic variables and unemployment rates, almost immediately, with no delay. Model 3 establishes that the AI is largely explained by the fertility rate variable, even though neither the AI indicator nor the TFR are connected in a strictly linear and direct way during this period. The use of a derived independent variable (TFR² = TFR*TFR) enables to explain the changes in the evolution of the AI. Between 1998 and 2002, the AI and TFR increased; the TFR rose from an extraordinarily low level, and the AI rose logically from this. From 2003 to 2007, the TFR continued to rise, but the proportion of the elderly population decreased. The opposite was true from 2008 onwards. Model 4 shows a relationship between the proportion of elderly persons (EI) on the one hand and the TFR and foreign immigration on the other, but this is less clear than that shown previously with the AI. The reason may be

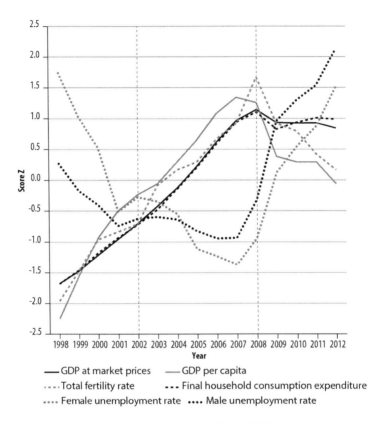

Figure 2.13 Growth, unemployment and fertility. Spain, 1998–2012

Source: Author's calculations based on INE data

the modification in the population age structure that characterised the sudden, substantial drop in the fertility rate in the years prior to 1998. The growth in the domestic product and the fall in male unemployment rates are directly related to the increase in the TFR and the arrival of foreigners. As a growth in the TFR has a direct effect on the decrease in the AI (P_{65+}/P_{0-19}), and an arrival of immigrants causes a fall in the EI (P_{65+}/P_{total}), it can be concluded that ageing is affected by changes in economic indexes. If we break down these analyses according to period, the conclusions are as follows:

For the early period (1998–2002): ageing was rapid, but at the end of the five-year period, it reached a local maximum linked to the start of the recovery of the Spanish economy, the increase in foreign immigration and the rise in the TFR.

In the pre-crisis period (2003–2007): there was a clear break in ageing; the upward trend of the TFR was maintained as well as that of foreign arrivals. This was the period of greater economic prosperity and higher employment rates.

Table 2.2 Growth, unemployment, fertility, migrations and ageing. Rates of variation and average values by five-year period. Spain, 1998–2012

	(2002–1998)/1998	Average (1998–2002)	(2007–2003)/2003	Average (2003–2007)	(2012–2008)/2008	Average (2008–2012)
Proportion of people aged 65 or over	0.177	↑ 79.56 %	−0.002	↓ 85.52 %	0.045	↑ 86.3 %
Ageing index	0.051	↑ 16.84 %	−0.022	↓ 16.79 %	0.052	↑ 16.96 %
Total fertility rate	0.087	↑ 1.212	0.062	↑ 1.338	−0.083	↓ 1.37
Foreign immigrants	6.747	↑ 264,866	1.143	↑ 696,317	−0.514	↓ 469,059
GDP at market prices	0.352	↑ 631,710 M€	0.345	↑ 914,476 M€	−0.054	↓ 1,051,182 M€
GDP per capita	0.130	↑ 19,020 €	0.079	↑ 21,020 €	−0.069	↓ 20,760 €
Final household consumption expenditure	0.322	↑ 368,686 M€	0.338	↑ 518,864 M€	−0.020	↓ 598,396 M€
Male unemployment rate	−0.383	↓ 20.29 %	−0.322	↑ 13.12 %	−0.946	↑ 19.89 %
Female unemployment rate	−0.394	↓ 9.96 %	−0.242	↓ 7.25 %	1.458	↑ 18.69 %

Source: Author's calculations based on INE data

To be read as follows: the rate of change in the proportion of the elderly between 1998 and 2002 is 0.177, which means that this index has increased by 17.7% since 1998, it's average value over the period being 79.6%.

In the critical period (2008–2012): the economic environment suddenly deteriorated. Ageing began again, the TFR resumed its fall and the foreign influx waned.

Characterised by profound changes in fertility and migrations, the pre-crisis and crisis periods are noteworthy in economic, social and demographic terms. Other than the ageing of the population, the crisis appears more like a correction of the previous, somewhat artificial period.

Box 2.1   The following diagram (Figure 2.14) illustrates the steps taken to verify the existence of explanatory statistical models of the variations in the ageing indexes during the period 1998–2012

GDP at market prices
GDP per capita
Final household consumption expenditure
Female unemployment rate
Male unemployment rate

Step 1

Total fertility rate
Foreign immigrants

Step 2

Ageing index
Proportion of people aged 65 or over

Step 1. Adjustment of the dependent variables - total fertility rate and total number of foreign immigrants - using multiple linear regression. The independent variables are the economic variables.
Step 2. Adjustement of the dependent variables : the proportion of the elderly population (EI) and the ageing index (AI). The independent variables are the total fertility rate (TFR) and the total number of foreign immigrants. The derived independent variables, TFR²=TFRxTFR, were calculated to explain the changes in inclination. Beyond the direct expression of the variables, delays of one and two years were posed assuming a phase-shifted temporal effect of the independent variables on the dependent variable. We also considered that the adjustment might be a curvilinear function. The regression technique used was that of linear least squares with Stepwise Forward selection of independent variables (Stata 14.0).

Figure 2.14 Steps of the model

Box 2.2   Relationship models of economic variables, fertility, migrations and ageing. Spain, 1998–2012

The four models that emerge are successive adjustments of the dependent variables of steps 1 and 2.

Model 1	Dependent variable: Total fertility rate		
	Standardised coefficients **Beta**[a]	**Sig.**[b]	**adjusted R²**[c]
(Constant)		0.000	0.916
GDP per capita (with a one-year time lag)	0.961	0.000	

Model 2	Dependent variable: Total number of foreign immigrants		
	Standardised coefficients		
	Beta[a]	**Sig.[b]**	**adjusted R[2c]**
(Constant)		0.000	0.945
GDP per capita	0.887	0.000	
Male unemployment rate	−0.311	0.000	

Model 3	Dependent variable: Ageing index		
	Standardised coefficients		
	Beta[a]	**Sig.[b]**	**adjusted R[2c]**
(Constant)		0.000	0.909
Total fertility rate	18.348	0.000	
(Total fertility rate)[2]	−17.589	0.000	

Model 4	Dependent variable: Proportion of persons aged 65 or over		
	Standardised coefficients		
	Beta[a]	**Sig.[b]**	**adjusted R[2c]**
(Constant)		0.005	0.600
Total fertility rate	25.807	0.001	
(Total fertility rate)[2]	−25.328	0.001	
Total number of foreign immigrants	−0.630	0.044	

[a] Comparable weighting of each independent variable in the model

[b] Significance of each coefficient ($p < 0.05$)

[c] Value of the adjustment of the multiple linear model

The same future in spite of different hypotheses

According to the United Nations[12] (2013), Spain could be, demographically, the fourth-oldest country in the world in 2050, with 34.5% of the population aged 65 or over, and Japan holding first place (36.6%). The projections by Eurostat (2014) and those by the INE (2012), based on other combinations of hypotheses, calculate proportions of 33.0% and 36.6% in 2052, respectively. Their differences notwithstanding, the evolutions in the age structure foreseen by these perspectives appear, in many ways, to be optimistic, particularly as regards the expected fertility levels. Although the hypotheses regarding mortality are very similar in the projections analysed, the differences in the other two phenomena are, on the contrary, much more marked (Table 2.3).

The evolution in the fertility rate upon which the perspectives are based continues the trend of the second half of the 2000s and indeed does not take the reversal linked to the economic crisis into account at all. They assume (in all

Table 2.3 Hypotheses of the demographic perspectives for Spain produced by the United Nations (medium variant, 2013), Eurostat (2014) and the INE (2012)

ISF	2012***	2017	2022	2027	2032	2037	2042	2047	2052
UN	1.50	1.57	1.63	1.67	1.71	1.74	1.77	1.79	1.81
INE	1.42	1.45	1.48	1.50	1.51	1.53	1.54	1.55	1.56
EUROSTAT	1.32	1.35	1.38	1.40	1.43	1.45	1.47	1.49	1.51
e_0	2012***	2017	2022	2027	2032	2037	2042	2047	2052
Male UN	78.76	79.52	80.26	80.96	81.64	82.29	82.94	83.57	84.19
Female UN	85.24	86.00	86.74	87.44	88.12	88.78	89.42	90.04	90.66
Male INE	79.09	80.30	81.43	82.49	83.50	84.45	85.36	86.22	86.88
Female INE	84.99	85.87	86.70	87.49	88.24	88.96	89.63	90.27	90.75
Male EUROSTAT	79.50	80.10	80.80	81.50	82.10	82.80	83.40	84.00	84.60
Female EUROSTAT	85.20	85.70	86.20	86.80	87.30	87.80	88.30	88.80	89.30
Projected net migrations	2010–2014	2015–2019	2020–2024	2025–2029	2030–2034	2035–2039	2040–2044	2045–2049	2050–2054
UN	599,997	499,998	500,002	500,002	449,998	499,997	500,000	499,999	450,001
INE*	−836,877	−620,584	−397,951	−229,494	−98,915	16,080	128,763	235,576	303,253
EUROSTAT**	−986,145	−407,374	−226,855	195,660	585,657	933,451	1,224,563	1,406,955	1,497,233

* INE 2010–2014 and 2050–2054: average of the available annual data (2012–2014 and 2050–2051) of projected immigrants and emigrants

** EUROSTAT 2010–2014: average of the available annual data (2013–2014) of the projected net migrations

*** For EUROSTAT data from 2013

projections, whether of the United Nations, Eurostat or the INE) that the fertility rate in Spain can only rise – an optimistic hypothesis to say the least. As regards migrations, the United Nations Population Division assumes that Spain can only maintain a strong net attraction, a plausible hypothesis, but one contingent on a rapid return to sustained economic growth. Regardless of the underlying combinations of hypotheses, all the projections demonstrate the inevitability of the Spanish population ageing, with a third of it likely to be 65 years or over in 2052. Less pronounced ageing could be achieved through particularly intense foreign influxes, a rise in fertility rates to very high levels,[13] or even particularly selective mortality, a hypothesis never contemplated in the official projections. The ageing trend could be accompanied by a decline in the total population and a fall in the number of individuals of working age. The outcome could be additional difficulties financing pensions, with a resulting decline in the living conditions of the elderly. All projections assume that the trend towards a lengthening of the schedule of mortality will be maintained, as this trend is long-standing. In a context of shrinking budgets allocated for public health, a consequence of the continued crisis or of sustained economic stagnation, an increase in mortality induced by a deterioration in the population's state of health[14] is a remote and perhaps too rapid scenario. Under certain conditions (selective mortality), it might even have the effect of slightly limiting the extent of the demographic ageing to come.

The effect of the fertility rate on ageing seems to be more important. The long-term trends in the primary determinants of the fertility rate (average age at first birth, average age at marriage, proportion of children born outside marriage, proportion of interrupted pregnancies (VTP), proportion of women with higher education, etc.) mostly contribute to a decline in the TFR. Meanwhile, family support policies or those favouring the reconciliation of family and professional lives, already relatively modest before the crisis, have all been reduced. Moreover, the unemployment level remains very high, temporary jobs are increasing and poverty is spreading, thus all the conditions are in place for reproduction to stagnate at very low levels, unless Spain can recover from the crisis quickly and lastingly.

Even more than the fertility rate, migrations are closely dependent on the health of economies. According to the *Estadística de Variaciones Residenciales* [Residential Variation Statistics] published by the INE – which has recorded foreign entries into Spain since 1998 – nearly 7.5 million people entered between 1998 and 2013 (the latest year for which data are available), with a peak of 920,534 entries during 2007 alone. In Spain, which was a country of emigration for a long time,[15] the migration factor has undoubtedly changed. However, the latest data show a collapse in immigration (307,000 foreign entries in 2013 – i.e., 24,000 fewer than in 2000, the first year of the wave of foreign entries, and 615,000 less than in 2007) and an intensification of emigration: either foreign citizens returning to their native country or searching for another host country, or Spaniards looking for jobs they can no longer find in their country. In a context of global economic crisis and increased international mobility, Spain does not have the capacity of its competitors to attract new immigrants and retain its own citizens. The sustained economic growth currently experienced by several Latin American countries[16] is limiting the number of potential candidates for emigration and may prompt foreign citizens in insecure situations in Spain to return home.

For all the reasons stated earlier, ageing in Spain is very likely to continue its advance at a more sustained pace than that projected by the United Nations, Eurostat or the INE. Indeed, another scenario is possible, that of the current poor economic situation being maintained, resulting in worsening health care and support for the dependent elderly and, ultimately, a rise in mortality that could check the ageing process. But is this really a desirable scenario?

The current Spanish population's age structure is the result of numerous and profound changes in behaviours that have taken place for over a century and of more recent events – the 2008 crisis – that will probably have a lasting impact. There is little evidence to indicate that the future holds anything but an ageing trend for Spain. The uncertainty lies not in the trend but in the magnitude of future ageing and in the ability of Spanish society to meet the immense challenge it faces!

Notes

1 The analyses conducted and the comments expressed are those of the text's authors alone.
2 Certain data are only available until 2013.
3 For example, the 2015 Nobel Prize winner for Economics, Angus Deaton (2012), devoted his opinion column in the newspaper El País, of March 11, 2012, to the crisis and its consequences: 'Life in times of austerity'.
4 Voluntary termination of pregnancy is considered to be another element to be included in the SDT, according to Van de Kaa (2002, pp. 9–10)
5 EI = (P65+ / Ptot) * 100; proportion of persons aged 65 or over.
6 AI = (P65+ / P0–19) * 100; ageing index.
7 SI = (P85+ / P65+) * 100; super-ageing index.
8 In Spain, where the number of foreign citizens was estimated at less than 200,000 in 1981, there were, according to the INE, 5,751,487 of them in 2011 and some 700,000 less (5,072,680) in 2013.
9 Uxó González, J. (2015), in Expansión. www.expansion.com/diccionario-economico/crisis-economica.html
10 Claessens and Kose (2009, p. 52).
11 CIS: Centro de Investigaciones Sociológicas (Centre for Sociological Research). Indicador de confianza del consumidor. Mes de octubre. Evolución de indicadores, *Estudio n°3.003*. Octubre 2013.
12 This is the medium variant.
13 The TFR would have to reach 7.5 children per woman in order for the proportion of those aged 65 or over in 2051 to be at the same level as in 2001 (16.9%); in order for the AI (P65+/P15–64) to also be at its 2001 level (24.7%) in 2051, the fertility rate would have to be between 10 and 11 children per woman (Zamora López, 2005).
14 On this subject, see Legido-Quigley et al. (2013).
15 The Spanish Ministry of Labour recorded more than 4.7 million departures between 1885 and 1940 and more than 1.7 million between 1946 and 1975. By comparison, only 0.3 million emigrants were recorded between 1976 and 2000.
16 According to IMF data, all countries of South America, except Argentina, Brazil and Venezuela, are expected to register a growth of more than 3.0% in their domestic product in 2015.

References

Arbelo Curbelo, A. (1962). *La mortalidad de la infancia en españa, 1901–1950*. Madrid: Consejo Superior de Investigaciones Científicas – Dirección General de Sanidad.
Caldwell, J. C. (2008). *Three fertility compromises and two transitions. Population Research and Policy Review*, 27(4), 427–446.

Castells, M., Caraça, J. M. G. and Cardoso, G. (Eds.). (2012). *Aftermath: the cultures of the economic crisis*. Oxford: Oxford University Press.

Claessens, S. and Kose, M. A. (2009). What *is a recession? Finance and Development*, 46(1), 52–53.

Cliquet, R. L. (1991). *The Second Demographic Transition: fact or fiction?* Strasbourg: Conseil de l'Europe.

Coleman, D. (2004). Why we don't have to believe without doubting in the 'Second Demographic Transition' – Some agnostic comments. *Vienna Yearbook of Population Research*, 2, 11–24.

Davis, K. (1945). The world demographic transition. *Annals of the American Academy of Political and Social Science*, 237, 1–11.

Deaton, A. (2012). La vida en tiempo de austeridad. *El País*.

Delgado, M. and López, F. Z. (2006). La contribución de las mujeres extranjeras a la dinámica demográfica en España. *Sistema*, (190–191), 143–166.

Delgado, M., Meil, G. and Zamora-López, F. (2008). Spain: short on children and short on family policies. *Demographic Research*, 19(27), 1059–1104.

Delgado, M. and Zamora-López, F. (2004). Españolas y extranjeras: su aportación a la fecundidad en España. *Economistas*, 99, 88–97.

Delgado, M., Zamora-López, F., Barrios, L., Camara Izquierdo, N., Alberdi, I. and De Rose, A. (2009). *Fecundidad y trayectoria laboral de las mujeres en España*. Madrid: Instituto de la Mujer.

Delgado Pérez, M., Barrios, L. and Zamora López, F. (2006). Déficit de fecundidad en España: factores demográficos que operan sobre una tasa muy inferior al nivel de reemplazo. *Revista Española de Investigaciones Sociológicas*, 115, 197–226.

Díez Nicolás, J. (1985). La mortalidad en la guerra civil española. *Boletín de la ADEH*, III(1), 41–55.

Grusky, D. B., Western, B. and Wimer, C. (Eds.). (2011). *The Great Recession*. New York: Russell Sage Foundation.

Kirk, D. (1996). Demographic transition theory. *Population Studies*, 50(3), 361–387.

Landry, A. (1934). *La Révolution Démographique: études et essais sur les problèmes de la population*. Paris: Sirey.

Legido-Quigley, H., Otero, L., Parra, D. la, Alvarez-Dardet, C., Martin-Moreno, J. M. and McKee, M. (2013). Will austerity cuts dismantle the spanish healthcare system? *British Medical Journal*, 346, f2363.

Lesthaeghe, R. and Surkyn, J. (2004). When history moves on: the foundations and diffusion of a Second Demographic Transition, in: *Paper presented at the Seminar on Ideational Perspectives on International Family Change*. Ann Arbor: Population Studies Center – Institute for Social Research – University of Michigan.

Livi-Bacci, M. (2001). Comment: desired family size and the future course of fertility, in: Bulatao, R. A. and Casterline, J. B. (Eds.), *Global Fertility Transition* (pp. 282–290). Supplement to PDR, Vol. 27. New York: Population Council.

Nadal, J. (1984). *La población española (Siglos XVI a XX)*. Barcelona: Ariel.

Notestein, F. W. (1944). Problems of policy in relation to areas of heavy population pressure. *The Milbank Memorial Fund Quarterly*, 22(4), 424–444.

Notestein, F. W. (1945). Population: the long view, in: Schultz, P. T. (Ed.), *Food for the World* (pp. 36–57). Chicago: University of Chicago Press.

Pascua, M. (1934). *La mortalidad infantil en España*. Madrid: Departamento de Estadísticas Sanitarias de la Dirección General de Sanidad.

Pérez-Agote, A. (2008). La secularización de los Españoles, in: Pérez-Agote, A. (Ed.), *Religión y política en la sociedad actual*. Debate social. Madrid: Editorial Complutense: Centro de Investigaciones Sociológicas.

Puyol Antolín, R. (1988). *La poblacion española*. Madrid: Editorial Sintesis.

Reques Velasco, P. (2006). La población de las comunidades autónomas españolas: transición demográfica, estructura actual y retos futuros, in: Fernández Cordón, J. A. and Leal Maldonado, J. (Eds.), *Análisis territorial de la demografía española: 2006* (pp. 85–114). Madrid: Fundación Fernando Abril Martorell.

Sobotka, T. (2008). The diverse faces of the Second Demographic Transition in Europe. *Demographic Research*, S7(8), 171–224.

United Nations, Department of Economic and Social Affairs and Population Division. (2013). *World Population Prospects: The 2012 Revision*. New York: United Nations.

Uxó González, J. (2015). Crisis económica. *Expansión*. Retrieved from www.expansion.com/diccionario-economico/crisis-economica.html

Van de Kaa, D. J. (1987). Europe's Second Demographic Transition. *Population Bulletin*, 42(1), 1–59.

Van De Kaa, D. J. (2002). The idea of a Second Demographic Transition in industrialized countries, in: *Paper presented at the Sixth Welfare Policy Seminar of the National Institute of Population and Social Security* (p. 34). Tokyo (Japan). Retrieved from www.ipss.go.jp/webj-d/WebJournal.files/population/2003_4/Kaa.pdf

Van De Kaa, D. J. (2004). Demographic revolutions or transitions. A foreword, in: Frejka, T. and Sardon, J.-P. (Eds.), *Childbearing trends and prospects in low-fertility countries: a cohort analysis*. European Studies of Population. Dordrecht: Kluwer Academic Publishers.

Van De Kaa, D. J. (2008). *Demographic transitions*. The Hague: Netherlands Interdisciplinary Demographic Institute.

Zamora López, F. (2005). La España que viene. *Papeles de Economía Española*, (104), 330–346.

3 From multifaceted transition to rapid ageing

Morocco at the dawn of a new era

Muriel Sajoux

After having experienced a particularly robust population expansion during the twentieth century, Morocco, like the majority of southern countries, is displaying a major demographic mutation as it enters the twenty-first century, with numerous economic and social issues: the ageing of its population. This is the result of a rapid demographic transition: the Moroccan population increased seven-fold in just over a century, rising from 5 million inhabitants in 1900 to close to 34 million in 2014 (HCP,[1] 2015). This growth was sustained until the early 1970s as a consequence of the falling mortality rate; it then slowed as the fertility rate declined. In just a few decades, Moroccan demographic dynamics has undergone a radical transformation. This chapter analyses the development of this rapid transition's main factors by highlighting both the differences between men and women according to their place of residence and the complexity of the mechanisms involved. Studying the fluctuations in the fertility and mortality rates allows us to understand the demographic transition's effects on the ageing of the Moroccan population and thus to measure the ongoing metamorphosis. Morocco, a young country, has seen a broad and rapid increase in the proportion of senior citizens and their numbers. Putting this into perspectives allows us to identify the various issues with which Moroccan society will have to contend in order to respond economically and socially to the rapid ageing to come.

Gaining years of life: mortality and places of residence in Morocco

The decrease in the probability of dying young has been the main engine for Morocco's rising life expectancy at birth. Indeed, recent decades have seen a remarkable fall in child mortality. The child mortality rate (amongst children under five years of age) was cut by three in 30 years,[2] dropping from 118 per 1,000 live births in the early 1980s to 36 per 1,000 births in 2010. During this period, the marked differences in mortality between rural and urban areas were widely reduced, as the abnormally high death rate of children in rural regions is now a third higher than that in urban areas (these differences reached their highest point in the 1990s, during which period it was twice as high). Nevertheless, the drop in young age mortality is not the sole reason for the increase in the lifespan; other age groups have benefited from the rapid spread of advances in sanitation and medicine, women giving birth in particular, but also those over the age of 60. Though they vary by gender and place of residence, these gains in years for seniors have allowed the period of 'old age' to become an increasingly long stage in the life cycle.

Life expectancy at birth: male/female differences and urban/rural disparities

The fall in the mortality rate in Morocco has led to a considerable increase in life expectancy. This was only 43 years in 1952, but it increased to 75 years by 2010 (Table 3.1). Disparities in life expectancy between places of residence, whilst still present, are tending to narrow. In 1980, life expectancy at birth for urban men (63 years) was 14% higher than that of rural men (55.4 years). Thirty years later, this relative difference had halved: life expectancy at birth for urban men (76 years) was 7% higher than that of rural men (71 years). For women, the relative difference decreased even more, going from 13% in 1980 (a life expectancy at birth of 65 years in urban areas and 57.6 years in rural areas) to 5% in 2010 (78 years in urban areas and 74 years in rural areas).

It is during the 2000s that life expectancy amongst women in rural areas rose rapidly thanks, in particular, to the significant drop in maternal mortality. In rural areas, this rate fell 45% over the course of about ten years, from 267 maternal deaths per 100,000 live births in the period 1994–2003 to 148 in 2009–2010 (Bencheikh and Fassi Fihri, 2012). However, this cannot alone explain the significant reduction in the difference in female life expectancy between places of residence, since the maternal mortality rate in urban areas fell by 61% between these two periods, going from 187 down to 73 maternal deaths per 100,000 live births. The difference in life expectancy by place of residence also results from a lengthening of the period of old age which is now seen in both in rural and urban areas and which involves women more than men.

Life expectancy at older ages: towards a lengthening of the period of 'old age'

As the idea of old age is a social construct (Caradec, 2015), it is impossible to determine a single threshold which is valid for any time or place. However, in demographics the average overall length of 'old age' can be calculated based on the life expectancy at 'older' ages greater than or equal to 60 years. According to the United Nations estimates, life expectancy at 60 in Morocco, which is in the order of 19 years in the 2010s, should exceed 23 years by 2050 (Table 3.2). The number of years left to live after 60 has not stopped growing.

The scale of the phenomenon also varies according to the place of residence. Indeed, the lifespan of men over 60 living in urban areas is 21.3 years, compared to 17.5 years in rural areas, the differential thus being 3.8 years (Table 3.3). Amongst women, this is lower, being 2.4 years. A similar configuration exists for life expectancy at 70 years: this is over three years higher amongst men in urban areas and two years higher amongst women.

Table 3.1 Life expectancy at birth in Morocco, by gender and place of residence, from 1952 to 2010 (in years)

Area	Urban		Rural		Urban/rural comparison		Overall		
Year	Males (1)	Females (2)	Males (3)	Females (4)	Males (1)/(3)	Females (2)/(4)	Males	Females	Overall
1952	–	–	–	–	–	–	–	–	42.9
1962	57.0	–	43.0	–	–	–	–	–	47.0
1967	50.1	–	47.2	–	–	–	–	–	48.2
1980	63.0	65.0	55.4	57.6	1.14	1.13	58.1	60.2	59.1
1987	67.8	71.8	61.1	63.0	1.11	1.14	63.7	66.4	65.0
1999	70.6	74.9	65.6	67.5	1.08	1.11	67.5	71.5	69.5
2010	76.0	78.0	71.0	74.0	1.07	1.05	73.0	76.0	75.0

Sources: United Nations and surveys and reports by the Centre d'Etudes et de Recherches Démographiques (CERED*) [Centre for Demographic Studies and Research] and the High Commission for Planning (HCP).
1952: United Nations. 1962: EOM 1961–1963, Enquête à Objectifs Multiples [Multiple Objectives Survey].
1967, 1980, 1999: CERED and HCP. 1987 et 2010: ENDPR 1986–1988 et 2009–2010, Enquête nationale démographique à passages répétés [National multiround demographic survey].
* This Moroccan demographic research centre is attached to the High Commission for Planning.

Table 3.2 Life expectancy at 60 (in years), Morocco, 1960–2050

	1960–1965	1980–1985	2010–2015	2045–2050
Males	14.0	15.2	18.5	22.4
Females	15.1	16.8	19.7	24.1
Overall	14.6	16.0	19.1	23.3

Source: Population Division of the Department of Economic and Social Affairs of the United Nations Secretariat, World Population Prospects: The 2015 Revision

Table 3.3 Life expectancy at older ages, Morocco, 2009–2010

Age x	Life expectancy at age x urban area		Life expectancy at age x rural area		Urban/Rural comparison		Life expectancy at age x the whole country	
	Males (1)	Females (2)	Males (3)	Females (4)	Males (1)/(3)	Females (2)/(4)	Males	Females
60	21.3	22.7	17.5	20.3	1.22	1.12	19.5	21.6
65	17.0	18.3	13.4	16.1	1.27	1.14	15.3	17.3
70	12.9	14.0	9.7	12.0	1.33	1.17	11.4	13.1
75	9.3	10.1	6.6	8.5	1.41	1.19	8.0	9.4
80	6.3	6.8	4.5	5.7	1.40	1.19	5.5	6.3
85	4.2	4.4	3.3	3.9	1.27	1.13	3.8	4.2
90	3.1	3.2	2.8	3.0	1.11	1.07	3.0	3.1
95	2.5	2.5	2.5	2.5	1.00	1.00	2.5	2.5

Source: Bencheikh and Fassi Fihri (2012, pp. 38–40)

*This data should be treated with caution, as errors in age reporting may have affected some of the results. These errors are probably more common in the older age groups, since the individuals concerned were born during periods in which civil registration was not necessarily carried out immediately after birth, and even at times many years after birth.

Measured in relative terms, the difference in life expectancy between places of residence is, 22% at 60 years of age for men and then increases in line with age. It peaks at 75 and 80 years of age: life expectancy for men living in urban areas is then 40% higher than that of men living in rural areas. The widening in this relative difference between 60 and 80 years of age can be partly explained by the rural populations' relative lack of access to health care. As regards rural abnormally high death rate, the impact of this lack increases as individuals are ageing and are being exposed to multiple illnesses with increasing frequency. Amongst women, this relative difference also increases between 60 and 80 years of age, but is lower than amongst men at all ages, remaining within a narrower range of 12% to 19% (Table 3.3).

Differences in living conditions and access to health care are one of the main reasons for the higher rural mortality at older ages. Not only do 'older' individuals have greater difficulties obtaining treatment in rural areas but also in country areas they may have generally received less medical care throughout the lives. They thus more frequently enter 'old age' with undiagnosed illnesses. The fact that the differential in life expectancy between the two places of residence is less for women than men should be studied in greater depth. One explanation for this could be that women generally have a different relationship with their health and bodies than men, in particular thanks to the benefit of the gynaecological and obstetric treatment they receive. Nevertheless, this cannot be the sole reason, as women currently aged between 60 and 70 spent the majority of their reproductive lives in the 1960s to the 1990s. And yet, even at the end of the 1990s, there were still marked disparities in reproductive health care between the two places of residence.[3] Although the increase in the average length of 'old age' is a major advance, it undeniably represents a considerable issue for Morocco as the country was late in considering the management of this phenomenon. This development of 'advanced age' is also accompanied by a rapid fall in the fertility rate, which also contributes to the ageing of the population.

Ageing from the bottom of the age pyramid: a fertility transition reflecting multiple mechanisms

Moroccan towns and countryside: from divergence to convergence as regards fertility rates

Whilst Moroccan women were giving birth to an average of 7.2 children in the 1960s, the current total fertility rate (TFR) is 2.2 children per woman. Although the fertility rate in Morocco began to fall in the 1960s, it should be noted that until the mid-1970s, this general trend was, in reality, only the result of a drop in urban fertility, as rural fertility rates remained very high (Figure 3.1). The rural fertility rate began to fall later, decreasing by 1.5 children per woman between 1977 and 1991. Subsequently, over the course of the 1990s, the rural fertility rate dropped much more rapidly than it had done previously; thus, between 1991 and 2004, the rural TFR decreased by 2.4 children per woman (from 5.5 to 3.1). The rural fertility rate has fallen steadily ever since from 2.7 children per woman in 2010

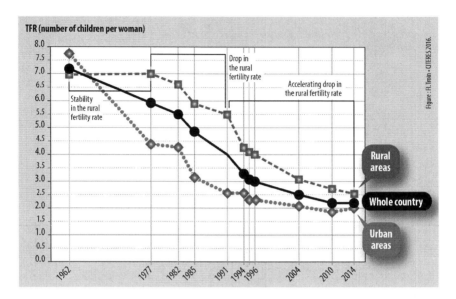

Figure 3.1 Evolution in the fertility rate in Morocco, by place of residence, 1962–2014

Sources: Surveys by the Ministry of Health for 1962, 1977, 1985, 1991 and 1995; Surveys on standards of living for 1996; RGPH for 1982, 1994, 2004 and 2014; ENDPR for 2010.

to 2.55 in 2014. As for the urban fertility rate, this is now below the generation replacement level, as it reached 1.8 children per woman in 2010 and is around 2.01 children per woman in 2014.

The rise in the urban fertility rate between 2010 and 2014, measured by the national multiround demographic survey of 2009–2010 and the 2014 general census of population and habitat, respectively, should be studied in-depth. Nevertheless, it is clear that over the last five decades, the fertility rate in Morocco has dropped according to a different timetable in the two places of residence. Having displayed an increasing differential until the early 1990s (in 1991, urban and rural fertility rates were, respectively, 2.5 and 5.5 children per woman), reproductive behaviours in the two places of residence converged rapidly, as a consequence of an accelerating drop in the rural fertility rate: the difference in birth rates between the two areas was only 0.54 children per woman in 2014.

The progression of the fertility transition across the whole of the Moroccan territory is also illustrated by the decrease in the differences in fertility between regions. Thus an analysis of the evolution in fertility rates at a regional level (Sajoux and Chahoua, 2012) shows that inter-regional differences reduced noticeably between 1982 and 2004. A study of both places of residence shows that the maximum fertility rate difference (that between the minimum and maximum TFR values) was halved between 1982 and 2004, falling from 3.2 to 1.5 children per woman.[4] The results of the 2014 census, which were presented in the new administrative division into 12 regions introduced in early 2015, display a maximum difference in fertility rate of one child per woman. The highest fertility rate (2.9 children per

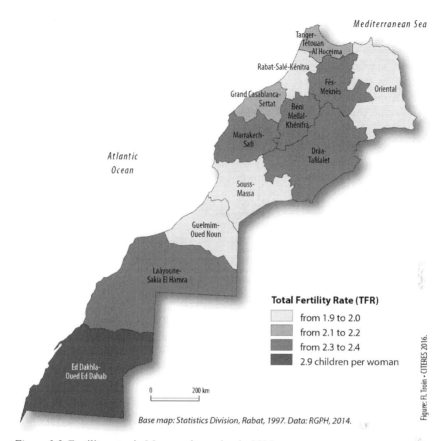

Figure 3.2 Fertility rates in Morocco by region in 2014

woman) was recorded in the Ed Dakhla-Oued-Ed Dahab region (the most southerly Saharan region). The lowest was recorded in the Oriental region (1.9 children per woman). Other than the aforementioned Saharan region, the fertility rate in Morocco's regions ranges from 1.9 to 2.4 children per woman (Figure 3.2).

Evolution of the determining factors related to fertility:
confirming the convergence of urban and rural behaviours

In a context in which procreation is only socially acceptable within the framework of marriage, two key elements have contributed to the drop in fertility: the fall in the average age of women at first marriage and the spread of the use of contraceptives amongst married couples. In the early 1960s, the average age of women at first marriage was fairly similar in both places of residence: 17.2 years in rural areas and 17.5 years in urban areas. By 1987, it had risen notably in urban areas, as it was then 25.4 years and 21.5 years in rural areas. It subsequently increased in a more sustained fashion in rural areas than in urban areas: a difference of 1.6 years between the two places of residence was noted in 2004. Women were then marrying for the first time at an average age of 27.1 years in urban areas and 25.5 in rural areas. Between 2004 and 2014, the difference in age at first marriage between urban and rural women remained almost identical (1.5 years in 2014), but a fall in this age at first union was observed for the first time in both places of residence, marking thus a halt in the uninterrupted rise seen in previous years. In 2014, the average age of women at first marriage was 26.4 years in urban areas and 24.9 in rural areas. As for the use of contraception by women within marriage, this was considerably higher in urban than in rural areas, with levels of 36% and 9.7%, respectively, in 1979–1980. Twelve years later, although this level has risen more than threefold in rural areas, there was still a marked difference between the two places of residence: 55% in urban areas and 33% in rural areas in 1992. In 2003–2004, these levels were only six percentage points apart: 66% in urban areas and 60% in rural areas. In 2011, the difference was only 3.4 points: contraceptive use amongst married women had reached 68.9% in urban areas and 65.5% in rural areas (Ministère de la santé, 2012). The adoption of the ideas of family planning and limiting family size appears to have permeated both places of residence in a similar fashion.

The recent unprecedented drop in women's age at first marriage may indicate that a maximum threshold has been reached, both in terms of delaying these first nuptials and of dropping fertility rates. If these trends continue, fertility rates are not expected to fall below their current levels of just over two children per woman nationally. This is nearly the same level as the current French fertility rate (1.96 children per woman in 2015). Though this is not sufficient to explain the similarity of fertility levels between the two countries, it is nevertheless interesting to note that Morocco and France have particularly close ties on the migratory and/or economic fronts. The human exchanges[5] resulting from these ties may contribute to an increasingly shared vision and behaviour as regards procreation and the size of nuclear families. Indeed, there are clearly more similarities in reproductive behaviours between France and Morocco than between France and Spain (1.32 children per woman in 2014) or between Morocco and Algeria. The latter indeed displayed a fertility rate of 3.1 children per woman in 2015[6]: since 2000, when it had dropped to 2.2 children per woman (Ouadah-Bedidi et al., 2012), the Algerian fertility rate has steadily increased.

If, in years to come, fertility rates in Morocco are confirmed as being stable at around two children per woman, this will mean that their role as an engine of the process of ageing from the bottom (of the age pyramid) has reached its maximum power. As a consequence, most of the demographic ageing to come will be the result of decreasing mortality rates and large numbers of those who were born during periods with higher birth rates than today reaching 'advanced age' (those who will be between 60 and 80 years of age in 2030 were born between 1950 and 1970 and those who will reach this age group in 2050 were born between 1970 and 1990).

The fertility transition in Morocco: complex and multifaceted

Having analysed the fertility transition in Morocco, Youssef Courbage (1996) argued that 'Morocco is ranked in the lowest quartile of countries in terms of female illiteracy, but in the highest quartile as regards its fertility rate'. This apparently paradoxical configuration indicated a possible disconnection between Morocco's fertility transition and traditional socio-economic determining factors. This is largely due to the singular character of the rural fertility transition which questions the traditional model of demographic transition (Sajoux, 2001). Indeed, the decrease in rural fertility accelerated greatly in the early 1990s. However, several socio-economic indicators demonstrated that Morocco's fertility transition could not be considered as falling under the 'traditional' theory in which fertility rates and development are linked by an inverse relationship. For instance, rural women's access to education lagged considerably behind that of urban women during this period, yet, improving levels of education is often considered a crucial prerequisite for reducing fertility rates. In 1994, when rural fertility rates were already beginning to fall rapidly, nearly nine out of ten rural women were illiterate. This was only the case in five out of ten urban women. In 1994, illiteracy rates amongst women aged between 25 and 34 (those in the age group with the highest birth rates) were particularly high in rural areas: 92.6% for those aged 25–29 and 95.2% for those aged 30–34. Access to education thus cannot explain the considerable decrease in the fertility rate of women in these age groups in comparison to previously recorded levels. It is more likely to be due to the desire of women (but also of couples) to increase their offspring's chances of obtaining an education, an education which they had not received. This may in part explain the considerable reduction in the fertility rate within a largely illiterate population. By devoting their resources – which were much lower than those of their urban counterparts – to a limited number of children, they increased the household's possibility of investing in each one of them, particularly as regards education. Thus a compromise between quantity and quality of children is introduced within the socio-economically underprivileged population. The singular character of the rural area as regards the link between female education and dropping fertility rates suggest, together with other elements (Sajoux and Chahoua, 2012), that one part of Morocco's demographic transition process approaches patterns of Malthusian poverty.

The consequences of these rapid evolutions in Morocco's fertility and mortality rates are visible in the population's age composition. The population is ageing, with changing dependency ratios and increasing numbers of the elderly, creating new challenges for those Moroccan policymakers responsible for implementing suitable public policies.

Rapid ageing and changing profile of the elderly population: issues for public policies

Projections and territories of ageing

The results of the 2014 census indicate that the relative proportion of those aged under 15 has dropped below 30% for the first time and that the proportion of those 60 and over is touching 10%. Though Morocco is still a relatively young country, it is clearly less so than in the past. The proportion of those under 15 was 1.5 times higher in 1982 (42.2%) than it is today (28%). At the same time, the Moroccan population has begun a rapid ageing process. Between 2004 and 2030, the proportion of those aged over 60 should have practically doubled, and between 2004 and 2050, it should have tripled. By that date, nearly one inhabitant in four should be over 60 in Morocco – i.e., the same proportion as in France today. Thus in less than five decades Morocco will experience an ageing process comparable with that experienced by France over two centuries.[7] From the end of the 2030s, the relative proportion of those aged 60 and over should be greater than that of those under 15– an unprecedented situation in Morocco's demographic history (Figure 3.3).

In territorial terms, there are variations as regards ageing. The results of the 2014 census indicate that 6 out of 10 individuals over the age of 60 live in an urban area. As a proportion of the population of each of the two places of residence, the percentage of the elderly population is a little higher in rural areas (9.9%) than in urban areas (9.4%). In regional terms, the ageing process is more significant in the regions of Beni-Mellal-Khénifra (10.6%), Oriental (10.3%) and Fès-Meknès (10.2%) (Figure 3.4).

Whilst the fertility rate in the Oriental region (1.9 children per woman, the lowest in the country at regional level) may partly explain the more marked ageing of that region, the emigration of those of working age has also probably played a part. The same is true for the two other regions mentioned earlier. A detailed analysis of the reasons for the regional differentials in ageing would be a rich source of information, not only to understand the relative importance of each type of factor (mortality and birth rates, structural effect, migration) but also to better determine the contrasted realities of the elders' living conditions at a local level.

Welfare system and number of elderly people

In absolute numbers, the population aged 60 and over should triple in just over three decades, going from 3.2 million in 2014 to 10 million in 2050 (Figure 3.5). The speed of this evolution follows a similar pattern to that observed in many

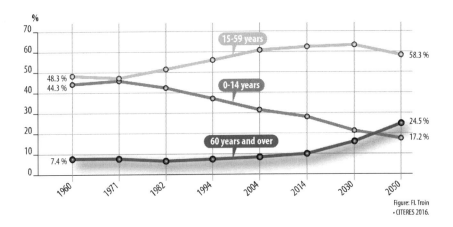

Figure 3.3 Population structure by broad age groups in Morocco

Sources: For 1960, 1971, 1982 and 1994 > CERED, 1998, p. 83–84; 2004 > HCP, 2005, p. 15; 2014 > HCP, 2015; 2030 et 2050 > HCP projections.

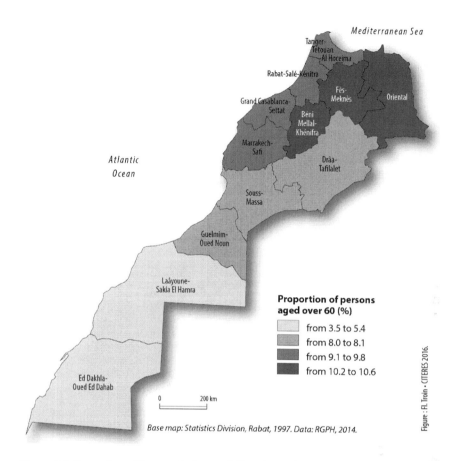

Figure : Fl. Troin • CITERES 2016.

Base map: Statistics Division, Rabat, 1997. Data: RGPH, 2014.

Proportion of persons aged over 60 (%)
- from 3.5 to 5.4
- from 8.0 to 8.1
- from 9.1 to 9.8
- from 10.2 to 10.6

Figure 3.4 Proportion of the population aged 60 and over in Morocco, by region, in 2014

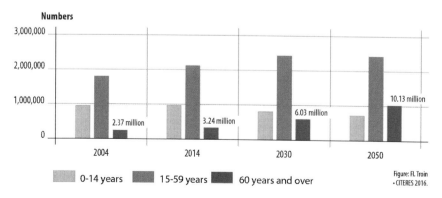

Figure: Fl. Troin • CITERES 2016.

Figure 3.5 Population numbers by broad age groups, Morocco, 2004–2050

Sources: 2004 > HCP, 2005, p. 15; 2014 > HCP, 2015; 2030 and 2050 > HCP projections.

African countries (Sajoux et al., 2015). As for the number of the 'very elderly', aged 75 and over, their number should almost quadruple, going from nearly 748,000 in 2014 to 2.87 million in 2050. Thus the age structure of the elderly population should change, and the average age of the elderly as a whole should increase.

The increase to come in the numbers of the elderly will require substantial effort on the part of public authorities to gradually, but nonetheless swiftly, adapt health-care systems and medical treatments into configurations which are suitable for meeting the needs of an increasingly aged population. This evolution is to be closely linked with an overall reflection on the evolution of the Moroccan welfare system. Currently, a limited proportion of the elderly population is covered by a retirement system (Box 3.1), and many still lack access to medical coverage which fully addresses the elders' health needs (Box 3.2). Although it is essential that demand for care for the elderly must be affordable, it is equally important that what is on offer is adequate. In its recent report on the elderly in Morocco, the Conseil Economique Social et Environnemental [Economic Social and Environmental Council] (CESE, 2015) highlighted the need to 'urgently develop gerontology

---

Box 3.1   An ageing population, partially and unequally covered as regards pensions

In Morocco, pension schemes are contributory and concentrated on formal sector employees. Several systems coexist, with differing legal statuses, methods of management, resources and benefit procedures. There are three mandatory regimes: the *Caisse Nationale de Sécurité Sociale* [National Social Security Fund], which covers the staff of private companies and duly declared agricultural workers; the *Caisse Marocaine des Retraites* [Moroccan Pension Fund], which covers public administration employees; and the *Régime Collectif d'Allocation de Retraite* [Collective Retirement Benefit Scheme] which covers the contracted staff of public administrations and the staff of some public institutions. As for the *Caisse Interprofessionnelle Marocaine de Retraite* [Moroccan Inter-professional Pension Fund], it provides cover for private sector staff on a voluntary and supplementary basis. Currently, there is no universal, non-contributory pension system. According to the latest world report on social protection (International Labour Organization (ILO), 2014), less than 40% of all those of legal retirement age (60 years) were collecting a pension. The results of the 2006 Enquête Nationale sur les Personnes Âgées (ENPA) [National Survey of the Elderly] indicate a much lower proportion: only 16.1% of respondents over 60 years of age stated that they received a pension (HCP, 2008) and there are significant disparities in cover rates by gender and place of residence. Moreover, many retirees are experiencing economic difficulties due to the modest level of their pensions. It is very common for the elderly without a pension to continue to work, particularly in rural areas. In early 2016, the governing Council adopted a bill amending and supplementing the law establishing the civil pension system. According to the terms of this bill, the legal retirement age for civil servants will increase from 60 to 63 by 2019.

Box 3.2   Social welfare and health in old age

Senior citizens experience greater health risks as is shown, for example, by the preva-lence of various chronic diseases as well as by the degree of difficulty encountered in performing various everyday activities (Fassi Fihri, 2009). At the same time, health insurance only covers a small proportion of the elders: according to the results of the 2006 Enquête Nationale sur les Personnes Âgées (ENPA) [National Survey of the Elderly], only 13.3% of senior citizens reported having health cover. This proportion is seven times lower amongst the rural elderly than amongst their urban counterparts: 3.2 compared to 22.4%. Recently established and founded on principles of social assistance and national solidarity in favour of the destitute, the *régime d'assistance médicale* (RAMED) [medical assistance scheme] provided care for just over 0.7 mil-lion people over 60 years of age in 2013 – i.e., 23.5% of senior citizens (Agence Nationale de l'Assurance Maladie (ANAM) [National Health Insurance Agency], Royaume du Maroc, 2014). This means that, although the number of beneficiaries of RAMED has not yet stopped rising, nearly a quarter of the country's senior citizens were experiencing severe economic difficulties, since they fulfilled the conditions for coverage under this assistance system. Developing health-care proposals adapted to the needs of senior citizens appears to be crucial. Using a 2004 study which as-sessed the health facilities in the city of Fez, M. Fassi Fihri (2009) wrote, 'Hospitals suffer from the lack of specialised geriatric structures suited to managing the specific needs of the elderly. Furthermore, there is no multidisciplinary approach for resolv-ing the multiple problems associated with the elderly. Finally, members of healthcare staff are unfamiliar with the characteristics of elderly patients and they are not con-sidered in the care on offer.'

and geriatrics', to 'improve the elderly's access to health services, particularly in rural areas' and to 'improve their medical and paramedical treatment' in order to ensure the elderly's well-being and state of health. The current deficits in these fields, coupled with the scale and speed of demographic changes to come, suggest key issues ahead. Although this is a considerable challenge, the associated oppor-tunities for employment and growth are far from being negligible.

Evolution in the profile of the elderly population: illustrations of changes to come

The way people are ageing is partly based on the individuals' past trajectory (Cara-dec, 2015). Those who are current adults or young adults and who will become elderly in 2050 will have had a variety of experiences marked by a certain number of inequalities (access to education, employment, health, etc.). However, given the major economic and social evolutions experienced by Morocco in a relatively short time, there are several factors which underline the fundamentally different char-acteristics of current senior citizens from future generations of the elderly. Hence, beyond the purely demographic evolution, the elderly Moroccan population should experience significant changes in many of these characteristics in the next decades.

An increasingly educated elderly population

The current elderly population is characterized in particular by a level of education that is, on the whole, low. Thus, in 2014, 70.5% of those aged 60 and over had not attended school, 11.9% had finished primary school, 9% secondary school and 2.4% had received higher education (HCP, 2015). Those aged 80 and over in 2014 were born before 1935; those over 70 were born before 1945, and those over 60 were born before 1955. Accordingly, even the youngest current senior citizens were of school age at a time when school was very far from universal, which explains why more than two-thirds of them have no education. For its part, the 2006 national survey of the elderly highlighted significant disparities in the elderly population: this survey indicated that whilst the overwhelming majority of the elderly (81.7%) had no education, this situation was more frequent amongst women than amongst men (94.3% compared to 68.1%) and more frequent amongst rural residents than urban ones (90.2% compared to 74.1%).

In contrast, those who will be between 60 and 70 years of age in 2030, and therefore over 80 in 2050, were born between 1960 and 1970. They thus belong to generations who reached the age of ten at a time when progress had been made as regards schooling in Morocco, in particular in urban areas, even though significant gender inequalities still persisted. In 1982, the enrolment rate for the population aged between 8 and 13 years was 53.5% nationally, 36.8% in rural areas (23.2% of girls compared to 49.4% of boys) and 78.1% in urban areas (74.1% of girls compared to 82% of boys). As for those who will be between 60 and 70 years of age in 2050, they were born between 1980 and 1990. Compared to previous generations, a much larger proportion of them will have had access to education. According to the 1994 census, the enrolment rate amongst the population aged 8 to 13 years was 62.2% nationally (43.4% in rural areas and 83.9% in urban areas). In 2003–2004, 80.4% of children between 7 and 12 years of age attended school (92% in towns and 68.9% in rural areas). In other words, amongst those who will reach 60 years of age in 2050, no more than two out of ten will be uneducated, compared to seven out of ten today. Considerably more educated, in 2050, the elderly will certainly have very different expectations and lifestyles than can be observed in today's senior citizens. They are likely to make greater demands on public authorities as regards how the latter ensure dignified living conditions for the elderly. At the same time, thanks to their level of education, it will certainly be easier to make the future elderly receptive to health prevention messages. This is a major opportunity which public institutions could seize in order to implement preventive policies for various illnesses, aimed at current adults and young adults. One example of this is high blood pressure, whose prevalence increases sharply with age, increasing the risk of stroke, myocardial infarction and heart failure, etc. The adoption of prevention strategies by the future elderly is likely to enable them to enjoy a healthier 'old age', and thus have a higher level of well-being. Such an option would at the same time generate future savings, on medical goods and services, and more widely in terms of welfare.[8]

Changing family configurations

Tomorrow's more educated senior citizens should also live in different family configurations to those of the current senior citizens. Due to dropping fertility rates, those reaching 'old age' in the 2050s will have family networks very different in size to current ones. The average number of direct lineal and indirect descendants should be very much lower. At the same time, it will become more frequent for two generations (in the sociological sense of the term) of 'senior citizens' to live together; if mortality at older ages continues to fall, the proportion of sexagenarians whose parents are octogenarians or nonagenarians should indeed rise. As regards marriage, those over 60 years of age, and to an even greater extent those over 70, belong to generations for whom marriage was almost universal. Yet the rate of celibacy at 55, referred to as permanent celibacy, has gradually increased. It reached 5.9% in 2014 (compared to 3% in 2004), being 6.7% of women compared to 5.1% of men. It is 8% in urban areas compared to 5.9% in rural areas. It is very difficult to know whether permanent celibacy will increase further in the future. It may never much exceed the current rates in urban areas. Even though this proportion is likely to remain well below 10%, the fact remains that celibacy amongst senior citizens should be more common in the decades to come. Yet, in a context in which having children is socially acceptable only within the framework of marriage, this means that, in comparison with the current prevailing situation, a larger, though limited, proportion of senior citizens will have no direct descendants.

All these factors suggest that future senior citizens' family network that can potentially be mobilized will be very different to that of current senior citizens. This is a major change and it must be taken into account when planning the economic and social response to the demographic ageing to come. The way people are ageing depends on both the 'past trajectory' and the 'current life context, more or less rich in 'resources' (Caradec, 2015). Today, several sources of vulnerability characterize the elderly population in Morocco (Sajoux and Nowik, 2010). Although the demographic realities of old age in the 2030s and 2050s may be considered to be relatively well known, the way individuals will then address this phase of ageing (in terms of accumulated social and economic capital, state of health, etc.) is still an ongoing development and is on no account as yet determined.

Notes

1 The High Commission for Planning (HCP) of Morocco is mainly responsible for producing statistics and planning.
2 Sources: Surveys and reports by HCP and the Ministry of Health, including: ENPS I-1987 II-1992, Enquête Nationale sur la Planification Familiale [National Survey on Family Planning, Fertility and Health in the Moroccan Population]; ENSME 1997, Enquête Nationale sur la Santé de la Mère et de l'Enfant [National Survey on Mother and Child Health]; EPSF 2003–04, Enquête sur la Population et la Santé Familiale [Population and Family Health Survey]; ENDPR 2009–2010, Enquête Nationale Démographique à Passages Répétés [National Multi-round Demographic Survey].
3 This can be illustrated by the fact that during the period 1994–1996 (ENSME 1997) almost 64% of rural women who were pregnant did not have an antenatal consultation compared to 22% of urban women. As regards the proportion of home births, this was 73.4% in rural areas compared to 24.5% in urban areas.
4 The approach used was based on the administrative division into 16 regions in place from 1994 to early 2015. In 1982, the country was divided into seven regions. The analysed results were obtained by recreating an identical division for 1982 to that used in subsequent censuses.
5 For example, the French make up the largest foreign community living in Morocco; it is a third larger than the Algerian community and almost six times greater than the Spanish community (HCP, Royaume du Maroc, 2009, pp. 23–24). Moreover, 'Of all Moroccan

nationals living abroad in 2005 nearly 32.6% were in France, the traditional immigration country, representing 37.9% of those living in Europe. Spain and Belgium were in second and third position respectively, with 18.4% and 12.9% of the Moroccans immigrants in Europe [. . .] ' (Mghari, 2007).

6 Office National des Statistiques, Démographie algérienne 2015, n°740, 16 p., www.ons. dz/IMG/pdf/demographie2015.pdf

7 In France, the proportion of those 60 and over was 8.9% in 1800 and 24.5% in early 2015.

8 For instance, a study carried out by the Caisse Nationale des Organismes de Prévoyance Sociale (CNOPS) [National Fund of Social Welfare Organizations] on the population with acute high blood pressure between 2008 and 2014 amongst policyholders highlighted the significant growth in health-care spending on this illness during this period.

References

ANAM (Agence Nationale de l'Assurance Maladie) and Royaume du Maroc. (2014). *Rapport global annuel 2013 et Plan d'action 2014–2016 relatif au régime d'assistance médicale*. Rabat: ANAM.

Bencheikh, A. and Fassi Fihri, M. (2012). La mortalité au Maroc: principaux résultats de l'Enquête Nationale Démographique à Passages Répétés 2009–2010. *Les Cahiers du Plan*, (39), 30–40.

Caradec, V. (2015). *Sociologie de la vieillesse et du vieillissement*. Paris: Armand Colin.

CESE (Conseil Economique Social et Environnemental). (2015). *Les Personnes âgées au Maroc*. Maroc. Retrieved from www.ces.ma/Documents/PDF/Auto-saisines/AS-20-2015-personnes-agees-au-maroc/Av-AS-20-VF.pdf

Courbage, Y. (1996). *Transition féconde en contexte peu propice: le Maroc de 1962 À 1994*. Le Caire: Congrès Régional Arabe de Population.

Fassi Fihri, M. (2009). Etat de santé et morbidité chez les personnes âgées au Maroc, in: CERED (Centre d'Etudes et de REcherches Démographiques) (Ed.), *Les personnes âgées au Maroc: profil, santé et rapports sociaux, analyse des résultats de l'Enquête Nationale sur les Personnes Âgées (ENPA 2006)* (pp. 95–134). Rabat: HCP (Haut-Commissariat au Plan).

HCP (Haut-Commissariat au Plan). (2005). *Recensement Général de La Population et de l'Habitat 2004. Caractéristiques démographiques et socio-économiques*. Rabat: HCP (Haut-Commissariat au Plan).

HCP (Haut-Commissariat au Plan). (2015). *Recensement Général de La Population et de l'Habitat 2014: présentation des principaux résultats*. Rabat: HCP (Haut-Commissariat au Plan).

HCP (Haut-Commissariat au Plan) and Royaume du Maroc. (2008). *Enquête Nationale sur les Personnes Agées au Maroc 2006*. Rabat: HCP (Haut-Commissariat au Plan).

HCP (Haut-Commissariat au Plan) and Royaume du Maroc. (2009). *Les résidents étrangers au Maroc. Profil démographique et socio-économique*. Rabat: HCP (Haut-Commissariat au Plan).

ILO (International Labour Organization). (2014). *World Social Protection Report: building economic recovery, inclusive development and social justice*. Geneva: International Labour Organization.

Mghari, M. (2007). Profil démographique et mobilité géographique, in: CERED (Centre d'Etudes et de REcherches Démographiques) (Ed.), *Les Marocains résidant à l'étranger analyse des résultats de l'enquête de 2005 sur l'insertion socio-économique dans les pays d'accueil*, (pp. 19–72). Rabat: HCP (Haut-Commissariat au Plan).

Ministère de la santé. (2012). *Enquête Nationale sur la Population et la Santé Familiale (ENPSF-2011)*. Rabat: Ministère de la santé.

Ouadah-Bedidi, Z., Vallin, J. and Bouchoucha, I. (2012). La fécondité au Maghreb: nouvelles surprises. *Population et Sociétés*, (486), 4.

Sajoux, M. (2001). *Développement rural et transition démographique. Le cas du Maroc*, Thesis, Université de Pau et des pays de l'Adour.

Sajoux, M. and Chahoua, S. (2012). Transition de la fécondité et développement au Maroc: Un lien complexe et spatialement différencié. *Les Cahiers d'EMAM*, (21), 33–62.

Sajoux, M., Golaz, V. and Lefèvre, C. (2015). L'Afrique, un continent jeune et hétérogène appelé à vieillir: enjeux en matière de protection sociale des personnes âgées. *Mondes en développement*, 3(171), 11–30.

Sajoux, M. and Nowik, L. (2010). Vieillissement de la population au Maroc. *Autrepart*, 53(1), 17–34.

4 Half a century of ageing in France

Dynamics and specificities of the Mediterranean coastline

Yoann Doignon, Isabelle Blöss-Widmer and Sébastien Oliveau

Demographic and geographic studies of the ageing of the French population have too often left out analysis of the process in its different territorial variations. The more precise issue of the demographic dynamics of the coastline,[1] whose rate of population growth has nonetheless been particularly sustained over the past 15 years, has been studied more precisely in recent years only. Descriptions of the phenomenon or projection models of ageing in France are usually based on data collected at aggregate administrative levels (regions, departments) and focus on the increase in the proportion of the elderly, leaving out the increase in their number (gerontogrowth).[2] Indeed, 'the increase in the elderly population is never mentioned despite it constituting a major issue in planning policies' (Ghékière and Houillon, 2013, p. 60). This chapter proposes to 'make visible' and characterise particular areas of ageing in the French territory, showing how ageing studied at a detailed administrative level reveals local specificities, in particular on the Mediterranean coastline. The simultaneous consideration of the number of the elderly and their proportion, that is to say, their greater or lesser concentration in an area, makes it possible to point out parts of the French territory where 'lifestyles' and infrastructures are more noticeably organised around the specific needs of aged or ageing populations. Indeed,

> one wonders what policies should be followed to accompany this major demographic event [ageing]. Some territories are preparing to accommodate a growing number of elderly people by developing housing stocks, creating suitable structures, pioneering and promoting local services or inter-generational relations. The stakes are very high because in some municipalities the number of elderly and very elderly people is expected to increase significantly over the next two decades.
>
> (Froger et al., 2010, p. 2)

To anticipate the adaptation of areas to changing lifestyles, this chapter demonstrates the significant impact of residential population mobility on the ageing of the French coastal areas, particularly on the Mediterranean coastline. More broadly, it investigates the link between demographic ageing and the process of coastalisation.[3]

After a reminder of the rhythms and specificities of the French demographic ageing, the spatial dimension of ageing will be explored to reveal the close link between this process and the various mobilities of the populations observed. Synthetic mapping[4] of ageing differentiated at the level of the French cantons[5]– i.e., more than 3,700 spatial units, by considering the dynamics of the process over the last 40 years – makes it possible to highlight the existence of specific unexpected features of coastal areas. The methodological originality of the analysis consists in not having isolated a priori given areas of the territory[6] before implementing the necessary statistical tools, but on the contrary in having integrated all the French cantons into the study for an *ex-post* interpretation, 'letting the data speak for themselves' (Gould, 1981). Moreover, the demographic indicators analysed include natural growth (births and deaths) and long-term migration trends (indications of the cantons' greater or lesser attractiveness since 1968), thus allowing a 'dynamic' study of the ageing of the areas.

Ageing and areas: French rhythms and specificities

National ageing, local ageing

In 2014, mainland France had 11 million people aged 65 or over – i.e., about 18% of its total population. In the world ranking of the oldest countries in the world, France is in twenty-third position[7]: one in two inhabitants is over 40 years old, compared to 28.5 in the world as a whole. Since 1950, when it occupied the seventh place worldwide (with a median age of 34.5), France's population has aged considerably (Figure 4.1), after a period of relative rejuvenation (1950–1975).

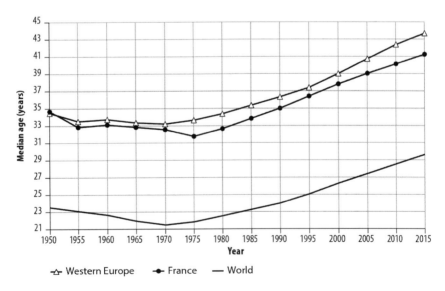

Figure 4.1 France, Western Europe, the world, 1950–2015, changes in the median age of the population

Sources: United Nations, Department of Economic and Social Affairs, Population Division (2015). World Population Prospects: The 2015 Revision, DVD Edition

However, its population has aged much less quickly than other countries, including some Mediterranean countries such as Italy (now in third position behind Japan and Germany), Greece (eighth position) or Spain (twenty-first position), whose positions in the world ranking have risen over the last 60 years. While the continuation of French ageing is programmed[8] by its age pyramid (the baby-boom generations arriving at old age), the phenomenon is nevertheless reduced in comparison to its European neighbours by its sustained and stable natural growth over 40 years: around 4% on average each year (Figure 4.2).

This remarkable natural growth is due to the fact that France is one of the most fertile developed countries in the world (Figure 4.3). Its fertility gives rise to births which offset the deaths of its ageing population. Natural growth (excluding migrations) is alone responsible for about three-quarters of its total growth, depending on the year: it is France's specificity within the European demographic space (Héran, 2004). 'France, uniquely amongst the developed countries, has been able to count on a more or less constant supply of births during the last forty years' (Ambrosetti and Giudici, 2014).

Despite this, in France, as elsewhere in Europe, the proportion of older people keeps growing, as does the median age, which has been rising inexorably since 1975 (Figure 4.1). Indeed, in Europe,

> the acceleration of demographic ageing took place in the second half of the twentieth century, with the end of the first demographic transition and the entry into a second phase: fertility gradually decreased until reaching the level of 1.6 children per woman, while at the same time life expectancy at birth reached 79.6 years.
>
> (Ambrosetti and Giudici, 2014)

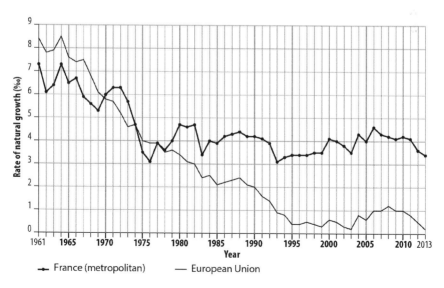

Figure 4.2 France, the European Union, 1960–2013, changes in the rate of natural growth
Sources: Eurostat

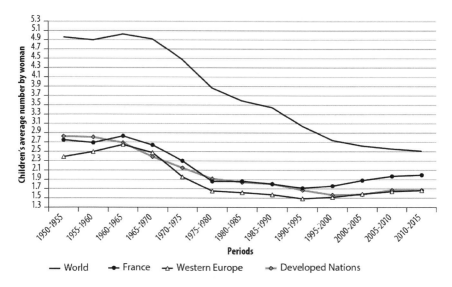

Figure 4.3 France, Europe, the world 1950–2015, changes in the total fertility rate (TFR)

Sources: United Nations, Department of Economic and Social Affairs, Population Division (2015). World Population Prospects: The 2015 Revision, DVD

The diversity of ageing situations becomes more pronounced the more detailed the administrative division becomes. The proportions of the elderly thus vary greatly from one end of France to the other and their rates of change since the mid-1970s are very different. Some simple calculations, based on INSEE data[9] at departmental level in 2014 (second French administrative level, see Figure 4.4), show that the proportion of people aged 65 years or over in one part of the country can be double that in another – i.e., 30% compared to 15%.[10] At a more detailed level, in the cantons (Figure 4.4), it is not uncommon to find more than 40% of the population aged 65 or over, some even having one in two inhabitants aged over 65. In this type of canton, the population profile is thus that of a pensioner in one out of two cases. At the other extreme, there are regions mainly composed of working persons such as executives, higher or intermediate-level intellectual professionals or employees in which only 5% to 6% of the population are aged 65 or over. The reality of the ageing of the different regions is therefore very heterogeneous. Some departments, such as Paris, have even become younger: the proportion of older people is lower today than it was 40 years ago. If we look at it more closely, by breaking the period down, ageing is sometimes a recent phenomenon, due to the possibility of relative slow-downs or rejuvenation observed since the end of the '60s. Counter-intuitively, it is also not always the areas with the highest proportions of the elderly which have experienced the biggest increases. The ageing of certain areas is in fact particularly rapid due to very unfavourable net migration (the departure of young people and the arrival of pensioners) which combine with negative or poorly sustained natural growth. This is, for example, noticeable in some departments of Eastern France or around the capital (with a dramatic increase in the proportion of older people by more than 80% in 40 years).

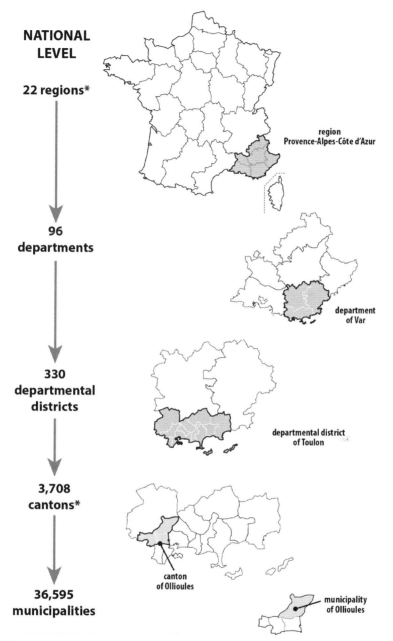

NATIONAL LEVEL

22 regions*

region
Provence-Alpes-Côte d'Azur

96 departments

department
of Var

330 departmental districts

departmental district
of Toulon

3,708 cantons*

canton
of Ollioules

36,595 municipalities

municipality
of Ollioules

* With the law enforcement NOTRe and the departmental reform in August, 2015, France counts from now on 13 regions and the level of cantons disappeared.

Figure 4.4 Complete administrative division of France

Source: IGN (National Institute of Geographic and Forester Information) France, GEOFLA 2-0, mars 2015

As for the 13 departments of the French regions bordered by the Mediterranean,[11] whilst they all have a higher proportion of the elderly than the average, the rate of increase is not unusual because these departments attract younger migrants[12] while retaining their native populations.

The population of France, whilst continuing to grow, is concentrated 'in the southern and western regions' (Léon, 2008, p. 137) – i.e., 'in the south of France' – whilst ageing affects the northern half of the country, except for the Ile-de-France region (Omalek, 2001). These changes are related to migratory movements. The consequences of these migrations on the ageing of these areas should, if possible, be assessed by taking into account the age of the migrants. Thus the southern regions, from Aquitaine[13] to the Provence-Alpes-Côte d'Azur region, have been particularly attractive for the past 30 years to populations of all ages, which has relatively slowed down their ageing. Retired people have seen other regions in western or central France as attractive – for example, those returning to their native region. However, they have not always retained the young people who had been attracted to study there, leading to an acceleration in the ageing of these regions which were already older than the national average. This is particularly the case in Brittany.[14]

The two ways of looking at demographic ageing of different areas: the proportion of the elderly and their concentration

Demographers usually show the ageing of a country's population by calculating average or median ages as well as the proportion of the elderly in the population as a whole. Since the beginning of this chapter, we have basically used the proportion of the elderly to illustrate the general degree of ageing of the territories. Indeed, according to academic definitions, 'the increase in the proportion of the elderly within a population reflects its ageing' (Demopaedia, 2013). Although this calculation is necessary to measure the weighting of the older generations within the population, it is not enough to describe and understand the precise dynamics of the ageing process of different areas. Indeed, ageing is also a matter of the absolute number of elderly people – i.e., the growth of the older population (gerontogrowth) and their concentration in particular areas of the country. The importance of taking into account the number to complete the proportion of elderly people is illustrated in Figures 4.5 and 4.6 – i.e., the population density map and the map of the proportion of elderly people in France (shown here in 2007). These maps represent the average values of the different areas using greyscale, regardless of the number of inhabitants living there. However, the greater part of France is sparsely populated, whereas the high-density areas, with the high population concentrations, are primarily urban. The result is a false view of the demographic dynamics of France, since it is primarily the large sparsely populated areas which attract the eye and not the small densely populated ones. Thus, for very many years, the attention of the uninformed public was polarised by the experts and their maps on the famous 'diagonale du vide' [literally: diagonal of emptiness] (Oliveau and Doignon, 2016). This refers to a broad, sparsely populated band, going from Eastern France to the south-west, the result of the rural exodus (of the nineteenth and

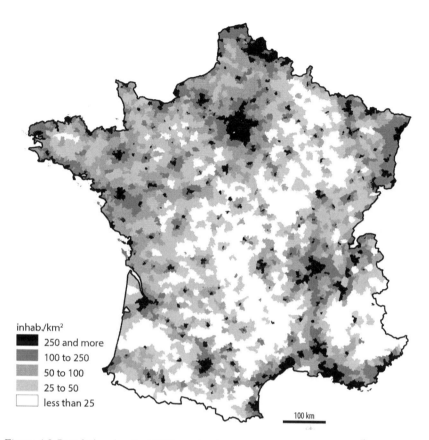

inhab./km²

■ 250 and more
■ 100 to 250
■ 50 to 100
□ 25 to 50
□ less than 25

100 km

Figure 4.5 Population density (2007, cantons)
Source: INSEE, Census 2007

twentieth centuries) and the metropolisation[15] which France has been experiencing since the second half of the twentieth century (Figure 4.5).

This map more or less coincides with that of the French areas most affected by demographic ageing (Figure 4.6), each appearing to be the negative of the other. Although considering the proportion of the elderly highlights the spatial influence of ageing on the country, it nevertheless wrongly suggests that it is in the rural areas that the highest absolute numbers of the elderly are concentrated. Indeed, the main urban areas have levels of elderly people below the national average, even though they have very high numbers of individuals. It is hence relevant to simultaneously map the absolute and relative ageing of the population.

Figure 4.7, which takes into account both the concentration and the proportion of the elderly, reveals an ageing France which is characterised by just as strong a presence of the number of the elderly in urban areas on the one hand (large circles) as in the Mediterranean coastal cantons. The highest numbers of elderly are in the large urban areas (Paris, Lyon, Nantes, Bordeaux, Toulouse, Strasbourg, Lille, etc.), but the percentage of elderly people in the population is lower there than

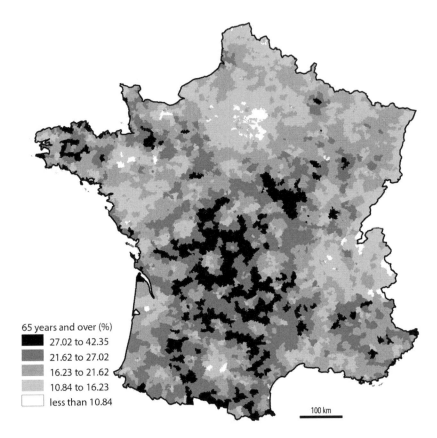

Figure 4.6 Proportion of people aged 65 or over (2007, cantons)

Source: INSEE, Census 2007

elsewhere (light grey and white). As for the coastal cantons,[16] these are marked by a significant presence of the elderly both in absolute terms (number of people, large circles) and in proportion (percentage of the general population, dark grey and black). One part of the Mediterranean coastline nevertheless seems to stand out from other coastal areas by having a smaller proportion of the elderly. Conversely, this map shows the interior diagonal from the south-west to the north-east ('diagonal of emptiness'), which is characterised by much lower numbers than elsewhere (smallest circles) reflecting the low population of these areas despite the high levels of the elderly.

This snapshot of the current situation of French ageing is original and clarifies the phenomenon at cantonal level. However, it is still insufficient to explain the demographic dynamics responsible and to further continue the deconstruction of areas which are remarkable from the point of view of ageing. Indeed, over the last 50 years, and particularly since the 1990s, as the growth and democratisation of modes of transport have reduced distances, individuals have been able to work farther from home and to change their place of residence more easily as required

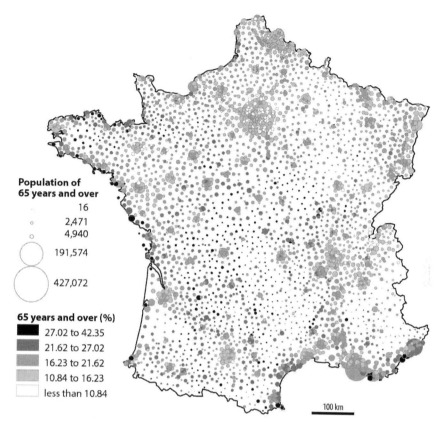

Population of 65 years and over

- 16
- 2,471
- 4,940
- 191,574
- 427,072

65 years and over (%)

- 27.02 to 42.35
- 21.62 to 27.02
- 16.23 to 21.62
- 10.84 to 16.23
- less than 10.84

100 km

Figure 4.7 Proportion and concentration of people aged 65 or over in France (2007, cantons)

Source: INSEE, Census 2007

by their life cycle. Accordingly, some areas have gained more population than others and have been very attractive destinations for migration.

To account fully for this dynamics and to permanently remove those representations which associate the concentration of the elderly and accelerated ageing too systematically,[17] it is necessary to simultaneously take into account their natural growth profile (surplus, zero or deficit in the birth-death balance), their migratory growth and the increase in the proportion of the elderly. The impact of migrations is indeed crucial to the dynamics of sub-national populations. Migrations also play a major role in structures by age and by sex. In the case of France, all the regional projections which manage to identify population concentrations in a particular part of the country – i.e., to indirectly estimate the most attractive territories – show this 'dual impact of migration' (Léon, 2008). On the one hand, migrations, through their number, do accentuate or temper the expected demographic changes in some areas. On the other hand, they have a direct effect on the ageing of the population which can be accelerated or slowed down by the age of the migrants and ultimately affect the fertility of the area under observation. Although in 2007 Arnaud Degorre and Patrick Redor entitled their paper 'The Departments of the South and the Atlantic Coastline Winners in the Game of Internal Migrations', only little is known indeed at levels of area analysis more detailed than department level (the second administrative level) about the precise and long-term demographic processes which led to such a differentiated ageing of the country. Little is known because the attractiveness of an area is closely linked to the fact that 'residential migrations follow household life cycles' (Degorre and Redor, 2007, p. 3), but also because the areas are differentiated both geographically and economically.

Ageing and coastalisation on the shores of the Mediterranean

The findings of the dynamic study of demographic ageing at cantonal level

To present a more detailed picture of the French cantons in order to understand the dynamics of their ageing, we developed an original methodology using automatic classification tools (Appendix 4.1). This typology is based on taking into account the natural dynamics of all the French cantons over a long period and their migration dynamics, while taking into account the concomitant changes in the proportion of the elderly. Mapping the profiles resulting from a classification[18] generally yields interesting results. Indeed, it can be seen that the statistical resemblances between cantons are accompanied by some spatial regrouping: similar cantons are often neighbours (Figure 4.8).

- **The profile hatched in black, the oldest (class 1)**, has had the highest level of elderly people since 1968. It is over-represented in the 'diagonal of emptiness' (low-density space, see Figure 4.5) and in some southern areas. These areas, mostly rural cantons, were particularly affected by a massive rural exodus. Young working persons migrated in large numbers, leaving behind the older population. This negative net migration resulted in an increase in demographic ageing, strengthened by the structural decline of the natural balance. It should be noted that in the last two decades, the net migration of these cantons has been less unfavourable than in the past. However, this has been insufficient to restore the natural balance because of the rather elderly profile of immigrants to these cantons.
- **The white profile (class 3)** represents the 'average' profile. It is composed of cantons which have aged at the average rate of all the metropolitan areas during the period.
- **The non-hatched profiles, in grey tones** (light grey, dark grey and black), mainly have in common the fact that they are **younger** than the cantonal average (white profile). They are organised concentrically around the major cities (Paris is a good example).

  - **The black profile (class 4)** reveals areas with very negative net migration since 1968 (more departures than arrivals) but paradoxically corresponds to younger areas. They are found in two types of cantons. **In urban**

centres (Lille, Paris, Nantes, Rennes, Lyon, etc.) on the one hand, where families are left to live farther away whilst younger students moved into the canton. On the other hand, this profile also covers various cantons which have experienced unfavourable economic conditions since the mid-1970s, such as some located in the northeast quarter of France.

- **The dark grey profile (class 5)** identifies **peri-urban areas**. These differ from the black profile because of the greater contribution of migrants of working age and families, which makes the natural and migratory balances observed throughout the period positive.
- **The light grey profile (class 2)** shows the **fringes of peri-urbanisation**. These are the last cantons affected by the spatial extension of urbanisation.

- **The profile hatched in light grey (class 6)** shows a unique spatial distribution. Mainly found in the southern half of France, it is situated near the Mediterranean and Atlantic coastlines, in the hinterland of urbanised areas. These are **areas** which were ageing but have **become attractive**. They have had a high level of immigration for 40 years. There is still an urban rationale, but

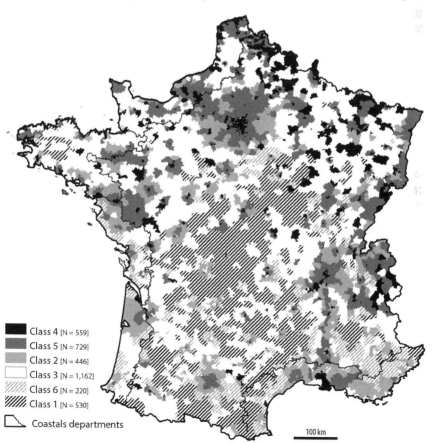

Figure 4.8 Profiles of French ageing since 1968 (cantons)
Source: INSEE, Census 1968, 1975, 1982, 1990, 1999, 2009

the areas are selected for their attractiveness and not for their proximity to the town centre: people are looking for pleasant spaces (coastlines, some valleys, etc.). This migration has also restored the natural dynamics. The combination of migratory and natural balances has resulted in a vigorous rejuvenation of the population of these areas.

The cartography displayed earlier shows a spatial organisation of the different types of cantons: the demographic specificities are also by area. Besides the classic contrast between urban, peri-urban and rural areas, specific coastlines are emerging, especially those of the Atlantic and of the Mediterranean.

Mediterranean specificity: ageing contained by an urban and peri-urban dynamics

To better demonstrate the Mediterranean specificity, we have recorded the incidence of different profiles for each of the four major French coastlines (North, Brittany, Atlantic and Mediterranean) (Figure 4.9). We defined the coastline as all the cantons situated within 50 kilometres from the shore.[19]

It should first be noted that none of the four coastlines can be superimposed on the profile of the rest of non-coastal France. This confirms how much the French coastline, regardless of its position, has a unique demographic dynamics. Coastlines have different characteristics when compared to the French average.

The ageing of the Mediterranean coastline shows a greater variety of profiles than other coastlines. While the Atlantic, Brittany and Northern coastlines account for between 35% and 50% of cantons with an average (white) profile of dynamics and demographic ageing, the Mediterranean coastline accounts for barely 12%. The light grey profile, which is characteristic of a distant fringe of peri-urbanisation, prevails on the Mediterranean coast with almost 30% of the cantons. This demonstrates that these districts have been continually attractive since 1968, thus holding

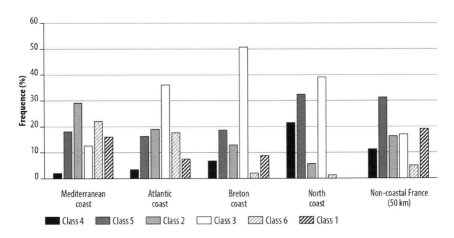

Figure 4.9 Ageing profiles for each French coastline, comparison with non-coastal France

Source: INSEE, Census 1968, 1975, 1982, 1990, 1999, 2009

back the demographic ageing. Moreover, in the Mediterranean cantons, the city centre (black) type profiles are rarer than on other coastlines, which demonstrates that the town centres of the urban Mediterranean are unique. The French Mediterranean coastal 'town' does not follow the same patterns as the municipalities in the rest of France. The dark grey profile, very common on the northern coastline, is not uncommon in the Mediterranean. These are peri-urban areas which have been dynamic for a long time but whose migratory attractiveness has been eroding since the beginning of the 1990s. The Mediterranean coastline is the one on which most of the cantons with the light grey hatched profile are concentrated (virtually absent on the Brittany and Northern coastlines) – i.e., areas which have become increasingly attractive since 1975, to the point that the pace of ageing is slowing. Since 1968, the natural contribution to growth has become less and less unfavourable and combined with the areas attractiveness to migrants has slowed down the rate of change in the proportion of those aged 65 or over in the population.

The predominance of these three profiles (light grey, dark grey and hatched light grey), symbolising the urban phenomenon (urban sprawl, peri-urbanisation, deconcentration...), is the major characteristic of the French Mediterranean coastline. Indeed, 7 out of 10 cantons belong to one of these three profiles, whereas this is barely 53% for the Atlantic coastline, 33% for the Brittany coastline and 40% for the North coastline. The Mediterranean coastline is above all dominated by an urban demographic dynamics, made of concentration and urban sprawl, through progressive deconcentration, as noted earlier by Christine Voiron (1999).

It should be noted, however, that 16% of the Mediterranean cantons still belong to the black hatched profile – i.e., cantons which continue to be the most elderly of the French cantons. Predominantly rural and located in the hinterland, their natural balance is very unfavourable and little counterbalanced by favourable migration trends. This profile does not exist in any of the Northern coastal cantons and exists to a much lesser extent on the other coastlines.

Thus, two major dynamics coexist on the Mediterranean coastline. One is marked by significant ageing, constant since 1968, characteristic of rural cantons in demographic decline. The other is experiencing an ageing slowdown, either because of a moderate but continuous historical attractiveness or because of more recent attractiveness, symbolic dynamics of urbanisation and peri-urbanisation.

Conclusion: the two 'Mediterraneans' of French ageing

As life expectancy increases, rising living standards and an earlier average age at retirement have allowed healthy retirees to start a 'new life', 'retirement migrations have increased considerably in industrial countries since the middle of the century' (Cribier and Dieleman, 1993, p. 449). France, like England, is a country with a long 'tradition of retirement migration', unlike Spain. As Jean-François Ghékière and Vincent Houillon note, 'demographic ageing accompanied by the growth of new categories of retirees is a factor contributing to the dynamics and demographic densification of the coastlines' (Ghékière and Houillon, 2013).

Young, more affluent urban retirees are looking for recreational areas (amenity migration), especially on the coastlines or near lakes, attracted by the sea, the mild climate and the landscapes. Others prefer to return to their native region. Although the propensity of pensioners to migrate varies from one period to another, this chapter has shown how, since 1968, the Mediterranean coastline, particularly on its eastern side, from Montpellier to Nice, has been characterised by attracting migrants of all ages (including many retirees) and retained its populations, resulting in a rather paradoxical change in the age structures of its areas. The urban and deconcentration phenomenon thus allows ageing to be relatively contained, compared with other areas affected by a very rapid ageing where there has been an exodus of the young population or even accentuated by the retirees' return migrations to their native region at retirement (Atlantic or Brittany coastlines).

On this part of the Mediterranean coastline, these two great demographic dynamics coexist, with both recently and historically attractive areas (Gastaut, 2009, p. 48) but, above all, with much more elderly areas with unfavourable demographic dynamics (Dukic, 2009, p. 77). Thus, **two 'Mediterraneans'**, spatially distinguishable, coexist. The first, going from Nice to Montpellier (2/3 of the coastline in length), is above all an urbanised coastline, urban/peri-urban in nature, whose demographic dynamics, contrary to popular belief, slows ageing more than it increases it. The second, on the last third of the Mediterranean coastline, with Montpellier behind it and going towards the Spanish border, has only a small number of important urban centres and is more characterised by rural areas, a large part of which belongs to the southeast border of the 'diagonal of emptiness'.

The impact of ageing on the spatial redistribution of populations must study the population mobilities at different ages. Their repercussions on lifestyles are to be assessed taking into account the number and concentration of the elderly using fine spatial scales. Residential migrations have a very important effect on the ageing of areas. We know that the greatest European and Mediterranean ageing is to be expected in areas which are not attractive to working populations. Despite the high cost of housing, the eastern part of the French Mediterranean coast has so far been able to attract and retain very diverse migrant profiles. This is due to urbanisation and peri-urbanisation supported by rather large pools of jobs and a pleasant living environment which is attractive to all ages and migrants from all over northern Europe. This highlighting of 'gerontogrowth' in the populations of the French Mediterranean coastline, which is less systematically associated with the concomitant rise in the proportion of the elderly in the population than elsewhere, raises the question of the long-term effects of the expansion of the 'Latin arc' and the 'Mediterranean arc' effects highlighted by researchers (Liziard, 2013a; Canicio, 1994, p. 15). This is the increasing concentration since the nineteenth century of a large number of elderly people primarily on the most sunny and urban coastlines and hinterlands of countries on the northern shore of the Mediterranean, as well as to the south and the east. Indeed,

> the majority of the Spanish, French and Italian coastlines are following this development model perfectly. It consists of a coastal concentration of the population and an inland decline, and continues with an extension of the coastal dynamics towards the near hinterland. This analysis confirms the existence

of a general model of coastalisation – with different timings and variable intensities of coastal concentration according to the zones studied.

(Liziard, 2013b, p. 54)

However, this coastalisation has an ambiguous relationship with ageing as we have demonstrated, in the French case, that the Mediterranean coast forms a specific group, even though it has been marked by the same acceleration of coastalisation as the other French coastlines since the 1960s.

'The process is still in its early years because, for the time being, only the first of the baby-boom generations have entered the upper part of the age pyramid' (Ghékière and Houillon, 2013, p. 92). Public management of demographic ageing of the regions, in its impacts on the lifestyles of all the inhabitants, must take into account individual needs and customs by providing appropriate responses. The regions of ageing vary widely from one part of the Mediterranean to the other, with the very isolated rural population in radical opposition to the overconcentrated regions in and on the periphery of urban areas, on the shores and in the hinterlands of the coastlines. The demographic ageing at work everywhere in the Mediterranean will only reinforce the local coastal spatial logics of territorial convergence in land, real estate, income or employment (Ghékière and Houillon, 2013; Canicio, 1994). In the long term, these phenomena, in conjunction with other economic and retirement conditions which are now less favourable than they used to be, could 'slow or even reshape migration flows' (Ghékière and Houillon, 2013, p. 92) enabling us to anticipate the emergence of unexpected new areas of attractiveness.

Notes

1 'The notion of coastline means those areas in direct contact with the sea or subject to its influence. It is difficult to define' (Ghékière and Houillon, 2013, p. 62).
2 'It is necessary to distinguish the notion of ageing from that of gerontogrowth. Gerontogrowth is defined as the increase in the number of elderly in the population (a decrease in elderly people being called 'gérontodécroissance' [literally: 'gerontodecrease']). It is mainly affected by the increase in life expectancy and migratory flows' (Dumont, 2005, p. 6). A French invention by G. F. Dumont, the English equivalent expression gerontogrowth is little used by the Anglo-Saxons, except by some gerontologists. However, the distinction which should be made between ageing and gerontogrowth can be found in some of the European Commission's works, such as that of Dimitriadis (2007).
3 The term 'coastalisation' refers to 'all the processes which induce the densification of coastal areas and the result of these processes' (Voiron Canicio, 1999, p. 103). For more details on this concept, see the thesis of Sophie Liziard (2013a).
4 Using an automatic classification tool: Ascendant Hierarchical Classification (AHC).
5 France has five administrative levels (from the 'région' [region] to the 'commune' [town]). The canton is one of the finest administrative divisions (level 4) before the town (level 5). Refer to Figure 4.4 for the various administrative networks of France.
6 In their article, Ghékière and Houillon (2013): 'We have chosen a limited area, a choice which is certainly debatable, but justified, taking into account only a part of the coastal fronts, namely the towns directly in contact with the sea' (p. 60) and further 'we did not integrate the hinterland towns because our objective was to clearly identify the areas where the seaside, amenity and attractiveness factors, appeared a priori determining in the process of ageing' (p. 62).

7 Calculations based on data from 'United Nations, Department of Economic and Social Affairs, Population Division (2015). World Population Prospects: The 2015 Revision, DVD Edition'.

8 The most likely demographic perspectives are that this median age will at best become stable in France (if fertility remains sustained) or that France will have the current ageing level of Italy, Japan or Germany in 40 years' time.

9 The French National Institute for Statistics and Economic Research.

10 Note, the proportion of those aged 65 and over amounted to 18.2% nationally in 2014.

11 The departments belonging to the regions Provence-Alpes-Côte d'Azur, Corsica and Languedoc-Roussillon.

12 In this chapter, we will use the term migrant to refer to those individuals whose continuing displacement cannot be fully and continuously monitored but for whom it is possible to compare an earlier residence with a current residence. See the demographic definition of the migrant according to the Multilingual demographic dictionary (Demopaedia, 2013): 'When one is not observing all migrations continuously, one can compare either the residence on a predetermined date or the previous residence to the current residence. In the first case, the term "migrant" refers to any individual whose residences at the beginning and the end of the period are different; leaving the residence at the beginning of the period, this migrant was an emigrant, on arrival in the current residence, an immigrant. In the second case where the question relates, in fact, to the last migration or change of residence whatever the date, any individual having had at least one previous residence different from the current one is an immigrant to the latter and an emigrant from the previous residence. When places of birth are known, any individual whose current residence differs from the place of birth is a non-native of the current residence. When the reason for the migration is of particular importance, one can qualify the migrant and speak of being an emigrant for political, religious or ethical reasons or an immigrant for political, religious or ethical reasons, as the case may be'.

13 Aquitaine, the third region in France (located in the south-west), owes 90% of its growth to its net migration. In this region, it is the section of the population aged 30 to 60 which contributes the most to demographic growth and slows down its ageing: in Aquitaine, people aged 60 and over are less likely than young people to move (Guichard, 2007).

14 On this subject, see Vye, D. (2011), Auzet, M. (2012) on the attractiveness of Brittany; and Besson et al. (2012) on the Provence-Alpes-Côte d'Azur region.

15 Organisation of the area around a city or an urban area (metropolis).

16 'Although a high proportion of people aged 60 or over is a general factor on coastlines, there is high variability in gerontogrowth at the local level' (Ghékière and Houillon, 2013, p. 61).

17 'Ageing and gerontogrowth prove to vary greatly according to the various fronts' (Ghékière and Houillon, 2013, p. 60).

18 Refer to Appendix 4.1 for details of the six classification profiles.

19 This distance of 50 kilometres is a good compromise for considering both the coastal cantons and those of the hinterland. The absence of a commonly accepted definition of 'coastline' requires this study to define a distance so as to present cantons which are coastal but include the hinterland at the same time.

References

Ambrosetti, E. and Giudici, C. (2014). L'Europe confrontée au vieillissement démographique. *P@ges Europe*. Retrieved from www.ladocumentationfrancaise.fr/pages-europe/d000 722-l-europe-confrontee-au-vieillissement-demographique-par-elena-ambrosetti-et-cristina/article

Auzet, L. (2012). Naître en Bretagne, être en Bretagne: un lien renforcé par les retours à la région natale. *Octant Analyse*, (28), 4.

Besson, V., Biau, O. and INSEE Paca. (2012). Portrait de la région Provence-Alpes-Côte d'Azur. *Dossier*, (7), 48.

Canicio, C. V. (1994). À la recherche d'un arc méditerranéen. *Méditerranée*, 79(1), 15–23.

Cribier, F. and Dieleman, F. (1993). La mobilité résidentielle des retraités en Europe occidentale. *Espace populations sociétés*, 11(3), 445–449.

Degorre, A. and Redor, P. (2007). Enquêtes annuelles de recensement de 2004 à 2006: les départements du sud et du littoral atlantique gagnants au jeu des migrations internes. *INSEE Première*, (1116), 4.

Demopaedia (Ed.). (2013). *Dictionnaire démographique multilingue, seconde édition unifiée, volume français*. United Nations – International Union for the Scientific Study of Population – Institut National d'Etudes Démographiques – Centre Population & Développement. Retrieved from http://fr-ii.demopaedia.org

Dimitriadis, D. (2007). *Opinion of the European economic and social committee on the family and demographic change*. Brussels: European Economic and Social Commitee. Retrieved from http://eur-lex.europa.eu/legal-content/EN/TXT/?uri=celex%3A52007AE0423

Dukic, S. (2009). Deux siècles d'immigration Languedoc-Roussillon. *Hommes et migrations*, 2(1278), 76–87.

Dumont, G.-F. (2005). Compte rendu de la séance du 20 janvier 2005, Séminaire Prospective Info: les enjeux territoriaux du vieillissement et du concept de gérontocroissance. Paris: Ministère de l'équipement des transports, de l'aménagement du territoire, du tourisme et de la mer.

Froger, V., Ghékière, J.-F. and Houillon, V. (2010). Vieillissement, changement social et paupérisation. *Espace populations sociétés*, (1), 95–108.

Gastaut, Y. (2009). Histoire de l'immigration en PACA aux XIXe et XXe siècles. *Hommes et migrations*, 2(1278), 48–61.

Ghékière, J.F. and Houillon, V. (2013). Le vieillissement démographique des communes côtières en France: un phénomène uniforme ? *Espace populations sociétés*, (1–2), 59–93.

Gould, P. (1981). Letting the data speak for themselves. *Annals of the Association of American Geographers*, 71(2), 166–176.

Guichard, N. (2007). L'Aquitaine au 3e rang des territoires de migrations. *Aquitaine e-Publications*, (1), 5.

Héran, F. (2004). Cinq idées reçues sur l'immigration. *Population et sociétés*, (397), 4.

Léon, O. (2008). Les projections régionales de population 2005–2030: concentration au sud et à l'ouest et intensité variable du vieillissement, le double impact des migrations. *Economie et statistique*, (408), 137–152.

Liziard, S. (2013a). Littoralisation de la façade nord-méditerranéenne: analyse spatiale et prospective dans le contexte du changement climatique. Thesis of Geography, Université Nice Sophia Antipolis, Retrieved January 15, 2017, from https://tel.archives-ouvertes.fr/tel-00927492/document

Liziard, S. (2013b). Littoralisation de l'Arc Latin: analyse spatio-temporelle de la répartition de la population à une échelle fine. *Espace populations sociétés*, (1–2), 21–40.

Oliveau, S. and Doignon, Y. (2016). La diagonale se vide ? Analyse spatiale exploratoire des décroissances démographiques en France métropolitaine depuis 50 ans. *Cybergeo: European Journal of Geography*. Retrieved July 21, 2016, from https://cybergeo.revues.org/27439

Omalek, L. (2001). Projections régionales de population pour 2030: l'impact des migrations. *INSEE Première*, 9(805), 4.

Voiron Canicio, C. (1999). Urbanisation et littoralisation sur les rives de la Méditerranée. In Sevin, O. (Ed.), *Les Méditerranées dans le monde* (pp. 103–112). Cahiers scientifiques de l'Université d'Artois. Arras: Artois Presses Université.

Vye, D. (2011). La ruée vers l'ouest ? *Espace Populations Sociétés*, (3), 603–616.

Appendix 4.1
Methodology

In an Ascending Hierarchical Classification (AHC), the statistical individual values (here the cantons) are grouped according to their similarity. Each class brings together a group of individual values whose characteristics are comparable and which deviate from those of the individual values of other classes. A standard profile can be drawn for each class, which indicates the average value of the class and compares it to the average of the entire population. The profiles resulting from the analysis present specific demographic situations. Six profiles are presented (Figure 4.10).

- The white profile (class 3) represents the 'average' profile. It is composed of cantons which have aged at the average rate of all the metropolitan areas during the period.
- The black hatched profile (class 1) is characterised by a natural change very much below the average (and is generally negative) in all periods. These are mainly more elderly cantons, whose natural change aggravates ageing. Since 1968, the migratory impact in this profile has been very secondary, although the negative migration balance has reversed slightly during the last two intercensal periods. It is in this profile that the number of people aged 65 or over is the highest, throughout the period.
- The cantons of the light grey hatched profile (class 6) show a positive change in the natural balance over the whole period, but insufficient to reach the average change in the cantons. The restoration of the natural balance is not yet sufficient to catch up with the cantonal average. At the same time, previously lower migratory movements became greater than the cantonal average from 1975 onwards. The cantons, displaying a high proportion of people aged 65 or over at the beginning of the period, are tending to become close to the average. If rejuvenation is not present, ageing slows down sharply.
- The light grey profile (class 2) is marked by a continuous increase in the natural balance during the period. Slightly below the average of the French cantons during the first period (1968–1975), the balance then becomes positive and rapidly deviates from the average. At the same time, net migration is experiencing some variations but still remains well above the average. Both balances reinforce each other resulting in a relative rejuvenation of the cantons in relation to the average over the whole period.

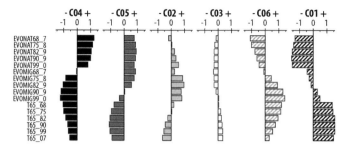

Every stick represents the distance of the average of every class to the overall average.
This distance is expressed in number of standard deviations of every variable.

Figure 4.10 Ascending hierarchical classification profiles

- The dark grey (class 5) profile is distinguished by a sustained natural dynamics throughout the period and a higher average migration dynamics at the beginning of the period which becomes lower from 1999 onwards. The cantons of this profile are therefore much younger than the average.
- The black profile (class 4) is marked by a very strong natural change at the beginning of the period, which slows down slightly throughout the period. The change in net migration is negative and has strongly intensified from 1975 onwards. These areas, younger than the average, show the rate of people aged 65 or over converging on the cantonal average. These cantons are ageing faster than the others but remain younger.

The variables used in AHC are the following:

EVONAT68_7: contribution of the natural balance to growth between 1968 and 1975 (in %)

EVONAT75_8: contribution of the natural balance to growth between 1975 and 1982 (in %)

EVONAT82_9: contribution of the natural balance to growth between 1982 and 1990 (in %)

EVONAT90_9: contribution of the natural balance to growth between 1990 and 1999 (in %)

EVONAT99_0: contribution of the natural balance to growth between 1999 and 2009 (in %)

EVOMIG68_7: contribution of net migration to growth between 1968 and 1975 (in %)

EVOMIG75_8: contribution of net migration to growth between 1975 and 1982 (in %)

EVOMIG82_9: contribution of net migration to growth between 1982 and 1990 (in %)

EVOMIG90_9: contribution of net migration to growth between 1990 and 1999 (in %)

EVOMIG99_0: contribution of net migration to growth between 1999 and 2009 (in %)

T65_68: proportion of people aged 65 years or over in 1968 (in %)

T65_75: proportion of people aged 65 years or over in 1975 (in %)

T65_82: proportion of people aged 65 years or over in 1982 (in %)

T65_90: proportion of people aged 65 years or over in 1990 (in %)

T65_99: proportion of people aged 65 years or over in 1999 (in %)

T65_09: proportion of people aged 65 years or over in 2009 (in %)

Part II

Contours of familial solidarities and change in multigenerational societies in the Mediterranean

Introduction

'The problem' of family solidarities in Mediterranean societies

Thierry Blöss and Michèle Pagès

The purpose of the second part of this work is to shed light on the dynamics of intergenerational relationships which the ageing process is tending to transform. This means 'considering private solidarities surrounding the elderly' (Nowik and Lecestre-Rollier, 2015). However, this also involves understanding how changes to life cycles and socio-economic developments in Mediterranean societies are altering the way families are organised, the place and status held by each generation and the role each plays. The context is the unprecedented situation in many societies, in both north and south, where the lengthening life expectancy is leading to increasing coexistence of the generations. All the more so in the absence of a guaranteed and effective public welfare system, families are trying to support their 'old' members, and all the more so in Mediterranean societies where the family is still playing its providential role. When 'crisis' occurs, are relationships between the generations of a family weakened, or on the contrary are they strengthened? Do they compensate for the Welfare States' limits? These issues have met with a wide range of responses from various analyses: evidence that there is no overwhelming causal explanation in this field. Nevertheless, there are various dimensions to the concept of family solidarity. Using the survey data available, the various chapters will try to identify lifestyle transformations and thus highlight the structural and functional dimensions of relationships between generations.[1]

Supporting the elderly is sometimes a source of conflicts and negotiations between family members. More broadly, new kinds of solidarities and family commitments are emerging throughout the life cycle, which are both redefining relationships between the generations and revealing new social reproduction issues. The insecurity of the new generations of young adults and the uncertainties about lifestyle linked to an extended old age are in fact signs of a profound transformation in the life cycle. In many societies, the life cycle is now based more on a new form of intergenerational dependence and less on a clear separation between age groups. The chapters which make up this part of the work will thus help us to understand that these intergenerational solidarities are reciprocal indeed: this reciprocity is often unequal and is part of a generalised dynamics of exchange, to the extent that each generation is finding that they are both carers and cared for, sometimes at the same time.

This part of the work mainly consists of an analysis of this 'generational situation' and takes into account the latest developments in the course of social existence. With demographic ageing, the intermediate generations, referred to either as 'sandwich generations' (Miller, 1981) or pivot generations (Attias-Donfut, 1995), are seeing their strategic role developing and sometimes becoming decisive. Of the generations in play, they seem to be the ones most often asked to provide assistance. Furthermore, against a background of sustained and repeated economic crises, these intermediate generations are seeing their situation being significantly transformed and their social function becoming more complex. They are somehow required to intervene in the health and autonomy problems of the older generations at the same time as assisting younger generations grappling with 'great difficulties' as they attempt to enter adult society.

Despite its limitations, explaining these lifestyle changes by reference to the economic 'crisis', often linked to the oil price shocks of the 1970s and more recently to the financial and banking failures in the late 2000s, does show that all the generations are affected by socio-historical change to some extent. These developments are not only affecting those wishing to enter the labour market and who are seeing their opportunities for entry reduce but also those already in the labour market. The latter are finding themselves, according to their professional strengths and to their age and gender, more easily pushed out of the market. In times of economic crisis, the 'sacrificed' generations are therefore very many as soon as the effects of the crisis can be gauged from the social characteristics of the individuals concerned (whether in terms of educational level, professional qualification or age and gender). Thus, in times of crisis, young people see their educational qualifications socially devalued or downgraded and the main losers are the working-class youth left behind by the school system. In times of crisis, still, adult women and older males are the weakest links in an increasingly competitive labour market. In times of crisis, finally, each generation appears more differentiated or fragmented, bearing witness to the deep social inequalities within each and, more fundamentally, to 'the reproduction of a differentiated and hierarchical social structure' within the production mechanism 'of successive generations' (Mauger, 2011).

One of the most significant consequences of the increase in individual life expectancy is undoubtedly the advent of a multigenerational society where at least three generations, and increasingly four, coexist. This trend represents a real and unprecedented social challenge for most societies. However, in reality, the emergence of such a multigenerational society falls outside any quantitative simplification which would have a maximum number of generations living actually together and interacting in everyday life. Far from this ready-made intergenerational solution, the reality of family relationships in an extended family is usually limited to binomial intergenerational exchanges where the intermediate generation (comprising mature parents) is seen as a go-between. When it comes to intergenerational solidarities, there are clearly major stakeholders, whether carers or cared for, and secondary stakeholders or links. Extreme intergenerational relationships between great-grandchildren and great-grandparents (where four generations coexist) are indeed generally limited to sporadic affectionate exchanges. What happens when five generations take up the challenge?

Mobilised families and welfare states: the temporal approach to the relationships between private and public solidarities

Southern European societies are thus rapidly ageing societies; the issue of managing ageing is becoming even more acute because fertility rates are low and the State finances have been bled dry (Van de Velde, 2015). If current family solidarities are obviously one resource to be shared in this context, another resource is the *sine die* prolongation of work after formal retirement age. When an individual has been employed in the formal sector, the transition to retirement sometimes means a substantial drop in income. Carrying on with professional work after the legal retirement age can actually subsume much contrasted social situations. There is indeed no similarity between, on the one hand, an unavoidable transition to another job on retirement when the previous, low-skilled and low-paid post did not bring in sufficient funds on which to live, and, on the other hand, continuing a professional activity in order to maintain a standard of living comparable to that enjoyed before retirement. In the first case, further work is necessary for survival; in the second, it is a way to maintain resources or living standards.

It is clear that elderly people's employment situations differ greatly between societies, depending on the importance of informal work in the different countries' economies. By definition, there is no retirement age where the informal sector exists, and as people grow old, they continue to work as best they can in order to survive. In societies where institutionalisation of the official and codified labour market has led to statutory recognition of the retirement age, the latter has continued to rise in recent years, putting an end to the historical pattern of continuous lowering attributed to social progress. Paradoxically, in societies where implicit labour-market rules have continued to disadvantage older workers, the retirement age has been continuously raised, thus forcing people to work for longer before receiving their pensions.

This phenomenon is undoubtedly one of the most notable changes to the ageing process and one of the similarities between societies. Although resulting from very different factors, depending on whether the labour market is formal or informal, active ageing is gaining ground.[2] Paradoxically, in a context where Welfare States are finding it increasingly difficult to preserve their pensioners' standards of living, which were set in the past during most prosperous financial times, this represents both a limit – or a major regression – on the principle of the right to retire and a way of preserving the elderly's financial independence. The gradual raising of the statutory retirement age in most countries is a true 'cultural revolution' insofar as, particularly for Southern European countries, this radical change in direction comes after decades of state compensation for older workers leaving the labour market early in the name of safeguarding employment (Guillemard, 2013). It therefore represents a recent and notable reversal of social forms of contemporary ageing even if it does not coincide with the true age of retirement from the labour market. Indeed, the individuals are still many to leave the labour market before the legal age, in nearly every country, because of the difficulties involved in carrying on working. The phenomenon is even more obvious in Southern European countries where the imposed[3] working conditions strongly limit elderly people's ability to continue in the labour market.

Given the scale and acuteness of the 'social problem' of ageing, it comes as no surprise that several chapters highlight and analyse the effect of the recent economic and financial crises on the role of the Welfare State, on public policies relating to supporting the ageing and on ageing people's family lifestyles. Can it be said that there is a division of roles between the family and the State in the care of the elderly? This question is especially difficult as analyses involving different countries show, primarily, that the latter often have nothing in common in terms of protection. The argument is therefore most often: all things being otherwise unequal. Two rather dissimilar State models, however, have been noted in studies involving Europe. On the one hand, there are the Northern European countries with their 'social-democratic schemes' (Esping-Andersen, 1990), characterised by most of the interventions coming from the State, as for instance, regarding care of the dependent elderly, for which the family comes in a way to play a secondary role. On the other hand, there are the Southern European countries, where there is minimal or even negligible State intervention and the elderly person's family is the cornerstone of their care.

The question of the division between public action and private assistance is certainly a difficult, if not inappropriate, one. In any case, it cannot be summarised by some logic of compensation. For example, it cannot possibly explain the situation in France where, historically, an active social protection policy has co-existed with no less active family support: a mature, working, adult child who has to look after a dependent elderly parent assumes the role of family caregiver and becomes the true hub of daily assistance. This is recognised by law and encouraged financially by the State (through monetary benefits). Not to mention that the 'unattainable' division of roles between State and family is constantly revived by the macroeconomic backgrounds of the societies we wish to compare. Indeed, the boundary between State and family is not historically invariable. It fluctuates according to the conjunction of circumstances.

Over the past few years, the notion of economic crisis with all its difficulties (unemployment, social and job insecurity, reduction in living standards) has been the main explanation put forward throughout the world to explain the changes in family support behaviours: both their limits and their ability to adapt and extend. In theory indeed, financial difficulties objectively put to the test the forms of family support, rendering the protagonists more vulnerable, whatever their age. In practice, strengthened forms of solidarities exist alongside failures, proving that a simplistic explanation has no place here. The economic crisis has also been invoked to justify changes in the level of 'social protection' which States are prepared to continue providing, or not. The primacy given to the economic crisis as a causal explanation in understanding the relationship between State and family is undoubtedly of a reductive nature. For example, it does not fully explain the differences in social and cultural norms governing solidarity relationships within the family at different stages of life and which are characterised by a longer period of intergenerational cohabitation in Mediterranean societies, whatever the economic background. Economic crisis or not, cultural trends are emerging which suggest a preponderance of, or greater emphasis on, family feeling and on close intergenerational relationships: in short, on what some would call a 'family-oriented' model

(Esping-Andersen, 1990) or a 'familialisation' of life paths leading to strong intergenerational solidarity and complementarity between family members (Van de Velde, 2015).

However, despite its limits, the notion of economic crisis does allow us to understand how societies differ from each other when faced with such a situation. It also demonstrates for example that, in Mediterranean societies, when economic difficulties become more pronounced the predominant role played by family support leads to a strengthening in the practices of material mutual aid. Depending on one's stage of life, intergenerational cohabitation takes on different forms and meanings. It may involve young adults living with their parents for even longer, due to the increasing difficulty of joining the work force. At the other end of the age spectrum, it may mean dependent elderly people being supported at home by their children. Thus, in times of crisis, instances of cohabitation exponentially increase and take on new forms. The following chapter analyses the situation in Spain and demonstrates how, with the crisis making the conditions for adults more precarious in Spain through soaring levels of unemployment, resorting to intergenerational cohabitation to alleviate the crisis actually means for adults returning to live in the homes of their elderly parents. Although the elderly in Spain are vulnerable, they are bolstering the position of adults who are in an extremely precarious social situation. Here, too, the economic crisis has led to, and strengthened, the family-oriented nature of Mediterranean lifestyles, by ushering in new kinds of intergenerational solidarity. These are contributing in concrete terms to the reduction in the number of households noted by demographers as the generations cohabit.

Similarly, depending on the country in question, the age and forms of social protection differ and are not progressing at the same pace. For example, low pension coverage and high levels of inequality amongst retirees in Morocco, together with the lack of health care often experienced by the elderly, are leading to significant mobilisation of families. This is often problematic due to a reduction in family size and the socio-economic conditions of the young who are affected by unemployment. An analysis of the Mediterranean social protection model in Italy shows the importance of the family's role in limiting the imbalances experienced by the elderly and reveals the flaws in intergenerational redistribution despite the numerous reforms undertaken by the State.

As there is no obvious, radical explanation, in the light of the various studies undertaken (Attias-Donfut and Litwin, 2015), it should be noted that social differences in the practices of intergenerational family support are not distributed along a north/south divide, whether we refer to the European region, or more specifically to the Mediterranean. Although similarities and thus inevitably differences come to light from international comparisons, these findings do not allow us to establish a strict relationship between the level of social protection offered by a country's public policies and the vitality of forms of intergenerational family support. In all cases, the logic of monetary compensation, once an assumption, is far from being established, thus demonstrating that no clear correlation exists between the characteristics of a Nation-State and those of family support behaviours.

Ageing, both individually and collectively, has mainly been defined as a process which poses a problem, one with negative repercussions. When it comes to solidarities, the approach taken by social science researchers has not been immune to this tendency. Socio-economic studies have particularly highlighted the limits of Welfare States in guaranteeing public solidarity measures for problem categories – among which the elderly – through financing social protection schemes (retirement, health, dependency risk, etc.). What some do not hesitate to label as implosion of the Welfare State, in a context of globalisation (Baverez, 2013), is in reality and in a less black-and-white view a fairly mixed range of Welfare State systems which, in recent decades, have shown their limits as regards guaranteeing their citizens social protection, whatever their level of social provision, since a Nation-State is 'never more than partly a Welfare State, and sometimes a very small part' (Merrien, 2007). Welfare States undergo constant change: alterations in lifestyles (choice, marriage, fertility, etc.) and the ageing of populations are probably the main factors which are forcing social States founded under different socio-demographic conditions to adapt (Barbier and Théret, 2009). These adaptations are expressed by the difficulties States experience in maintaining their level of commitment as regards social protection, all things being otherwise unequal. What distinguishes Welfare State systems in neighbouring societies, such as those of the Mediterranean, are above all the profound differences in their own histories, but also in their development. European Union injunctions, for example, (in countries affected by this supranational institution) have had little harmonising effect.

However, in Mediterranean societies the action of the States as regards public solidarity is not limited to the measure of their protective intentions or of their financial commitments. It also usually involves persuasive a moral action which tends to strengthen and enhance the role of families in solidarity work. In these societies resorting to the family is even more widespread as the fact that there is little or no alternative has been internalised (family mobilisation in southern countries generally occurs within a Welfare State system which is only weakly active). It is also recognised as essential and even natural by public authorities.

The specificity of Mediterranean lifestyles can thus be analysed through the ways in which intergenerational relationships are forged throughout the life cycle and by how they are regarded:

> In comparison with the rest of Europe, lifestyles are very different in the south. In Italy, Spain and Greece it is unusual for a couple to live alone (without another cohabitant). Sharing accommodation (that of the pivot generation who are mainly in their fifties) with adult children and/or elderly parents is observed in two-thirds of cases, contrary to other countries where half of those couples interviewed lived alone.
>
> (Ogg and Renaut, 2006a)

In this area, France lies mid-way between these two worlds. In comparison with European countries, Mediterranean countries share a common sense of family which considers the duty of supporting one's own as a predominant value, particularly when the assistance given is domestic or involves the care of others. It is likely, as underlined by Jim Ogg and Sylvie Renaut (2006a), that 'the current social policies in each country affect the position' (or opinion) 'held by populations as regards the Welfare State'. In other words, 'faced with insufficient institutional means, significant family mobilisation is observed as well as a strong consensus about the idea that supporting elderly parents is more the role of the family than that of the State'.

Social transformations in life cycles tend to call into question the place of each member in the family and, in some way, redistribute the roles of each. They require a

> new kinds of family solidarities linked to a change in intergenerational rela-
> tionships. This is caused both by the difficulties young people experience en-
> tering the labour market and those experienced by older people in continuing
> to work, in dealing with long illnesses and, later, in paying for dependency
> care, especially in care homes.
>
> (Weber, 2015)

Who should take care of whom in the family? Answers to this question will differ depending on the situation. Certainly, family obligations are, above all, moral
in nature. What a parent owes to their children, or vice versa, can be interpreted as
a collection of emotional outlooks which vary in different individuals according
to their social characteristics (gender and class). Being a good parent or a caring
and grateful child comes, in reality, from an imposition process which leads to
the creation of different rules of behaviour for men and women. Many societies
rely on this family support obligation principle in defining their public solidarity
actions, thereby establishing what we might call the principle of subsidiarity. This
means that public solidarity only intervenes if private solidarity (within the family
network) has failed. In reality, this principle of subsidiarity is seldom in operation
because some societies give social rights to individuals regardless of any family
support to which they may have access. In addition, and above all, even when
no family support is available, public assistance remains unsuccessful in most
societies. Here, we are touching not only on the limits of the Welfare States but
also more fundamentally on their social identity. And although the legal standards
applied to the family (which embody society's morals) include a wealth of provisions about the respective rights and duties of spouses, parental authority and
the reciprocal obligations of family members, these principles and practices can
vary greatly from one country to the next. In this respect, Mediterranean societies
value family solidarities. They share a fragmented and uncoordinated approach to
family policy, with the State delegating the responsibility to families for the well-
being of their members (Damon, 2007).

The existence or even the identity of a Mediterranean social State model may
therefore rely more heavily on its own state of mind or family-oriented ideology
in ultimately considering the family as the main stakeholder in intergenerational
solidarities rather than on its intervention methods, even if we must recognise
that the two features are linked. This model, which Manuela Naldini (2003) calls
'family and parental solidarities and which is based on the existence of strong
intergenerational and parental relationships throughout the life cycle', is thus

characterised by the ineffectiveness of social measures for income support and employment and by insufficient public services for children and the elderly, thus suggesting that it is the responsibility of families to look after them. More fundamentally, this model assumes that the reciprocal responsibilities and obligations in the family will extend to the wider family: between spouses, from parents to children, etc. This is the model implemented in Italy, which has also spread to other Mediterranean countries, particularly to Spain (Cousins, 1995) under the influence of the Church – a genuine agent of social control (Conti, 2014). Its patriarchal vision has resulted in encouraging family obligations and solidarities, not to mention curbing 'any form of public intervention relating to social reproduction and care, particularly as regards the implementation of services for children and the elderly' (Naldini, 2002). Thus it is no surprise that in times of crisis the practices of family mobilisation are intensifying (from parents to their adult children struggling to enter working life, from mature children to their elderly parents stricken by issues of material autonomy or health problems, etc.) even though it is not amongst those most disadvantaged that this phenomenon is most clearly seen, far from it.

Class and gender relationships: combined effects to better identify generational situations

'When we talk about generation, we quickly forget any other differentiating factor' (Chauvel, 2014). This warning brings us to understand that the changes affecting social positions and the roles of each generation in a context of both increasing life expectancy and financial insecurity at various times of life (youth, adulthood, old age, etc.) are to be highly differentiated according to the social classes of the individuals in these positions. This warning is taken literally by the authors of this work who show in this section that internal social inequalities in each generation relate mainly to the mechanisms for the reproduction of the social structure (primarily class and gender).

Indeed, each generation has its own constraints which partly correspond to the societal context defining its own living conditions. However, each generation defines itself also and above all in relation to the other generations which either precede or follow. It therefore belongs to a family order which crosses generations and whose purpose is primarily the social reproduction of its members. It is this position, experienced differently depending on the members' social characteristics and the capital at their disposal, which will determine the nature of intergenerational relationships (exchanges or transactions), and also their scope and, more fundamentally, their issues. From this point of view, ageing which is a key aspect of changes along life cycle is a factor in social inequalities in both intragenerational and intergenerational relationships. Family solidarity, and the way it is practised, differs from one generation to the next, from one social background to another, and between genders. Thus these behaviours are established according to socially differentiated logics – i.e., which reveal the differences in the situations of the generations and the social positions held by the individuals and which function as regulatory frameworks.

The role of the family is unchanged by the ageing of the population and on a daily basis comprises a variety of behaviours involving transmission, exchange and mutual support. This variety of intergenerational social relationships (between children and parents, parents and grandchildren, etc.) thus does not escape the social reproduction process insofar as class membership and also gender both continue to strongly determine the strategic abilities of each member of the line. In these conditions, and 'very logically', women are far more on the front line than men when it comes to providing material support and care for an elderly parent. Gender is thus shown to be a key factor in determining the extent and nature of this assistance (Ogg and Renaut, 2006b). Still in these conditions and barring unforeseen events, those from wealthy backgrounds are distinguished by their efficient transmission of financial and/or cultural heritage between family generations.

According to a recently used assertion (Nowik and Lecestre-Rollier, 2015), family solidarities are put to the test by ageing insofar as this process tends to transform intergenerational social relationships without it being possible to distinguish stereotypical behaviour models. The 'problem' of ageing does not come down to the bleak vision of material support in daily tasks being provided for the elderly by their relatives. There are multiple social realities involved in ageing and thus they cannot be simply reduced to an increasing vulnerability of the elderly. A Galician proverb states that men die rich, beautiful and happy, thus summarising the social differences in living conditions awaiting the elderly according to their gender. Women, whose life expectancy is higher, comprise the majority of the ageing population. They are more prone to financial vulnerability and debilitating disease, as well as greater isolation. They mainly look after their husbands whilst the latter are alive yet, once widowed, they cannot expect to receive similar support in return. We can extend this sociological deconstruction by adding that thanks to the impact of social protection schemes and more prosperous professional careers, today's elderly are active and are expected to provide financial support to their descendants, particularly amongst the inheriting social classes. Who is helping whom? The answer to this question requires one to depart from any bleak vision which might see the ageing of senior citizens as an unbearable burden for their descendants, as well as with any populist approach which might see in contemporary old age a solution to the limits of the Welfare State. Such an answer requires in a more objective way that we understand the social logics which makes the family, in Mediterranean societies in particular, a system of unequal obligations in which the effects of gender, social classes and generations are combined.

Notes

1 Useful reference may be made to the classification established by M. Silverstein and V. Bengtson (1997) based on six dimensions: the structural dimension, which measures the distance between the homes of family members; the associative dimension, which combines the frequency of social contact and shared activities with family members; the emotional dimension, i.e. the sentimental and emotional closeness and intimacy between family members; the consensual dimension, relating to similar points of view as regards opinions, values and lifestyles; the functional dimension, which concerns the exchange of services and favours or financial support; the normative dimension, relating to the sense of obligation felt toward family members.

2 Over recent years (2000–2010), a general rise in the employment rate in the 55–59 age group can be observed (from 50% to 61% for the European Union of 27) as well as in the 60–64 age group (from 23% to 31%) even though the proportion of people aged 55 and over increased substantially in all member States during the same period as baby boomers reached old age.

3 'The Share survey confirms that France, together with the Southern European countries (Italy, Spain and Greece), is the country in which the quality of employment is considered as the worst by its older workers, particularly as regards career prospects and low recognition of their work. They also reported poorer working conditions than those enjoyed by their European neighbours. The results of the French survey on working conditions from 2005 are in accordance with this data. They show that almost 40% of employees aged 35 to 55 feel they will be "unable to carry on with their current job until they are 60". Reasons given range from roles involving physically demanding work (labourers) to tensions surrounding work organisation, unpredictable or excessive working hours and work intensity (office workers and managers)' (Guillemard, 2013, p. 49).

References

Attias-Donfut, C. (Ed.). (1995). *Les solidarités entre générations: vieillesse, familles, État.* Paris: Nathan.

Attias-Donfut, C. and Litwin, H. (2015). Comparaison de l'entraide familiale à l'échelle européenne: idées reçues, réalités et incertitudes. *Informations Sociales*, 2(188), 54–63.

Barbier, J.-C. and Théret, B. (2009). *Le système français de protection sociale.* Paris: La Découverte.

Baverez, N. (2013). Solidarité familiale, solidarités collectives à l'âge de la mondialisation, in: Fulchiron, H. (Ed.), *Les solidarités entre générations: Solidarities Between Generations* (pp. 683–692). Bruxelles: Bruylant.

Chauvel, L. (2014). *Le destin des générations: structure sociale et cohortes en France du XXe siècle aux années 2010.* Paris: Presses Universitaires de France.

Conti, F. (2014). L'Etat social dans l'Europe méditerranéenne: quelques considérations dans une perspective comparatiste, in: Brodiez-Dolino, A. and Dumons, B. (Eds.), *La protection sociale en Europe au XXe siècle.* Histoire. Rennes: Presses Universitaires de Rennes.

Cousins, C. (1995). Women and social policy in Spain: the development of a gendered welfare regime. *Journal of European Social Policy*, 5(3), 175–197.

Damon, J. (2007). Les politiques familiales en enjeux, in: Paugam, S. (Ed.), *Repenser la solidarité* (pp. 242–263). Le lien social. Paris: Presses Universitaires de France.

Esping-Andersen, G. (1990). *The Three Worlds of Welfare Capitalism.* Princeton: Princeton University Press.

Guillemard, A.-M. (2013). Le vieillissement actif: enjeux, obstacles, limites. *Retraite et société*, 2(65), 17–38.

Mauger, G. (2011). Préface, in: Mannheim, K. (Ed.), *Le problème des générations* (pp. 3–20). Paris: Armand Colin.

Merrien, F.-X. (2007). *L'Etat-Providence.* Paris: Presses Universitaires de France.

Miller, D. A. (1981). The 'sandwich' weneration: adult children of the aging. *Social Work*, 26(5), 419–423.

Naldini, M. (2002). Le politiche sociali e la famiglia nei paesi Mediterranei: prospettive di analisi comparata. *Stato e mercato*, (1), 73–100.

Naldini, M. (2003). *The family in the mediterranean welfare state.* London; Portland: Frank Cass.

Nowik, L. and Lecestre-Rollier, B. (2015). Quand le vieillissement repose sur les familles, in: Nowik, L. and Lecestre-Rollier, B. (Eds.), *Vieillir dans les pays du Sud: les solidarités familiales à l'épreuve du vieillissement* (pp. 19–53). Hommes et sociétés. Paris: Karthala.

Ogg, J. and Renaut, S. (2006a). Les quinquagénaires européens et leurs parents. De la famille ou de l'État, qui doit s'occuper des ascendants ? *Informations Sociales*, 6(134), 28–39.

Ogg, J. and Renaut, S. (2006b). The support of parents in old age by those born during 1945–1954: a european perspective. *Ageing & Society*, 26(5), 723–743.

Silverstein, M. and Bengtson, V. L. (1997). Intergenerational solidarity and the structure of adult child-parent relationships in american families. *American Journal of Sociology*, 103(2), 429–460.

Van de Velde, C. (2015). *Sociologie des âges de la vie*. Paris: Armand Colin.

Weber, F. (2015). Quelle famille pour les bénéficiaires de la protection sociale ? La subsidiarité des politiques sociales en question. *Informations Sociales*, 2(188), 64–65.

5 Public policies towards the family in Italy

An analysis of the evolution of the Italian welfare state and its impact on gender and generations

Elena Ambrosetti and Donatella Strangio

Almost 20 years ago, Ferrera (1996) published his seminal paper on the 'Southern Model' of welfare in social Europe, identifying four main characteristics of the welfare states of Italy, Spain, Portugal and Greece. According to Ferrera, the main traits of the Southern European welfare model (1996) are 1) an income maintenance system characterized by high fragmentation, dualism and corporatism; 2) the establishment of a universal National Health Service; 3) low state penetration into the welfare sphere and a mixture of public and non-public actors in this domain; and 4) the persistence of clientelism and the selective distribution of cash benefits based on 'patronage machines'. The main feature of this model is the strong focus on old-age pensions at the expense of unemployment, sickness benefits and family allowances measures (Andreotti and Sabatinelli, 2004). In order to compensate for such imbalances, Southern European welfare models are characterized by the significant presence and important role of the family acting as a 'social clearing house' (Ferrera, 1996). The system is largely based on a male breadwinner, family/kinship solidarity model, where the division of labour is gender asymmetrical and women have to provide the assistance and care essential for the family's welfare (Naldini, 2003). In this situation, women's participation in the labour market is generally low: as they are traditionally involved in the care of children and the elderly, they struggle to balance work and family life. Working women have often given up their jobs after the birth of their first child (Moreno and Marí-Klose, 2013). Several scholars have emphasized that the main factors which have influenced the evolution of Southern European welfare models include the importance of the prevailing culture and social norms in Catholic societies, in particular the gender division of labour, gender roles within the family and strong family values (Leon and Pavolini, 2014; Saraceno, 2003; Pfau-Effinger, 1998). Intergenerational solidarity expressed through late release from the parental home, frequent co-residence or spatial proximity with the parents after marriage, have been the main distinctive traits of the Southern European family for several centuries (Moreno and Marí-Klose, 2013). Intergenerational solidarity is used to protect young family members from economic crisis and unemployment; in return, when parents reach old age, they can rely on strong support from their children.

Over the last few decades, several factors have undermined the stability of the southern welfare model; for example, the economic turmoil which has affected Europe and, in particular, Southern European countries since 2008. Nevertheless, in order to analyse the evolution of the Mediterranean welfare model since its first definition by Ferrera in 1996 other factors of change should be taken into account together with the economic turmoil. These factors are largely linked to changes in the demographic, socio-economic and political/institutional situation in Europe during the last two decades. First of all, from the demographic point of view, the main consequences of the so-called demographic transition– i.e., low fertility and an ageing population – have dramatically evolved since the beginning of the '90s and they constitute a major challenge for the modern welfare system and for the relationship between gender and generations. Secondly, the socio-economic arena has also witnessed major changes during the last two decades: the level of female employment has increased and dual-earner families are now widespread in the Mediterranean. Employment in the service sectors has also dramatically increased and this, together with informal jobs, new vulnerabilities and new social risks, is one of the main characteristics of the globalized world economy. Finally, on the political and institutional side, Southern Mediterranean countries were under constant pressure as they entered the process of the European and Economic and Monetary Union (EMU) and had to respect rules imposed on them by European Union (EU) treaties.

Because of such changes, the southern model may be evolving into a new form. Evidence from previous studies has emphasized the capacity of some countries to evolve from this model and the persistence of more traditional behaviours in other countries (Leon and Pavolini, 2014; Naldini and Jurado, 2013; Naldini and Saraceno, 2008). In this respect, Italy seems to be witnessing strong resistance to updating its welfare structure and as a consequence the changes which have so far occurred have mainly been driven by EU reforms. In the following sections, we will examine the evolution of social policies in Italy over time, gender and generations in order to find out how and if Italian social policies took the aforementioned demographic, social and economic changes into account. Secondly, we will study the role of economic and institutional factors in the development of policies. Our aim is to understand how and if Italian social policies over the last 20 years have taken men and women's changing roles in society into account, both in the private and the public sphere, and if intergenerational redistribution[1] has evolved in a more egalitarian way compared to the past. Our chapter is organized as follows: the first section will deal with the major demographic changes since 1960. The second section is dedicated to the analysis of the Italian welfare model from an economic history perspective. The third section will analyse whether the Italian welfare model has changed over the years to take into account the main social, demographic and economic changes occurring in the last 20 years and their effect on gender and intergenerational equity.[2]

Main demographic changes in Italy

The Italian population has increased substantially during the last 60 years, from about 47 million inhabitants in 1951 to about 60 million in 2011. During the last few decades, Italy, like other Western European countries, has been affected by the first and second demographic transitions (Van de Kaa, 1987). The major consequences of these demographic transitions have been population increase, due to a non-simultaneous decrease in mortality and fertility (in the first transition), and profound changes in marriage and family formation patterns, which followed the legalization of divorce in several European countries (in the so-called second demographic transition). Nowadays, couples may decide to marry later or possibly forego marriage. As a consequence, in countries like Italy, where births outside marriage are still low compared to other European countries, fertility has fallen to very low levels (Salvini, 2011).

The decreasing trend in general and infant mortality, which started after WWII, has steadily led to high life expectancy rates at birth. Over the last 60 years, Italy has become a country with one of the highest life expectancies at birth (see Chapter 1 for further details). The number of marriages and the birth rate increased rapidly in Italy in the initial period after WWII. At the beginning of the 1950's the total fertility rate (TFR) was 2.5 children per woman and this increased during the so-called baby-boom period of the 1960s. It reached its maximum in 1967, when a rate of 2.7 children per woman was recorded (Baldi and Cagiano De Azevedo, 2005). Since then, the TFR has started to decrease: it fell to 1.4 in 1990, 1.24 in 2000 and 1.4 in 2013 (ISTAT). The marriage rate was quite stable until the 1970's when it started to decline. This trend continues today. At the same time, the divorce rate has increased (divorce became legal in 1970), but it remains quite low compared to other European countries. New patterns of family structure have emerged in Italy during the last few decades: the number of single and two-component families increased from the end of the '80s until the present day, and they now represent more than half the families in Italy. Families with three, four and particularly with five or more members have been constantly decreasing over the same time period (ISTAT, 2010). This new family structure is the result of a series of factors: first of all, an ageing population. More than half the families comprising only one member are of a woman over 60. The percentage of unmarried cohabiting couples (7%) and reconstituted households (7%) is still low in Italy which demonstrates the preference for more traditional family structures (marriage). The traditional late departure of the young from the family is still one of the main characteristic of the Italian family today.

An economic-historic perspective: the 'Italian' welfare model in the literature

The distortions or peculiarities of the Italian model

Since the '80s, a significant amount of sociological and political science literature has presented comparative abnormalities in Italian welfare as part of the more general weakness of the political, economic and social system (Ascoli, 1984; Ferrera, 1984). Some historical literature has begun to reconstruct the development paths of various social policies in detail (Costanzo and Migliavacca, 2015; Giorgi, 2004; Silei, 2003), although other aspects and the evolutionary dynamics of our welfare state still remain to be explored. The peculiarity of the Italian welfare system lies in the internal composition of its spending. In the period of 2000–2008, most of the social spending in Italy was absorbed by the 'old-age' sector (59.1% of the total against a European average of 43.7%), especially by the pension system (Figure 5.1).

The 'family', 'unemployment' and 'housing and social exclusion' sectors, 4.2%, 1.8% and 0.3%, respectively, appear markedly reduced in comparison to the European values of 7.8%, 5%, 7% and 3.3%. No such a distortion was recorded for any other country. Italy also has a second distortion: distributional. Within the various spending sectors, including pensions, there is a clear protection gap (in the access to benefits and their generosity) between different occupational categories. Although all the continental welfare states share a degree of segmentation and have some contrast between the included and the excluded, within Bismarckian and southern European systems, Italy is exceptional. From a historical perspective, Italy reached its peak in terms of double distortion in its welfare distribution (in terms of old age and unemployment) between 1980 and 1990. In the pensions' area, 'high' protection reached values greater than the EU average, while 'average' and 'low' protection were less. In the unemployment area, 'high' protection (layoffs or mobility) were only provided in Italy, whilst average protection was lower than the average EU value. Comparative research showed that functional polarization of spending had several peaks during the 15 years from 1985 to 2000. To find the roots of the double distortion, it is necessary to go back in time to pinpoint the historical period prior to 1985 when this distortion began to appear. The internal imbalance in social spending grew rapidly in Italy in the seventies, but the engine of distortion had been activated in the previous decade of the twentieth century. Whilst the expenditure pattern still appeared relatively balanced in the mid-'50s, at the end of the next decade, the imbalance was apparent and higher than that of other continental countries.

Which components of the expenditure were responsible for this imbalance? Between 1955 and 1980, a continued and pronounced decline in household spending was recorded in Italy. Within overall spending, unemployment benefits were substantially stable against inexorably rising pension expenditure. The latter was due to a constant improvement of the so-called guaranteed retirement pension;

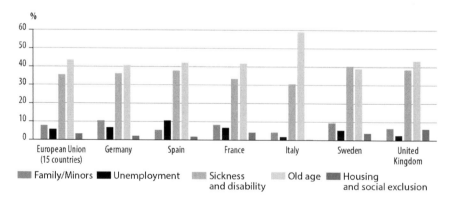

Figure 5.1 Social spending by sector, as a % of total social spending, average 2000–2008

Source: author's elaboration on Eurostat online database

minimum pensions remained stable, while the relative value of unemployment benefits and family allowances decreased significantly between 1965 and 1980 (Ferrera, 1984). On the basis of these considerations it is possible to state that the distortion of the Italian welfare model began in the '50s and gradually accelerated over the next two decades. This process was the result of choices made during the 'golden age' which unbalanced the age and distribution orientation of Italian welfare, orienting it towards pensions and former workers to the detriment of any risk associated with stages of life before retirement – i.e., of policies supporting families, children and the unemployed.

The birth of Italian welfare also suffered from other unbalances which have greatly affected its evolution since the end of WWII: the development of these characteristics is well documented in the literature (Naldini, 2003; Saraceno, 2003; Ferrera, 1996) and goes beyond the scope of our research. We will therefore only mention them briefly. The Italian welfare model traditionally left a lot of the responsibility with the family, so social policies, and those aimed at families, were not developed for some time. Social policies explicitly targeted at families and children were implemented for the first time in Italian history during Fascism (1922–1945) with the aim of maintaining the birth rate and the family. Even though the effects of these policies were limited (Saraceno, 2003), the impact and the echoes of such measures influenced post WWII governments to the point that later measures taken were cautious: 'perhaps a social reaction against the pre-war fascist preoccupation with the idea of increasing the population' (Ferrari, 1975, p. 426). Consequently, 30 years after the end of the war, in 1975, Ferrari noted that whilst the Italian population had witnessed profound cultural, social and economic changes in the '50s, '60s and the first half of the seventies, social policies from the pre-war period, particularly those directly related to marriage and fertility, remained intact. The post-war period was also characterized by strong political division between Catholic and secular parties (in particular the Left) on the role of the family, in the fields of sexuality and of equal opportunities for men and women (Naldini and Saraceno, 2008; Saraceno, 2003). The position of the Catholic Church should be particularly emphasized in this context. The Church had not been against the establishment of institutions and rules regulating the family; on the contrary, its position favoured the family being considered an entity to be treated separately from other institutions. Specifically, it should be an institution regulated by the Church (Saraceno, 2003). For example, from the very beginning of the debate on the establishment of public crèches and kindergartens, the Church and the Catholic parties lobbied together to fight against public education facilities. The latter were seen as being in opposition to Catholic education. Even the Communist party was affected by the Catholic orientation of the Italian people to the point that it did not intervene in such debates except in defence of working women (Saraceno, 2003).

Paradoxically, even though the importance of state policy in helping the creation of families was stressed in the new Constitution of 1948 (art. 31), as a result of the aforementioned political divisions, no specific measures were taken for long time. A constant lack of consensus on priorities and the aforementioned political and ideological division about issues concerning the family are amongst those characteristics which are peculiar to the Italian welfare model and which represent important sources of resistance to addressing structural reform. We will be discussing these in the following sections (Naldini and Saraceno, 2008). Another characteristic feature of the Italian welfare system is that, although the debate about the possibility of establishing a welfare system started in the '50s, the most important reforms were approved during the seventies,[3] a period of economic recession. The resources available for public spending were therefore very limited; because of the economic downturn, the problem of Italian public debt started to escalate from the seventies onwards.

Old and new challenges

Over the past three decades, the intensity and type of social needs have profoundly changed in all European countries. As already emphasized in the first section of this chapter (see also Chapter 1), the most disruptive change was undoubtedly the ageing population which hit Italy with particular intensity. In the wake of lower fertility rates and a gradual increase in life expectancy, the proportion of older people in the total population has constantly increased: in 1965, those over 65 accounted for 9.9% of the Italian population; in 2010, this was about 20.2% (EU average 17.4%). An ageing population has created not only a higher demand for services but also new types of needs, both on the part of the elderly (those who are dependent for example) and on the part of those family members (mostly women) who perform the care.

   A second change was due to the profound transformation of methods of production and the transition to a new post-industrial order. Technological innovation, the service sector, economic integration and globalization have resulted in striking upheavals in European labour markets. A steady decline in Fordist employment (i.e. stable and safe jobs, with permanent positions) has been recorded and this has not been fully compensated for by an increase in atypical employment. Italy has also recorded a sharp rise in unemployment and inactivity in those who are 'demoralized': these factors have become worrying structurally, especially in the Southern regions and amongst certain categories, such as young people, women and the over 50. The transformation of the labour market and income distribution has raised new questions relating to the need to define, on the one hand, adequate protection adapted to the new forms of flexible employment and, on the other hand, the need to support inclusion and increase worker employability, especially those who are most vulnerable.

   From the perspective of flexicurity (the so-called Jobs Act has recently been approved by the Italian Government) and more generally of the social investment state (Ferrera, 2010), social policies in several European countries, and now in Italy, are being established on a promotional basis rather than on a compensatory one. With the approval and implementation of a series of new measures their range has spread throughout the entire life cycle, starting in early childhood, when soft skills and human capital are created. In addition, whilst other European countries have found a balance between flexibility and social security because the political programs have become part of the ministries' agendas so that they will become a reality – e.g., fiscal policy for the family in Sweden, reforms to care services in the United Kingdom and the welfare mix for working men and women in France – in Italy, because of a greater rigidity in the labour market and immobility in the welfare state, the reforms are struggling to proceed in harmony because there has been no adjustment of the latter to support the former. The lack of coordination between these two policy areas prevents the achievement of a balance between flexibility and security (Ferrera, 2006; Della Sala, 2002).

A third aspect of change is that of gender relations within the family. Whilst in post-war industrial societies traditional families with a male breadwinner and a housewife were in the majority, the new post-industrial era is characterized by a greater variety of family typologies: families with two income earners, single parents, de facto unions and so on (Saraceno, 2008). We are witnessing new social relationships which are characterized by much more insecurity than in past European societies, with important consequences in terms of economic vulnerability and inclusion. As already emphasized in the first section of this chapter, Italy is less affected by these dynamics because they are inhibited by the 'syndrome of family values' but at the price of putting the family at increasing economic and social stress and making it more and more difficult to maintain.

Another ongoing trend since the '80s has been the increasing female participation in the labour market (Figure 5.2) in large part related to the expansion of services. Although this trend has encouraged the expansion of economically more secure, dual-income households, it has also created new tensions and often a work overload within the household, with serious repercussions on women and in particular on working mothers (Del Boca and Rosina, 2009). As a consequence, a new need has emerged in social protection systems, a need for collective support for the family and for measures which can mitigate this imbalance between work and private life: schemes and programs which are both child-friendly and mother-friendly (Esping-Andersen, 2002). In the absence of such policies, not only are working women subject to heavy penalties in terms of time, effort, career and salaries, etc., but they are often even forced into not entering

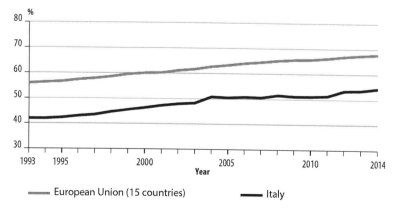

Figure 5.2 Female activity levels over time, Italy and Western Europe

Source: author's elaboration on Eurostat online database

the labour market: employment levels for women in Italy have increased much more slowly than in other countries despite the strong preference expressed by Italian women (Ferrera, 2008).

Italian families ensure subsistence and assistance for their members and are able to meet the needs of care not covered by the public system. However, they were only able to do that locally: people with special needs could only rely on the protection of the family living in close proximity. Informal care and domestic work are largely provided by women: a recent study revealed that amongst the population aged over 49, in Italy women are more likely than men to provide informal care to children and parents who are not co-resident and to take care of their grandchildren (Albertini and Pavolini, 2015). Under the burden of the pressure caused by the double distortion of Italian welfare (and the labour market), families have tended to react using local compensation strategies; for example, desperately searching for any possible connection with the guaranteed employment sector for a least one family member, or exploiting every possible niche in the underground economy. The latter amounts to 20% of the GDP in Italy. In the wake of these major social and economic changes, Italian welfare has had to face important challenges which we will explore in the next section.

Did Italian policymakers take into account the socio-economic transformations? Was the Italian welfare model recalibrated?

During the '80s, the political agenda started to reorient policy towards containing public spending dynamics and introducing structural reforms to curb pensions, on the one hand, and to change social security benefits on the other. Many Italian regions, aware of the system's shortcomings, began strengthening it through programs supporting families, focusing not only on transfers but also on services (Madama, 2010). Since 1992, a phase of reforms has started in all areas of social spending: subtractive in the pensions' area and additive in the unemployment and family assistance areas.

The major decisions taken between 1990 and 2012, in terms of policy measures, are in Table 5.1. It should be emphasized that the process of European convergence and the establishment of a starting date (1998) for EMU acted as a robust external constraint for the policy choices of Italian governments in the '90s, stimulating institutional change. After the launch of the EMU, many other instruments have allowed the EU to exert adjustment pressure on the Italian welfare state. The entry into the euro zone has represented a historic turning point for the Italian economic and social model, to the point that it might be argued that in the '90s the European Union saved not only the welfare system but also the entire country.

However, there were also other internal driving forces which pushed the governments into taking new social policy measures. First of all, the decline in fertility: as shown in the first section of this chapter, the total fertility rate reached its lowest values in the mid-'90s. At that time, Italy finally recognized itself as a low-fertility country (Naldini and Saraceno, 2008). Concerns about low fertility

Table 5.1 The main legislation adopted by Italian welfare (1990–2012)

Years	Pensions	Unemployment	Family/Assistance
1990's	**1992:** Amato reform	**1991:** Mobility allowance	
	1993: Ciampi reform	**1993–1994:** Increase of the mobility allowance	
	1995: Dini reform		**1997:** Law on children's welfare
			1998: Minimum insertion income (experimental), third child allowances, maternity care allowances
2000's		**2000:** Increase of the mobility allowance	**2000:** Framework law on social services and social assistance
			2001: Constitutional reform
	2004: Maroni/ Tremonti reform		
		2005: Increase of the mobility allowance	
	2007: Damiano reform	**2007:** Increase of the mobility allowance	**2007:** National Extraordinary Creches Plan and Long-term care fund
			2008: Purchases card
	2009–2010: Sacconi reform	**2009:** Redundancy Fund (CIG) in derogation	
	2011: Fornero reform	**2012:** Fornero reform	
		2015: Job Act	

Source: Author's elaboration

were no longer restricted to the sphere of demographers but emerged into political debates, in the mass media and in public opinion. The lack of work/family reconciliation measures, and the consequent low participation in the labour market, together with young people leaving the parental household later than in any other European country, and the consequent increase in age at first union and first child, are considered to be some of the main determinants of low fertility. Unfortunately, only a few measures to counteract such phenomena were taken despite the aforementioned increase in awareness of low fertility's consequences. Furthermore, Naldini and Saraceno (2008) argue that the political debate and the measures taken at the time lacked both gender and intergenerational equity dimensions. In fact, the reforms which addressed the labour market's flexibility, such as the Treu Act of 1997 and the Biagi Act of 2003, were specifically aimed at working women: the work/family reconciliation debate concerns only women and does not

affect the traditional, gender unbalanced, division of labour and family responsibilities. Men become protagonists of the fertility debate only because their late
entry into the labour market compared to other European countries might delay
their formation of a family and the birth of their first child.

Major reforms: family and childcare policies and pensions

As stressed by Léon and Pavolini (2014), during the '90s and the 2000s, four major
policy reforms concerning the family and children were implemented. The first was
law 285 of 1997 about children's welfare: this law established the National Fund for
Children and Adolescents. Its goal was to implement measures at national, regional
and local level to facilitate the promotion of the rights, quality of life, development,
individual achievement and socialization of children and adolescents. Amongst
other interventions, the law promoted care services. However, limited financial
resources were allocated. Thus, although it promoted the development of a variety
of initiatives, the law was not able to provide structural changes to care needs (Da
Roit and Sabatinelli, 2013). In 1998, a special family allowance was established
for low-income families with at least three minor children. In 2000, a new law on
parental leave was established (Law 53/2000) which included significant innova-
tions. Henceforth the timing of this leave was flexible as the law allowed it to be
taken within the first eight years after the child's birth. Parental leave is considered
to be an individual right and not a family right as it was in the past; working fathers
used to be entitled to parental leave in substitution for mothers. Each parent thus
has the right to take up to six months individually with a maximum length of ten
months per couple. A type of father's bonus of one month was introduced: in addition, if the father takes at least 3 months, it can rise to a maximum of 11 months
per couple. The new law on parental leave is considered as one on the major policy
shifts towards gender equality of the last 15 years: rights and responsibilities for
children should be shared between men and women. Nevertheless, if the law has
changed in favour of a more egalitarian gender division of childcare responsibilities, the behaviour of fathers and mothers is much more difficult to change. According to the data from the Italian Labour Force Survey of 2011 (ISTAT), only 6.9% of
working fathers with a child under 8 years old took parental leave at least once versus 45.3% of working mothers. The most important and promising reform approved
at the beginning of the 2000s was the Framework Law 328 of 2000. This has been
judged to be a fairly good law in terms of its principles and general aims because
it finally stated the 'idea that national 'basic levels of social intervention' (LEAs)
would be guaranteed everywhere in different policy areas and for several types of
intervention' (Leon and Pavolini, 2014, p. 355). In addition, the law defined the
responsibilities of the various levels of government (state, regions and municipalities) and set uniform basic standards and coverage levels to be achieved across the
country (Naldini and Saraceno, 2008, p. 744). However, the resources allocated for
implementing the reform were not sufficient. In addition, a constitutional reform
was approved in 2001 which transferred the responsibility for social services and
assistance almost entirely onto the regions and local authorities; henceforth, the
role of the state in these fields was greatly limited in consequence.

During the 2000s, reforms in social and family policies were much less relevant than in the previous decade. The Berlusconi government (2001–2006) introduced two new policies relating to children under 3 years of age. Law 53 of 2003 gave children aged two and a half the possibility of going to kindergarten (previous legislation had stated that the entry age was 3). The second intervention (inserted in the National Budget Planning Law of 2003) was the introduction of the possibility of funding for company crèches and similar childcare activities (Leon and Pavolini, 2014). The reforms adopted by the centre-left government (2006–2008) tried to invest in more traditional childcare facilities such as crèches: a National Extraordinary Crèches Plan was adopted in order to improve the coverage for children under three years old by 4% (Sabatinelli, 2010).

To conclude our analysis of social and family policy reforms in Italy we would argue that there is still a need for large structural reforms (Naldini and Saraceno, 2008): the lack of reform can be ascribed to several factors and obstacles resulting from sociocultural, economic and political factors. Even though governments and public opinion recognize the need for such reform, because of the major social and demographic changes which have occurred since the mid-Seventies, there is still a lack of change in attitudes and behaviour towards women and motherhood in Italian society. From the economic point of view, financial constraints such as the public deficit prevented Italy from implementing many structural reforms. In addition, the centralization of the pension system, which we will discuss next, hindered reforms in other sectors of public expenditure. Lastly, the current economic crisis is another inhibitory factor (Leon and Pavolini, 2014).

As strongly emphasized in the previous sections, another major challenge faced by Italian society since the '90s is that of an ageing population. Major reforms have therefore been implemented in Italy over the last 25 years in the field of old age (Table 5.1), particularly as regards pensions. The two major reforms of the '90s were the Amato reform of 1992 and the Dini reform of 1995: they changed the principle for calculating pension benefits (Natali, 2015). Until 1995, pension benefits were calculated on the basis of the years of contributions and the last wage earned (non-contributory system), while from 1995 onwards pension benefits were based on a combination of years of contributions and the actual amount of contributions paid (contributory system). These reforms were implemented slowly in order to directly affect only the younger workers and were thus continued though the Berlusconi reform of 2004 (reform Maroni-Tremonti). The main innovation in old-age benefits was an increase in the legal retirement age (Natali, 2015, p. 52). The reform also introduced new measures to increase the financial resources of public schemes, including the so-called solidarity contribution of 4% deducted from high-level pension benefits, an increase in the contributions paid by workers in new and more flexible jobs, and a further distinction between social insurance benefits and social assistance benefits. The Fornero reform adopted in 2011 accelerated the reforms legislated for in the 1990s. This raised the retirement age, linking it to longevity and moved it towards equalising retirement ages for men and women, and it will improve the mechanism for adjustments in the future, linking future benefits with gross national product. Finally, it tried to eliminate early retirement rights. From the gender and intergenerational perspective, the pension reforms can be considered as positive because their aim was to address intergenerational redistribution and to equalize the treatment of men and women within the social security system.

Economic consequences of the reforms

The '90s were a turning point in the amount of public expenditure allocated to each sector (Figure 5.3). Looking at the internal composition of expenditure, the proportion for pensions decreased by only four percentage points between 1995 and 2009, while expenditure for the family and children increased by only one point and a half and the expenditure for social safety nets remained almost unchanged.

The clear distortion of Italian welfare remains as, unfortunately, the weighting of old-age expenditure in relation to GDP remains high, even when compared to other EU 15 (euro zone countries) (Figure 5.4). In addition, the weighting of other social indicators within GDP increased (heath, family and children, social exclusion, unemployment), although in lower percentages compared to old age. As a result, those at risk of poverty and social exclusion in Italy and those experiencing severe material deprivation are mostly young adults and children, while those less exposed to these risks are people over 75 (Figure 5.5)!

In such a context, the family plays an important role in compensating for the imbalances of the welfare system in Italy: there are substantial transfers of

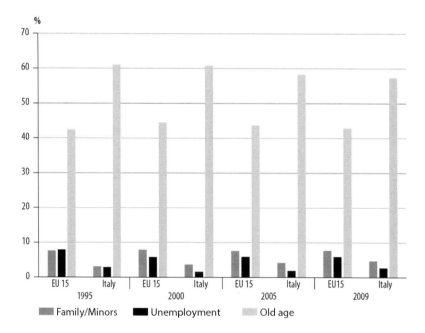

Figure 5.3 Social expenditure by sector (as a % of total social spending), Italy and EU-15, 1995–2009

Source: author's elaboration on Eurostat online database

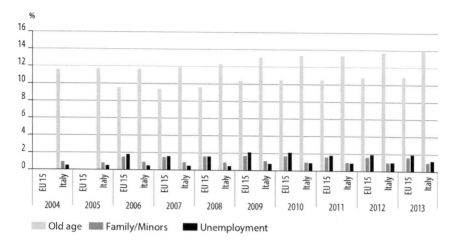

Figure 5.4 Proportion (%) of GDP for old age, family/children, unemployment, EU-15 (euro zone) – Italy (2004–2013)

Source: author's elaboration on Eurostat online database

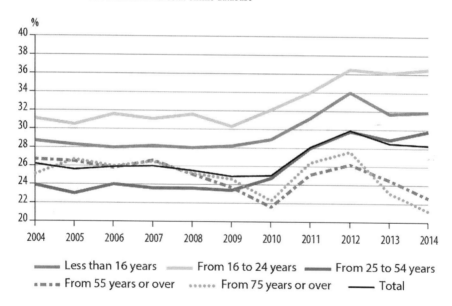

Figure 5.5 People at risk of poverty or social exclusion by broad age groups – Italy (2004–2013)

Source: author's elaboration on Eurostat online database

resources from parents to adult children even after they have left the parental home (Albertini and Kohli, 2013). However, in Southern European welfare regimes, the most used form of support is the prolonged residence of adult children with the parents; in exchange, adult children will later take care of elderly dependent parents. Financial transfers from parents to adult children and grandchildren are another important form of intergenerational private support which is very wide-spread amongst Italian families.

This is symptomatic of an economic model whose institutions need a strong shift to give hope to younger generations. However, the crisis which began in 2008 had a profound effect on the levels of growth and wealth in euro-area countries, particularly as regards Italy. It had an impact on its GDP, which has decreased steadily in recent years. In addition, the 2008 crisis dealt a severe blow to the economy and to Italian society, highlighting once again the persistent structural weaknesses of its welfare model. The financial emergency caused heavy political turbulence and the formation of a new government of technocrats led by Mario Monti. At the end of 2011, a new pension reform was launched (the aforementioned Fornero reform) in order to correct the still existing distribution anomalies and further contain the spending dynamics for the coming decades. In the summer of 2012, an ambitious reform of the labour market was approved which changed the institutional architecture of the social safety net system: the main reason these reforms covering the sustainability of the Italian model were addressed was the European Union.

Conclusion

Setting Italy within the context of the Southern European welfare model, this chapter has tried to explain the main peculiarities of the Italian model by taking a socio-economic perspective. We have argued that the Italian model is characterized by a double distortion. Firstly, in the internal composition of spending which is largely absorbed by the old-age sector, especially by the pension system, at the expense of the other sectors. Secondly, a distributional distortion; within the various spending sectors, including pensions, there is a clear protection gap between different occupational categories. Demographic change together with socio-economic transformations posed new challenges to the aforementioned Italian model. The most important factors which impelled Italian governments to reform the welfare system include lowest-low fertility; an ageing population; the profound transformation of methods of production and the transition to a new post-industrial order, with the consequent sharp rise in unemployment and inactivity; changes in family formation and gender relationships and the increasing female participation in the labour market. As a result, the political agenda of the '80s started to reorient policy toward containing public spending dynamics and introducing structural reforms to curb pensions, on the one hand, and on the other to change social security benefits. It should be noted that the process of European convergence and the establishment of a starting date (1998) for European Monetary Union acted as a robust external constraint for the policy choices of Italian governments in the '90s, stimulating institutional change. We have discussed the most important reforms in the family and childcare field and in the pension system, their effect on gender and intergenerational equity and on public expenditure. We have argued that although important new legislation has been introduced in the social and family policy fields over the last 25 years, including new responsibilities for fathers and relevant measures for gender equality, there is still a need for large structural reforms (Naldini and Saraceno, 2008). The lack of reform can be ascribed to several factors: little change in attitudes and behaviour towards women and motherhood in Italian society, financial constraints such as the public deficit and, lastly, the current economic crisis (Leon and Pavolini, 2014). The pension reforms introduced since 1992 are positive from the gender and intergenerational perspective and from the public expenditure perspective, because their aim has been to address intergenerational redistribution, equalize the treatment of men and women within the social security system and to cut public expenditure. These reforms were implemented under the financial constraints imposed on Italy by the European Union, and they have been slowed by the sharp decrease in the Italian economy since the beginning of the economic downturn of 2008 (Chiara et al., 2015). However, as stressed by Zannella (2015), Italian welfare is characterized by strong imbalances in transfers towards the elderly, by high youth dependency alleviated by the family and by a strong gender bias in terms of work, both in the market and in the home.

Notes

1 In modern welfare states, redistribution occurs not only between rich and poor but also between young and old, between generations. Intergenerational redistribution takes place in several ways through social policies: e.g. pension systems, the health care system (Prinzen, 2015).
2 'Intergenerational equity' may be defined as (1) equality of opportunity: i.e. equity between persons in the intergenerational transmission of economic status – or (2) equity in the intergenerational division of aggregate resources, considering all members of each generation as a group (Osberg, 1997).
3 The reform of pensions was adopted in 1969 but only fully implemented in 1978. In 1978, la Sistema Sanitario Nazionale (SSN) [the Italian National Health Service] was also introduced (Ferrera, 1996).

References

Albertini, M. and Kohli, M. (2013). The generational contract in the family: an analysis of transfer regimes in Europe. *European Sociological Review*, 29(4), 828–840.

Albertini, M. and Pavolini, E. (2015). Care policies in Italy between a national frozen landscape and local dynamism, in: Ascoli, U. (Ed.), *The italian Welfare State in a European perspective: a comparative analysis* (pp. 133–156). Bristol: Policy Press.

Andreotti, A. and Sabatinelli, S. (2004). Early childcare in Italy: path dependency and new needs. *EMES Italy Working Paper*, 23.

Ascoli, U. (Ed.). (1984). *Welfare State all'italiana*. Roma: Laterza.

Baldi, S. and Cagiano De Azevedo, R. (2005). *La popolazione italiana: storia demografica dal dopoguerra ad oggi*. Bologna: Il Mulino.

Chiara, A., Natali, D. and Sacchi, S. (2015). The europeanisation of the italian welfare state: channels of influence and trends, in: Ascoli, U. (Ed.), *The italian Welfare State in a European perspective: a comparative analysis* (pp. 259–281). Bristol: Policy Press.

Costanzo, R. and Migliavacca, M. (2015). 'Everythings needs to change, so everything can stay the same': the italian welfare state facing new social risks, in: Ascoli, U. (Ed.), *The italian Welfare State in a European perspective: a comparative analysis* (pp. 21–47). Bristol: Policy Press.

Da Roit, B. and Sabatinelli, S. (2013). Nothing on the move or just going private? Understanding the freeze on child- and eldercare policies and the development of care markets in Italy. *Social Politics: International Studies in Gender, State & Society*, 20(3), 430–453.

Del Boca, D. and Rosina, A. (2009). *Famiglie sole: sopravvivere con un welfare inefficiente*. Bologna: Il Mulino.

Della Sala, V. (2002). 'Modernisation' and welfare-state restructuring in Italy: the impact of child care, in: Michel, S. and Mahon, R. (Eds.), *Child care policy at the crossroads: gender and Welfare State restructuring* (pp. 171–190). New York: Routledge.

Esping-Andersen, G. (2002). *Why we need a new welfare state*. New York: Oxford University Press.

Ferrari, G. (1975). Law and fertility in Italy, in: Kirk, M., Livi-Bacci, M. and Szabady, E. (Eds.), *Law and fertility in Europe: a study of legislation directly or indirectly affecting fertility in Europe* (pp. 426–461). Dolhain: Ordina Editions.

Ferrera, M. (1984). *Il welfare state in Italia: sviluppo e crisi in prospettiva comparata*. Bologna: Il Mulino.

Ferrera, M. (1996). Il modello sud-europeo di welfare state. *Rivista Italiana di Scienza politica*, 1, 67–101.

Ferrera, M. (2006). *Le politiche sociali: l'Italia in prospettiva comparata*. Bologna: Il Mulino.

Ferrera, M. (2008). *Il fattore D: perchè il lavoro delle donne farà crescere l'Italia*. Milano: Mondadori.

Ferrera, M. (2010). The South European countries, in: Castles, F. G., Leibfried, S., Lewis, J., Obinger, H. and Pierson, C. (Eds.), *The Oxford handbook of the welfare state* (pp. 616–628). Oxford Handbooks in Political Science & International Relations. Oxford: Oxford University Press.

Giorgi, C. (2004). *La previdenza del regime: storia dell'Inps durante il fascismo*. Bologna: Il Mulino.

ISTAT (Ed.). (2010). *La misurazione delle tipologie familiari nelle indagini di popolazione*. Roma: ISTAT.

Leon, M. and Pavolini, E. (2014). 'Social investment' or back to 'familism': the impact of the economic crisis on family and care policies in Italy and Spain. *South European Society and Politics*, 19(4), 353–369.

Madama, I. (2010). *Le politiche di assistenza sociale*. Bologna: Il Mulino.

Moreno, L. and Marí-Klose, P. (2013). Youth, family change and welfare arrangements. *European Societies*, 15(4), 493–513.

Naldini, M. (2003). *The family in the Mediterranean welfare state*. London; Portland: Frank Cass.

Naldini, M. and Jurado, T. (2013). Family and welfare state reorientation in Spain and inertia in Italy from a european perspective. *Population Review*, 52(1), 43–61.

Naldini, M. and Saraceno, C. (2008). Social and family policies in Italy: not totally frozen but far from structural reforms. *Social Policy and Administration*, 47(7), 733–748.

Natali, D. (2015). Two decades of pension reforms in Italy shedding light on a series of mirror-images, in: Ascoli, U. (Ed.), *The italian welfare state in a European perspective: a comparative analysis* (pp. 49–70). Bristol: Policy Press.

Osberg, L. (1997). *Meaning and measurement in intergenerational equity*. Retrieved from http://citeseerx.ist.psu.edu/viewdoc/summary?doi=10.1.1.470.9009.

Pfau-Effinger, B. (1998). Gender cultures and the gender arrangement – a theoretical framework for cross-national comparisons on gender. *The European Journal of Social Sciences*, 11(2), 147–166.

Prinzen, K. (2015). Attitudes toward intergenerational redistribution in the Welfare State. *Kölner Zeitschrift für Soziologie und Sozialpsychologie*, 67(1), 349–370.

Sabatinelli, S. (Ed.). (2010). *Le politiche per i bambini in età prescolare in Italia e in Europa*. Milano: QUID IRS.

Salvini, S. (2011). La popolazione oggi in Italia, in: Salvini, S., De Rose, A. and Associazi-one Italiana per gli Studi di Popolazione (Eds.), *Rapporto sulla popolazione. L'Italia a 150 ani dall'unità* (p. 156). Bologna: Universale paperbacks Il Mulino.

Saraceno, C. (2003). *Mutamenti della famiglia e politiche sociali in Italia.* Bologna: Il Mulino.

Saraceno, C. (Ed.). (2008). *Families, ageing and social policy: intergenerational solidarity in european welfare states.* Cheltenham, Glos; Northampton, MA: Edward Elgar.

Silei, G. (2003). *Lo stato sociale in Italia: storia e documenti.* Manduria: Lacaita.

Van de Kaa, D. J. (1987). Europe's second demographic Transition. *Population Bulletin,* 42(1), 1–59.

Zannella, M. (2015). Reallocation of resources between generations and genders in the market and non-market economy: the case of Italy. *The Journal of the Economics of Ageing,* 5, 33–44.

6 Households of the elderly in Spain

Between solitude and family solidarities

Francisco Zamora López, Laura Barrios, Irene Lebrusan, Alain Parant and Margarita Delgado

The profound demographic and legislative changes which have been happening in Spain for several decades have substantially affected household structure.[1] Both the 2008 financial crisis – which was particularly severe in Spain – and its repercussions have played a role by encouraging better assistance and protection of the most vulnerable family members. Against a background of lasting crisis, with a welfare state forced to drastically reduce the level of its operations and support, the situation of women, the traditional providers of care and assistance within families, might deteriorate very rapidly and considerably. Their legitimate right to reconcile their family and professional lives might become increasingly difficult to achieve.

In Spain, the development of the welfare state was not accompanied by *defamiliarization* (Albertini, 2010) – that is to say, by a weakening of the solidarity characteristic of the Mediterranean family. It is true that the welfare state has done little in this regard, even though it has sometimes considered some complementary actions such as the Dependency Act, for example, (Act 39/2006 of 14 December). This act was originally ambitious but it suffered successive limitations related to the economic and social background, becoming practically devoid of meaning (Box 6.1).

Beyond a brief review of the general evolution of households in Spain between 1981 and 2011, this chapter intends to focus initially on analysing households containing at least one elderly person. The objective is to assess how the demographic ageing process, which has seriously affected Spain, has been able to change its structure. We also intend to highlight any regional differences. Nevertheless, the significant intensification of the phenomenon of residential isolation of the elderly, sometimes likened to a relational isolation,[2] also led us to include these rarely considered dimensions in the analysis since the particularly severe economic and social conditions derived from the 2008 crisis may have generated new models of coexistence and promoted the creation of alternative family solidarities. For this, three types of data sources were used: the population censuses of 1981, 1991, 2001 and 2011; the Labour Force Surveys (LFS) of 2002, 2007 and 2012; and the Instituto de Mayores y Servicios Sociales (IMSERSO) survey of the elderly in 2010.[3] This meant dealing with data covering a long period of time (censuses) and paying particular attention to the inter-census period of 2001–2011, in which the crisis occurred, in order to detect any new behaviours or changes in the composition of households associated with the economic recession.[4]

Box 6.1   'The Elderly and Dependency Act'

In 2006, a law promoting personal independence and care for people in situations of dependency was published (Act 39/2006) which aimed to improve the quality of life of those having difficulty carrying out key actions in everyday life, regardless of age, by promoting their independence within their usual living space. With respect to the initial project (detailed in Royal Decree 504/2007), the eligibility conditions were fist tightened in 2011 (Royal Decree 174/2011) and then again in 2013 (Royal Decree 1050/2013) when three levels of protection were introduced: a minimum protection, provided by the general state administration; supplementary protection, given by a State-Autonomous Community of residence partnership; and additional protection subject to the decision of the Community. This is a source of a profound regional inequality in the allocation of support as the financial capacities of communities vary a great deal.

Personal services are provided by the Autonomous Communities' social services network and consist in: services preventing dependence and promoting personal independence, hotlines, home care services, day and night centre services (which distinguish between two types of people: those under 65 and those aged 65 or over) and residential support services. Access to these services is directly related to the degree of dependency (moderate, severe or heavy dependency) and the applicant's economic capacity.

This Act envisages financial support for non-professional caregivers from the family circle (relatives by blood, marriage or adoption, up to third degree relatives), which amounts to setting down the principle of financial recognition of family solidarity. However, this provision does not consider the reality of dependency in the elderly as care must have been provided for a year before assistance is requested. The result is a real lack of protection and increasing household vulnerability, a source of even higher future spending.

Households of the elderly in Spain: increasingly composed of single people

Household structures are a visible synthesis of changes in the population's behaviour. In Spain, the behavioural changes occurring during the period considered were many and varied, including the steep fall in fertility from around 2.2 children per woman in 1980 to less than 1.2 in 1998–1999 and 1.3 in 2013. The drop in fertility has directly reduced the size of the nuclear family. Other phenomena have also been involved in the transformation of household structures: a rise in single-parent households (single mothers or fathers with children) from 7.1% in 2001 to 8.7% in 2011, resulting from an increase in marriage annulment, separation and divorce (including divorce of the elderly[5]) as well as from births outside marriage (from 4.0% in 1980 to 34.0% in 2010); an increased frequency of nuclear families in the 'empty nest' phase (the phase when the children have left home); an increase in one-person households, from 1.6 million in 1991 to 4.2 million in 2011, households which consist mainly of women (66.4% and 55.7%, respectively) who are in most cases widows.

The diversity of households has increased sharply[6] because of greater tolerance towards modern behaviour patterns and their recognition by the legislature. The average household size has reduced by about one person, from 3.53 in 1981 to 2.58 in 2011. In addition, although the majority of the Spanish population still lives in a nuclear family its influence has nonetheless decreased, from 87.4% in 1991 to 81.7% in 2011. The most significant transformation occurred in households where at least one member was aged 65 or over. Elderly people living alone accounted for 21.1% of the population aged 65 or over in 2011 compared to only 16.2% in 1991. This rise in residential isolation does not necessarily mean that such elderly people are isolated or lack relationships with relatives or close friends. Non-cohabitation may result from a desire for independence and individual autonomy. According to Meil (2011), in the CIS (Condiciones de vida de los mayores, 2008), when asked the question, 'in the event of assistance being required, with whom would you prefer to live?', only 11% answered, 'with my children'. A large majority (77%) said they would prefer to 'live at home with a caregiver or companion'. According to the 2010 IMSERSO survey, regardless of where they lived and the condition of their health, 87.3% of the elderly would prefer to live 'in their own home, even if alone'; only 5.5% would prefer to go to live 'in the house of one of their sons/daughters or another relative', and only 3.8% of them chose the option 'in a residence/institution for the elderly'. However, if the need for care was specifically felt, 15.4% of those interviewed would choose to stay at home, while 46.1% would prefer to go to live with a child or other relative and 18.3% would opt for a specialised home. Men would choose to live at home more than women (90.4% compared to 84.9%), even if alone, and would consequently be less likely to accept either going to live with a child or other relative (3.5% compared to 6.9%), living in a retirement home (3.5% compared to 4.1%) or sharing accommodation with a non-relative (1.4% compared to 2.1%).

Does this mean that women tolerate isolation less than men? They seem, at least, to fear it more than men, as is revealed by their responses to the question, 'For what reason does growing old worry you?' in the 2010 IMSERSO survey. Whilst 22.2% of men answered 'because of the isolation', women gave the same response in 30.5% of cases. Also, 30.7% of women (compared to 28.8% of men) stated that one of the 'main requirements of the elderly in modern society' is 'to avoid isolation'. That women's greater concern as regards isolation comes from the fact that they may experience it more often, having a longer life expectancy and thus a greater probability of becoming a widow, cannot be excluded.

The perception of isolation fluctuates within wide limits in the elderly population, depending on the size of the town in which they live. It appears to be less marked in towns of intermediate size (40.7% and 52.8% in towns with 10,001 to 20,000 inhabitants and 20,001 to 100,000 inhabitants, respectively); a low population density (villages with fewer than 5,000 inhabitants) reinforces it less than a very high density population (towns with more than 100,000 inhabitants). The proportions of the elderly feeling isolated then rise to 66.8% and 79.5%, respectively. Whether actual or only perceived, isolation does not have the same consequences for all elderly people. Up to 70% of them enjoy living conditions which allow them to be independent until the age of 80 (Esparza Catalán and Abellán García, 2008). Difficulties arise as age increases and alongside it the degree of dependency. According to the 2010 IMSERSO survey, although 51.3% of people aged 65–69 declare they have 'very good' or 'good' health, this percentage decreases with increasing age, reaching 36.5% for those aged 80 or over. Despite this, the increase in the number of people living alone has been more rapid for 85-year-olds than for the entire population aged 65 or over, rising from 17.1% in the 1991 census to 27.7 % in that of 2011, which contradicts the observations of some authors (Zueras and Miret Gamundi, 2013).

The reasons for this increase in the number of people living alone are diverse: the elderly's improved physical and mental characteristics, their relatives' reduced financial and/or human resources meaning they cannot go to live with them, an insufficient number of places available in residential homes to meet the growing demand and an increasing predisposition to living alone. Whatever the explanation for this rise in residential isolation amongst those aged 85 or over – there is no compelling argument – in 2011, this affected 18.8% of men and 38.0% of women. However, living alone does not mean being socially isolated: thus 67.5% of those aged 65 or over state that they have had daily contact with one of their children during the past 12 months, 37.4% with a nephew or niece and 22.1% with a brother/sister. Whether the decision to live alone is voluntary or not, it is nevertheless a situation which can be accompanied by the preservation of some level of family relationships. The question is to what extent this level of family relationships is likely to continue in a context of accelerated demographic ageing.

Between 1991 and 2011, the ageing of the Spanish provinces advanced notably, especially in the northwest quarter of the peninsula – Lugo, Orense and Zamora stand out, as in these provinces the proportion of people aged 65 or over was close to 28% – and in some central and northern provinces. In what seems a relatively aged Spain, a few coastal provinces emerge – Almeria, the Balearic Islands, Cadiz, Huelva, Las Palmas, Murcia, Guadalajara, Seville – with less than 15% of the population aged 65 or over (Figure 6.1). This differentiated regional ageing is essentially explained by the emigration of the younger people from the provinces which have aged the most and by the historically higher fertility rates of the provinces which have aged the least.

Figure 6.2 illustrates the proportion of people aged 65 or over living alone by province. There was a general rise in residential isolation between 1991 and 2011, except for the provinces of the far northwest, Murcia and the Canary Islands. The geography of the isolation amongst the elderly in Spain has no real logical explanation. Indeed, those provinces most affected by the phenomenon include some that are more rural than average and some that are more urbanised than average, some interior provinces but equally some coastal and island provinces. The link between population ageing and the proportion of the elderly living alone is also unclear. For example, some provinces in Galicia are amongst those provinces which have the most elderly but are nonetheless notable as having the lowest proportions of elderly living alone. It could always be assumed that the elderly receive more attention from their children but there is no evidence to support this claim.

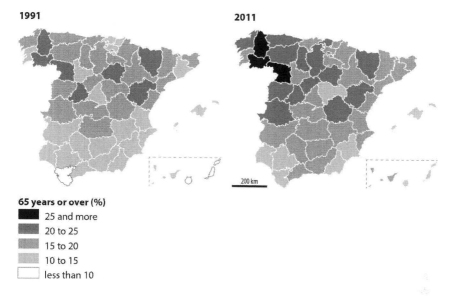

1991   2011

65 years or over (%)
- 25 and more
- 20 to 25
- 15 to 20
- 10 to 15
- less than 10

Figure 6.1 Proportion of people aged 65 or over in the total population of the provinces. Spain, 1991 and 2011

Sources: Compiled by the authors from the 1991 and 2011 censuses (INE); © Instituto Geografico Nacional

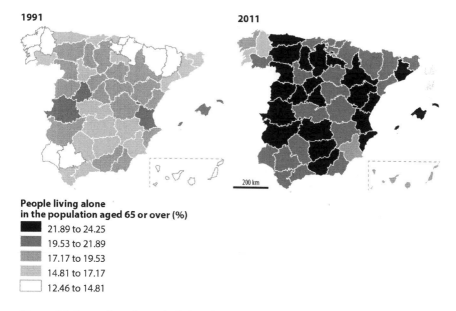

1991   2011

People living alone
in the population aged 65 or over (%)
- 21.89 to 24.25
- 19.53 to 21.89
- 17.17 to 19.53
- 14.81 to 17.17
- 12.46 to 14.81

Figure 6.2 Proportion of people living alone in the population aged 65 or over by province. Spain, 1991 and 2011

Sources: Compiled by the authors from the 1991 and 2011 censuses (INE); © Instituto Geografico Nacional

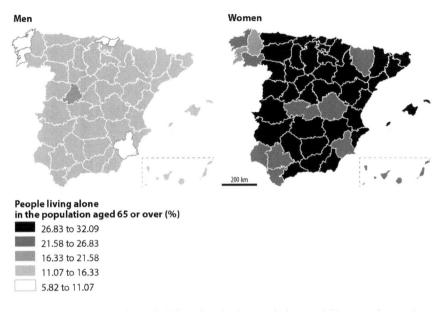

Men

Women

200 km

**People living alone
in the population aged 65 or over (%)**
- 26.83 to 32.09
- 21.58 to 26.83
- 16.33 to 21.58
- 11.07 to 16.33
- 5.82 to 11.07

Figure 6.3 Proportion of people living alone in the population aged 65 or over by province
and by gender. Spain, 2011

Sources: Compiled by the authors from the 2011 census (INE); © Instituto Geografico Nacional

Figure 6.3 shows that ageing and especially residential isolation in the elderly
have a clear gender dimension. Whichever province is considered, the proportion
of women aged 65 or over living alone unfailingly exceeds that of men. Their longer life expectancy at birth and the younger age when married explain the higher
risk of widowhood for women than that of men and, all else being equal, their
higher risk of living alone.

Although they should not be confused, choosing residential independence and
feeling isolated can nonetheless coexist amongst the elderly. To what extent has
'The Great Recession', to which reference was made in another chapter, affected
the size and composition of households and particularly the households of the
elderly? The data mentioned earlier do not allow us to account for the changes
which have taken place since 2008 in the households in which elderly people live,
whether they live alone or with others.

Changes in the structures of households with
elderly people in times of crisis

As we previously indicated, we chose a source which supplies data with greater
frequency than the censuses and which allows this type of analysis. This part of
the analysis of the changes in the households in which at least one person aged
65 or over resides is based on data from the LFS of 2002, 2007 and 2012. The

analysis starts from the hypothesis that those difficulties directly linked to the economic crisis experienced by Spanish households have not been without effect on cohabitation within households and that, as regards those in which the elderly live, these difficulties may have led to a regrouping of the family. Although the elderly constitute a vulnerable population, they have, nonetheless, generally maintained their income. As they generally own their homes, they are also a relative centre of stability for other family members.

The LFS data allow the number and proportion of households in which there are elderly residing to be estimated. In Spain in 2002, out of a little more than 14.5 million households, 34.6% contained at least one person aged 65 or over. In 2007, the total number of households had increased by 2 million, and in 2012, it reached 18 million. However, during that 2007–2012 period, the proportion of households with at least one elderly person stabilised at around 31.5%. In so far as the proportion of people aged 65 or over has been increasing throughout the decade, the fact that a lower proportion of households with at least one elderly person was noted implies that household size has increased and their composition has changed. In Spain, the average number of people per household decreased between 2002 and 2012, both for those containing a person aged 65 or over (whose size reduced from 2.32 to 2.11 individuals on average) and for those in which all members were under 65 (whose average size fell from 3.10 to 2.78). The question is whether the size reduction affected all households or more specifically elderly households.

Table 6.1 shows the distribution of individuals cohabiting with at least one person aged 65 or over according to household size. The most remarkable quantitative change concerned those who live in households composed of more than three members. Their proportion fell by 12 percentage points in total between 2002 and 2012, whilst that of households consisting of two people had the most significant increase.

One-person households

Regardless of the age of the individuals, the proportion of those living alone increased from 2002 to 2012. However, although this proportion was significantly higher at each date for the older population, its increase over the period

Table 6.1 Distribution of individuals who cohabit with at least one person aged 65 or over according to their household size. Spain, 2002–2012 (in %)

Household size	2002	2007	2012
One person	13.9	14.5	15.5
Two people	31.0	33.8	40.4
Three people	19.0	19.0	19.9
Four or more people	36.1	32.7	24.2
TOTAL	100.0	100.0	100.0

Source: Author's calculations based on LFS data (INE)

considered was more pronounced for the younger population: +50% and +11.5%, respectively, compared to +28% for all ages combined (Table 6.2).

Households composed of a single elderly person were still overwhelmingly female (Table 6.3), but their growth nevertheless slowed down over the period compared with that of households composed of only one man (+12% compared to +20%). Older men living alone are, like women, frequently widowers, but their numbers increased much less rapidly than that of separated and divorced men (+4.0% compared to +118%); their proportion within the total men living alone was equal to just under 50% in 2012 (compared to over 57% in 2002 and 2007).

Two-person households

The distribution of individuals living in two-person households with at least one elderly person is summarized in Table 6.1. In 2012, 40.4% of people who lived in households with at least one person aged 65 or over were part of this household category (i.e. a proportion ten points higher than in 2002). In comparison, only 17.6% of individuals living in a household without elderly people belonged to a two-person household – a household category which comprised a total of 23.5% of the population in 2012. Combined with that of one-person households, the extremely rapid overall growth in two-person households explains the decrease in the average size of Spanish households. Amongst the two-person households with at least one member aged 65 or over, the most common situations were those in which the two individuals were elderly, in a proportion of around 61% that has changed very little since 2002 (Table 6.4).

Amongst the households consisting of two people aged 65 or over, the most frequently encountered by far were those composed of a man and a woman (95.7% in 2012, one and a half points more than in 2002); the woman-woman combination was clearly decreasing (from 3.3% in 2002 to 1.9% in 2012), whilst the man-man combination, of little significance, represented only 0.5% in 2012. As regards the family ties identified in two-person households (Figure 6.4), the most significant change related to the increase of almost three points in households with two spouses between 2002 and 2012. This is linked to the population's increased life expectancy; this increase operated at the expense of one-person households. The second most common configuration was that of an elderly person living with a child (son/daughter), but without any increase over

Table 6.2 Proportion of one-person households by age. Spain, 2002–2012 (in %)

Age	2002	2007	2012
≥ 65	13.9	14.5	15.5
< 65	4.6	5.9	6.9
TOTAL	7.2	8.2	9.2

Source: Author's calculations based on LFS data (INE)

Field: The population of private households

Table 6.3 Population aged 65 years or over living alone in Spain by gender and marital status, 2002–2012

Marital status	2002 Sex			2007 Sex			2012 Sex		
	Male	Female	Total	Male	Female	Total	Male	Female	Total
Single	31.8	13.2	17.9	26.0	11.5	15.3	29.7	12.0	16.7
Married	2.9	0.6	1.2	6.4	1.4	2.6	6.0	1.6	2.8
Widowed	57.3	83.8	77.1	57.5	83.4	76.7	49.9	81.2	72.9
Separated or divorced	7.9	2.4	3.8	10.1	3.7	5.4	14.4	5.2	7.6
Total	100.0	100.0	100.0	100.0	100.0	100.0	100.0	100.0	100.0
(Absolute numbers)	(410,175)	(1,212,707)	(1,622,882)	(443,324)	(1,276,173)	(1,719,497)	(492,201)	(1,363,625)	(1,855,826)

Source: Authors' calculations based on LFS data (INE)

Table 6.4 Distribution of two-person households according to the number of people aged 65 or over. Spain, 2002–2012 (in %)

Number of members aged 65 or over	2002	2007	2012
Two people ≥ 65	61.3	61.5	62.4
One person ≥ 65	38.7	38.5	37.6
Total	100.0	100.0	100.0

Source: Author's calculations based on LFS data (INE)

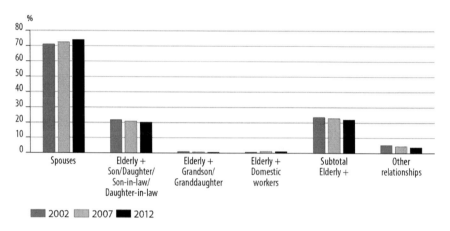

Figure 6.4 Family composition of two-person households. Spain, 2002–2012

Source: Compiled by the authors from LFS (INE)

time, which would have been a sign of more frequent family regrouping in a context of social and financial restrictions.

Three-person households

The proportion of individuals living in three-person households with at least one elderly member increased slightly, though it was still less than 20%. Nevertheless, it was lower than that noted for all three-person households (Table 6.1). This category of households appeared – and this is only logical – more diverse than the previous one and included a generally younger population. This was due to the extremely low proportion of households entirely composed of people aged 65 or over. The most common combination of individuals was that of two spouses, at least one of whom was 65 or over, plus an offspring (see Figure 6.5). The two spouses + mother/father type can equally involve a young couple living with an elderly relative, an elderly father/mother or an elderly couple living with an obviously elderly ancestor. Moreover, a resurgence of households combining an elderly person and one or more of their descendants was observed; this type of household, whose proportion decreased from 2002 to 2007, represented 12.6% of the total households in 2012.

To summarize and to broadly characterise the structure of households containing people aged 65 or over, we would say that 75.8% of those who were cohabiting

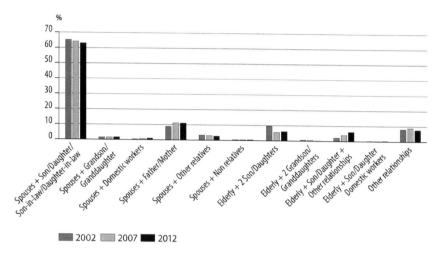

Figure 6.5 Family composition of three-person households. Spain, 2002–2012
Source: Compiled by the authors from LFS (INE)

with elderly people in 2012 were living in households of less than or equal to three people, compared to 63.9% in 2002. Amongst these households, the most common were composed of two people; more than 61% of these were two people aged 65 or over, presumably couples, followed by households consisting of one person and their offspring, and the other types were a very small minority. In three-person households, characterised by a greater variety of situations, the principal type was still that combining an elderly person or an elderly couple and one or two of their offspring. Finally, one household in six was composed of a single person.

If we consider the changes occurring from 2002 to 2012, we should first note a slower increase in the proportion of elderly households composed of a single person than that of the proportion of elderly people in the total population. Conversely, we noted a significant increase in the proportion of elderly individuals living in households composed of two people and, in particular, of those comprising two elderly individuals, as well as a stable proportion of the elderly living with a child. For three-person households, there was a clear increase in those combining one or two elderly people and one or two offspring. Although these results are consistent with family regrouping – our initial hypothesis – the trend nonetheless appears to be very weak and statistically insignificant; a greater number of surveys and observations are required to support the assertion.

The Great Recession seems to have only marginally exerted an effect on the composition of Spanish households. We know that changes in behaviour must be profound to have a significant and lasting impact. It is perhaps too early to assess the changes caused by a crisis which has not yet been overcome, and we will perhaps have to wait a few years to draw definitive conclusions (Börsch-Supan et al., 2013). This does not prevent us from discovering how elderly people have been able to mitigate the effects of the crisis, for example, through the support they were able to give to those who were more affected: their children and grandchildren (Puga, 2011).

Elderly households and family support

Without ignoring or wanting to minimise the diversity of the expression of family solidarity, nor its direction in Spain, the analysis of which is not the subject of this brief study (Puga, 2011), and although aware of the bidirectional flow of solidarity (Albertini and Kohli, 2013; Meil, 2011; Litwin, 2010; Attias-Donfut and Ogg, 2009; Albertini et al., 2007), we will here focus on the support dispensed by the elderly. The IMSERSO 2010 survey provides us with some elements which can increase our understanding of the support the elderly provided to their family members in the midst of the recession, although the effects of this crisis will only be fully appreciated in the future.

In 2010, elderly people spent an average of €501 a month on housing (21.0%); food, clothing and footwear (46.9%); medication (4.0%); leisure (3.2%); financial support for family members (5.5%); telephone fees (7.7%) and external assistance with domestic work and/or care (11.8 %). Housing, food and external assistance represented nearly 80% of the elderly's expenditure and the 5.5% (i.e. €27.60) dedicated to financial support for family members was particularly remarkable. If we consider that the net monthly income is on average €506, the expenses appear, by necessity, a close match, the savings capacity being virtually zero. That the elderly dedicate a part of their financial resources to family support under these circumstances, as small as it may seem, is fairly eloquent evidence of family solidarity. About 20% of elderly people confirm that they support a child financially: 1% a grandchild and 0.7% support a brother or nephew; the effort is globally significant.

There are some differences by gender and age of the contributor. Women dedicate a little less on average to financial support for family members than men (€23.60 compared to €32.70), which is hardly surprising since 30% of them have no income (compared to 0.1% of men). Similarly, the younger elderly (aged 65–69) devote more money in absolute (€31.80) and relative (6.6%) terms to supporting relatives than the more elderly (€21.70 and 3.8%, respectively); this result is somewhat consistent with what is known about the monthly average income of the ones and the others (€557 and €534). It should also be noted here that expenditure on external assistance (domestic and care services) increases with age and accounts for over a quarter of total expenditure of people aged 80 or over compared to less than 2% for those aged 65–69. In another area, that of housing, it is worthy of note that in Spain ordinary housing predominates – that is to say, housing designed to be inhabited by one or more people who are not necessarily united by ties of kinship and do not constitute a community.[7] Considered as an element of stability, homeownership is highly sought after. Although it is not the determining factor for a household's quality of life for those who can afford it (since they have sufficient income), it can constitute an accelerator of poverty for the most financially disadvantaged tenants. The proportion of homeowners tends to increase with age, as does the number of households with no payments to be made (repayments of loans, rent). In 2011, the proportion of people owning their own home amounted to 79.0% (a decrease compared to the year 2001 when it stood at 82.2%), but for elderly people, it peaked at 84.0%. In recent years, mortgage debt has increased for the entire population (from 15.6% in 1991 to 22.8% in 2001 and 32.9% in 2011) as well as for the elderly: in 1991, 4.9% of homeowners had mortgage pending payments compared to 5.4% in 2001 and 7.0% during the last census.[8] The average expenditure on housing[9] is more than twice as high for private tenants than it is for homeowners (EAPN-ES, 2012). Ten percent of the elderly live in rented housing, a proportion which increases with age: 10.7% for those aged 75 or over and 11.7% for those aged 85 or over.

The importance of the property assets of the elderly in the financial and housing strategies of their offspring is undeniable, but difficult to demonstrate with data: mortgage guarantees which make the creation of new households possible, *inter vivos* transfers, transformation of second homes located in the periphery of large cities into main residences, etc. Concerning housing transfers, the proportion of housing inherited increased, reaching 20.5% in 2014 compared to 11.0% in 2007,[10] while that of housing put on sale decreased. As highlighted by Lebrusan and Hillcoat-Nallétamby (2014), parental support to children affected by the crisis goes well beyond hospitality and cohabitation. As evidence of intergenerational solidarity, it is extremely diverse: sharing meals, financial support, not necessarily abundant but frequent, endorsements, supporting the education of grandchildren, health care, etc.

Conclusion

Over the last few decades, Spain – one of the European countries most severely affected by the financial crisis of 2008 and its aftermath – has experienced very profound changes. In a context of accelerated demographic ageing, primarily resulting not only from the sudden steep fall in the fertility rate but also fostered by the ongoing lengthening of life expectancy at birth, household structures have been substantially transformed. The rise of households consisting partly of elderly people has been accompanied by a rise in one-person households (mostly women), which the crisis seems to have somewhat slowed. Despite its strength and durability, intra-family solidarities have hardly been affected by the crisis, in particular, those which descend from the elderly to the younger members.

Nonetheless, ending the crisis now – positively – appears to be an urgent necessity because the family solidarity reserves, already largely depleted, are not inexhaustible. In addition, Spain, in the coming decades, will have to deal with a very rapid and sustained demographic ageing, which is a phenomenon whose socioeconomic effects, only glimpsed until now, will be very widely multiplied.

Notes

1 At this point we will mention the steep fall in the fertility rate, the rapid increase in life expectancy and the liberalisation of divorce laws, the recognition of homosexual marriage, the consolidation of the rights of children born outside marriage and the decriminalisation of the voluntary termination of pregnancy.
2 In this regard, see La Soledad en España, the very recent study by Juan Díez Nicolás and María Morenos Páez (2015).
3 This study was conducted nationally (except for Ceuta and Melilla) in a simple random sample of 2,500 people aged 65 or over, interviewed by telephone.
4 Another source, although very useful for international comparisons, the SHARE survey (Survey of Health, Ageing and Retirement in Europe) was ruled out in the case of Spain due to the extremely low number of people aged 65 or over interviewed.

5 Within the population who were divorced, separated or whose marriage had been annulled, the proportion of people aged 60 or over has more than doubled from 1998 to 2013, from 4.3% to 8.7% for men and from 2.6% to 5.7% for women (source: INE: National Institute of Statistics).
6 We must also mention here the increase in the number of homosexual couples from under 10,000 in 2001 to nearly 55,000 in 2011, following the vote and the enactment of Act 13/2005.
7 Definition from the glossary of the 2001 Census (INE).
8 Data from the 1991, 2001 and 2011 censuses (INE).
9 Regular expenditure for the payment of housing, excluding maintenance expenses.
10 Statistics on the law of succession in the property (INE).

References

Albertini, M. (2010). La ayuda de los padres españoles a los jóvenes adultos. El familismo español en perspectiva comparada. *Revista de Estudios de Juventud*, (90), 67–81.
Albertini, M. and Kohli, M. (2013). The generational contract in the family: an analysis of transfer regimes in Europe. *European Sociological Review*, 29(4), 828–840.
Albertini, M., Kohli, M. and Vogel, C. (2007). Intergenerational transfers of time and money in european families: common patterns – different regimes? *Journal of European Social Policy*, 17(4), 319–334.
Attias-Donfut, C. and Ogg, J. (2009). Évolution des transferts intergénérationnels: vers un modèle européen ? *Retraite et société*, 2(58), 11–29.
Börsch-Supan, A., Brandt, M., Litwin, H. and Weber, G. (Eds.). (2013). *Active ageing and solidarity between generations in Europe: first results from SHARE after the economic crisis*. Berlin: De Gruyter.
Díez, N. J. and Morenos, P. M. (2015). *La soledad en España*. Madrid: Fundación ONCE – Fundación Axa.
EAPN-ES (European Anti Poverty Network-ES). (2012). *Nuevas propuestas para nuevos tiempos*. Madrid: EAPN-ES.
Esparza Catalán, C. and Abellán García, A. (2008). *Encuesta de discapacidad, autonomía personal y situaciones de dependencia (EDAD 2008). Primeros resultados*. Madrid: Instituto de Mayores y Servicios Sociales – Consejo Superior de Investigaciones Científicas.
IMSERSO. (2010). *Encuesta de personas mayores 2010*. Madrid: IMSERSO.
Lebrusan, I. and Hillcoat-Nallétamby, S. (2014). Older people's living arrangements in a context of economic crisis: comparing household structures in northern and southern european contexts – United Kingdom and Spain, in: *Paper presented at the ENHR Conference*. Edimbourg.
Litwin, H. (2010). Social networks and well-being: a comparison of older people in mediterranean and non-mediterranean countries. *The Journals of Gerontology Series B: Psychological Sciences and Social Sciences*, 65(5), 599–608.
Meil, G. (2011). *Individualización y solidaridad familiar*. Barcelona: Obra Social 'la Caixa'.
Puga, M. D. (2011). La fortaleza de la familia como pilar ante la crisis socioeconómica, in: Centro de Estudios del Cambio Social (Ed.), *Informe España 2011: una interpretación de su realidad social* (pp. 182–236). Madrid: Fundación Encuentro.
Zueras, P. and Miret Gamundi, P. (2013). Mayores que viven solos: una panorámica a partir de los censos de 1991 y 2001. *Revista Española de Investigaciones Sociológicas*, (144), 139–152.

7 Family solidarities and old age in Morocco

New realities, new challenges

Muriel Sajoux and Mohammed Amar

In the coming decades, Morocco will experience a genuinely complete demographic transformation: the proportion of elderly people in the population will grow very rapidly, both in relative terms and in terms of numbers. According to the projections of the Office of the High Commissioner for Planning,[1] the proportion of the population aged 60 and over should rise from 10% of the total population in 2015 to 24.5% in 2050. Thus in only 35 years, the relative proportion of the elderly is expected to increase as much as it did in more than a century and a half in France. Morocco is also expected to experience a particularly strong gerontogrowth – growth in the number of the elderly: by 2050, the number of people over the age of 60 is expected to have nearly tripled.[2] As for those aged 75 and over, their number should almost quadruple during this period, rising from 0.764 to 2.87 million people. As a result of the demographic transition process,[3] the ageing of the Moroccan population will be accompanied by a reduction in family size. This situation of a rapid ageing of the population is bringing numerous challenges for Moroccan society.

In most developing countries, the ageing process is mainly taken care of by families (Nowik and Lecestre-Rollier, 2015). They are the main suppliers of the response to the needs of advanced age, particularly given the often limited and, above all, variable support of the social welfare system. In this chapter on the role of family solidarity in ageing in Morocco, we will consider the way family solidarity is expressed and organised in order to identify the possible difficulties and limitations which families may encounter as well as the sources of any hidden weaknesses. We will base this on the results from censuses or large surveys conducted on a national scale and also on data collected using a qualitative approach (Appendix 7.1). We will first discuss a few key issues concerning the context in which these solidarities are deployed.

Family and living conditions in Morocco: general features

The importance of the family is well established in Moroccan society's value system. R. Bourqia (2010) points, for example, to the central role of the parental blessing:

> The duty of children to support their elderly parents is part of the search for this parental blessing which accompanies the individual throughout his/her life. Having offspring and the efforts exerted to raise them is both an emotional and a material investment which places children in a situation of debt towards their parents.

The data from the world values survey of 2011[4] reveal that the family was considered 'very important' in Morocco by nearly 91% of those interviewed. Nevertheless, in recent decades the mode of 'making a family' has changed.

Socio-demographic changes and evolutions in the Moroccan family

In a context where procreation is only socially feasible in the framework of marriage, we will begin by considering the transformation in matrimonial behaviour in order to understand the changes which have occurred within the Moroccan family.

An ever more delayed first marriage

The increase in the average age at first marriage has been particularly important. For women, this rose from 17 years of age in 1960 to 22.2 in 1982 and then returned to 25.8 in 2014, the same level as in 1994, after having reached 26.3 in 2004. The average age at first marriage for men has also increased: from nearly 23.9 years of age in 1960 to 27.1 in 1982 and 31.4 in 2014. This increasingly late union is due to many factors, mainly socio-economic ones. Although it is a reflection of factors related to the 'modernisation' process (an increase men and women's educational levels, urbanisation, increased participation of women in the labour market, etc.), it is also related to the socio-economic difficulties faced by young people wishing to start a family (unemployment or job instability, cost of housing, etc.) which may force them to delay marriage. However, it is worth noticing that although the average age difference between men and women on entering marriage decreased between 1960 (from 6.6 years) and 2004 (to 4.9 years), it has since increased, reaching 5.6 years in 2014. It thus appears that even if women now marry almost nine years later, on average, than they did in the early 1960s, within marriage, it is still socially important and desirable for a husband to be many years older than his wife. Thus, whilst being subject to some form of 'modernisation' through delayed first union, Moroccan marriage retains 'traditional' features through this difference of around six years in the average age of men and women at first marriage.

Family endogamy in decline but still present

Although family endogamy has declined in recent decades, and is lower in Morocco than in other Arab countries,[5] this also demonstrates an attachment to 'traditional' patriarchal values. This type of union is seen as a factor in maintaining family cohesion and/or protecting inheritance. It can take various forms and may be manifested as marriages between first cousins or distant cousins. The results of the 2009–2010 ENDPR[6] reveal that about one-fifth of non-single people married a relative the first time (20.6% of women and 22% of men). Three-quarters of endogamous marriages are contracted between first cousins. Nevertheless, it should be noted that changes are underway: the rate of female endogamy decreased from 33.7% in 1987[7] to 29.3% in 1995[8] and to less than 21% in 2010. Over the past two decades, the proportion of marriages contracted with a first cousin has remained almost stable (16.3% in 1995 and 15.5% in 2010), whilst the proportion of marriages with a distant relative has significantly declined, decreasing from 13% to 5.1%.

Low divorce rates and permanent celibacy rising

The question of the dissolution of marriage by divorce was relatively little integrated into the surveys conducted in Morocco. Nevertheless, it is possible to say that the proportion of women whose first marriage ended in divorce was 10.5% in 2010[9] compared to 15.2% in 1995 (Lfarakh, 2012). According to the 2009–2010 ENDPR, remarriage appears to be less common amongst women than amongst men: 14.5% of previously married men and 8.5% of previously married women remarried after divorce or widowhood. Although marriage is still extremely important in Moroccan culture, it is proving to be less universal than in the past. Thus, between 1994 and 2010, the proportion of single people aged 50, called the 'permanent celibacy rate', doubled for men (from 2.9% to 5.8%) and was multiplied by eight for women (0.8% to 6.7%).

Declining fertility and spreading of the nuclear family model

Although the fertility rate decreased from over 7 children per woman in the early 1960s to 3.3 in 1994, it now stands at 2.2 children per woman (2.5 in rural areas and 2 in urban areas). Thus, in 2014, the fertility rate in Moroccan urban areas is the same as in France. This substantial decline in fertility means that in just two generations, the nuclear family model has become widespread in Moroccan society. Although the family is still its main pillar, certain aspects have undergone major transformations or even mutations. In order to understand the scope of family solidarity, how it is expressed and how its resources are deployed, various key features of current living conditions in Morocco need to be mentioned.

Living conditions in Morocco. An overview

Significant socio-economic progress, persistent regional disparities

Morocco has experienced considerable changes over the course of a few decades which have affected the lives of its inhabitants. One of these is urbanisation: the urbanisation rate doubled between 1960 and 2014[10] (from 29.1% to 60.3%). The symbolic milestone of 50% was reached a little over 20 years ago. Indeed, the 1994 census revealed that the urban population already represented more than half of the country's population; the urbanisation rate had by then reached 51.4%. The decline in illiteracy is another major change. Whilst the illiteracy rate of the population aged 10 and over was 65% in 1982 (78% for just the female population and 51% for men), it had decreased by half, to 32%, in 2014 (49.1% for women, 22.1% for men). Nevertheless, significant regional disparities remain. The rate is twice as high in rural areas as in urban areas: 47.7% compared to 22.2%. Regional disparities are also very marked: for instance, nearly one woman in two is illiterate in the Beni Mellal-Khénifra region compared to one in three in the Grand Casablanca-Settat region.

The basic household equipment has also increased, and this has had an impact on family daily life; yet here too significant territorial disparities still persist. Thus, as regards connection to the electricity grid, there is a ten-point difference between residential areas: in 2014, 95.3% of households in urban areas were connected compared to 85.3% in rural areas (this proportion was only 43.2% in rural areas in 2004). The rural-urban disparity is even greater as regards access to the drinking water network: 91% of households are connected in urban areas compared to 38.3% in rural areas (this proportion was only 18.1% in rural areas in 2004). One final example: more than one urban household in two has a modern bathtub or shower compared to less than one household in ten in rural areas. Regional disparities are also apparent in the provision of health care. 'Analysis of the ratio of the number of ESSB[11] per inhabitant shows fairly strong regional disparities with up to five-fold differences. Nine out of 16 regions have an ESSB ratio per inhabitant below the national average' (CESS, 2013).

Employment and unemployment rates, gender and age disparities

Within the population aged 15 and over, the employment rate[12] was 48% in 2014, but it was almost three times higher for men than women: 72.4 compared to 25.3%. These figures were 68.2 and 17.8% in urban areas and 78.7 and 36.9% in rural areas. Thus, for the moment, the level of women's participation in the labour market still appears to be well below that of men. In urban areas, more than 82% of the female population aged 15 and over are unemployed. The employment rate of urban women is highest in the group aged 25–29, reaching 29.1%. As we will see later, this low participation of women in economic activity is undoubtedly linked to their place in family solidarity and to the fact that they play a leading role within the family as the caregiver when the need arises.

The unemployment rate is 9.9% for the general population and is slightly higher amongst women than men: 10.4 compared to 9.7%. It is at its highest in the urban areas (14.8%): women's unemployment rate is nine points higher than that of men (21.9 compared to 12.8%). The urban youth unemployment rate for those aged between 15 and 24 is particularly high at 38.1% (46.8 for women and 35.2 for men). The rate is 20.9% for those aged between 25 and 34 (30.8 for women and 17.8 for men). The difficulties young people face when entering the labour market are making the ties which should create family solidarity more complex. Many young adults facing unemployment and job insecurity receive financial support from their elders and only belatedly, and with difficulty, attain a certain economic independence. The fact that having a degree is no protection from unemployment makes this situation particularly hard.

Family solidarity in ageing: diverse modes of expression

Elders are both providers and recipients of support

Family solidarity relates to the generations as a whole. According to the nature of the support studied and the financial constraints of the family, the generations may appear as recipients and/or providers of support. The role of the elderly is part of this pattern and they are by no means only the recipients of support within families. The National Survey of the Elderly (ENPA), conducted in 2006 by the Office of the High Commissioner for Planning (HCP, 2008), was thus able to show that 46.9% of those over 60 are providers of material support (as donations in cash or in kind), with the proportion being 65.9% for men and 29.5% for women (Azam-mam, 2009). The survey also points out that 44.6% of the elderly are exclusively beneficiaries of family support, 32.9% are both providers and recipients, 13.9% are only providers and 8.5% are neither. The proportion of elderly women who are exclusively beneficiaries of support is 62% whilst 42.2% of elderly men are both recipients and providers, reflecting a gender-related disparity. Being a provider and a recipient of support can affect each generation simultaneously since intergenerational cohabitation, although changing, is still part of the current family reality.

Little residential isolation of the elderly and frequent intergenerational cohabitation

Statistical approach to residential isolation and cohabitation

At the moment, few elderly people live alone in Morocco. Households with one elderly person living alone actually declined between the early 1980s and the 2000s (7.1% in 1982, 5.1% in 1994 and 4.5% in 2004). The results of the 2014 census show that this percentage increased 0.7 points in 10 years to reach 5.2%. Nearly three-quarters of the elderly living alone are women. Although the residential isolation of the elderly remains extremely limited for the moment, analysis of the isolation shows a clearly marked gender gap. At the same time, analysis of the change in the size of those households containing at least one person aged 60 or over does not seem to show an obvious reduction in intergenerational cohabitation between 1982 and 2004, even if it is not exactly what this change measures (Nowik et al., 2012). For their part, the data from the 2006 ENPA reveal that the average size of households containing one or more elderly people is 5.8, which is slightly higher than the average size of all households recorded in 2004 (5.2 people per household nationally[13]). The average size of this household type in just urban areas was 4.9 people in 2006 – i.e., it was almost equivalent to the average size of urban households measured by the 2004 census, namely, 4.8 people.[14] In rural areas, the average size of households having one or more elderly members was 6.7 in 2006 compared to 6 for all rural households in 2004.[15]

According to the 2006 ENPA, 58.9% of the elderly live in households of five or more people, 21.6% in households of three or four, 12.7% in two-person households and 6.8% live alone.[16] Elderly people living in couples (or in polygamy where spouses are part of the same household) represent only 6.9% of all the elderly, this proportion being higher for elderly men (8.7%) than for elderly women (5.7%). Situations where the elderly live alone or only with their spouse are relatively rare. Significantly more frequent (27.1%) are situations where the elderly person lives in a household which also comprises non-single children, their spouses and/or their children.[17] An even higher proportion, 31.3%, live in extended households[18] (Azammam, 2009). The importance of intergenerational cohabitation can also be illustrated by the fact that nearly half of the elderly who had grandchildren lived with at least one of them. Although intergenerational cohabitation is a reality in Moroccan society, care should be taken when interpreting its level. This cohabitation is partially maintained due to socio-economic factors unfavourable to either one or the other of the generations, since the young often have difficulty in finding employment and young couples frequently have difficulty in finding independent housing.

Beyond the statistics, coexistence corresponds to numerous situations

Cohabitation may be particularly necessary because of economic difficulties encountered by the elderly living in modest circumstances, as is illustrated by the case of Abdellatif, aged 76, married with five surviving children (three daughters and two sons), 12 grandchildren and 1 great-grandchild. When he was 61, he and his wife Khadija (who is about 10 years younger than him and is also his first cousin) left the small town where he had been working during the last period of his working life and settled in Meknès with their eldest son. The latter is now nearly 50 and works as a technician. His monthly salary is 4,000 dirhams. He has been married for a long time but has no children. All four live in the same house: Abdellatif and his wife on the ground floor, his son and his wife upstairs. Meals are taken together. Their youngest son, in his 40s, works in a factory and lives 40 kilometres away; he is married and has a daughter in primary school. He 'earns a modest salary, 2500 dirhams'. Their three daughters are all married and do not work. Their eldest daughter, now a little over 50 years old, lives in a village to the south of Agadir. Her husband 'works the land'. She has five children and is a grandmother. Their second daughter, in her 40s, lives in a small town 30 kilometres from Meknès where her husband is a retailer; they have three sons either studying or training. The youngest of his three daughters, soon to be 40, lives in the same city as the youngest son. Her husband works in a café, and they have three children. Abdellatif was only a member of a social security fund for part of his working life and has a monthly income of only 1,500 dirhams. Although he is one of the minority of Moroccan elderly to receive a pension, his revenue is insufficient to cover his needs and those of his wife, especially since the latter suffers from diabetes. The medication costs 1,600 dirhams per quarter and only 650 dirhams is reimbursed. 'Sometimes it's my son (the one they live with) who pays; my other son has too small a salary, he can't help us'. Abdellatif adds, 'We can't do other than live with our son'. This son is the one who has the best professional situation, although this is modest, but, more importantly, he has no dependent children. Although the offspring of Abdellatif and Khadija are relatively numerous, the available financial resources to support them are limited due to the modest situation of each one and to the fact that, apart from the son with whom they live, they are supporting their own family; in particular, they have expenses linked to education and their children's studies. It is also interesting to note that Abdellatif believes that cohabiting with his son and daughter-in-law runs smoothly because of family endogamy.

There can also be cohabitation of a sexagenarian offspring and an octogenarian parent (or sometimes even one in their seventies) as part of the continuance of an ancient family pattern. This is the situation of Abdelhamid and his family. He is a former officer aged 64 who has been retired for a few years. He lives with his wife and their youngest daughter, aged 17, who is a student, and with his mother, an octogenarian. This cohabitation is nothing new: Abdelhamid's mother, who is also the maternal aunt of his wife, has always lived with them. His wife is still actively employed as a teacher and, since Abdelhamid often moved during his military career, it was his mother who looked after their children (three boys and a girl) when they were young. Financially, Abdelhamid's pension and his wife's salary give them a sufficient income. They have medical cover for themselves and their two children, still students, but this cover does not apply to his mother. The whole of her medical expenses, which are significant because of her rheumatism, are borne by them. In this example, the grandmother, now in her 80s, had in the past given significant and much valued support; in return, the support she currently enjoys is particularly reflected by this continued cohabitation and by the meeting of her financial and material needs. It is on the integration of the different ways family solidarity is expressed that we are now going to focus.

Polymorphic family solidarity: interlocking and multi-stakeholder

Our own field observations allowed us to study how various forms of assistance are expressed and how they are interwoven. From our analysis, it appears that family solidarity is very much a part of elderly people's lives and is expressed in many ways, both in terms of the different family (or household) member's needs and of the availability and capabilities of each member. They play a particularly important role because of the so far limited nature of the public solidarity which is specifically aimed at the elderly.[19] In particular, they often play an essential role in covering health-related risks by bearing all or part of the cost. In general, the wide variety of ways family solidarity is expressed leads us to talk about the *polymorphism* of private solidarity (Sajoux and Amar, 2015; Sajoux and Lecestre-Rollier, 2015). Indeed, intergenerational cohabitation situations are usually combined with other forms of solidarity. This is illustrated by the case of Nadia, 63 years old and a widow for 12 years. She lives with her daughter, herself a widow (her husband was in the army), and two of her grandsons, aged 11 and 13. All four live in the house of her daughter whose income is barely sufficient. Being diabetic and having heart problems, Nadia must take daily medication and have regular tests. As she has no medical cover, she must pay for her treatment herself. It is her children (she has four children in total and nine grandchildren) who help her cover the cost.

The diversity and the interconnectivity of the different forms of family solidarity can also be seen in the situation of Malika and Bouchra, a mother and a daughter, both 'elderly' and living under the same roof. Malika (whose exact age is unknown) married very young, like many women of her generation; only 15 years or so separate the mother and daughter. Malika has six sons and two daughters. As for Bouchra, she has no children. Both are widows and receive no income.

The house in which they live belongs to one of Malika's sons, and thanks to money from her other sons, who have good professional positions, they can cope with the various expenses. Without their support, she and her daughter would find themselves in very great difficulty.

Whether or not there is intergenerational cohabitation, intra-family material support appears to be essential in the lives of most of the elderly encountered but not unequivocally so, in the sense that they can be recipients but may also be providers of this type of support. Moreover, the exchange of visits and favours also varies according to each person's needs and abilities: assistance for the parents and grandparents with shopping, housework, travel, dealing with public services or medical bodies, etc., as well as assistance for the children (preparation of meals, a presence in the home, etc.) and especially for the grandchildren (care for the youngest children, care for school children at lunch time, after school and during holidays). To sum up, we can speak of a 'tangle of inter- and intra-generational solidarity' (Lecestre-Rollier, 2015), which is in essence *interlocking* and *multi-stakeholder*.

Challenges of the current modes of organisation of family solidarity

Focusing on only the needs of the elderly, it is clear that current family size allows the tasks and roles to be distributed between the children supporting their elderly parent(s): for example, one finances all or part of the housing, another bears the cost of medical care and a third provides assistance in carrying out daily activities, which can be very important when the assisted elderly person is dependant. The burden of support is thus divided, which provides relief to each of them individually (Sajoux and Lecestre-Rollier, 2015). Yet, in only a few years' time, the families who will have an elderly to support will be much smaller than they are on average today. It follows that the family solidarities observed today may no longer be organised in the same way. It is likely that families will simply not be able to cope if they are not supported by suitable public measures. Only those with enough money will be able to call on the private sector, for example through the use of personal services companies. If such a configuration should become a reality, we might then observe an extreme polarisation of the ageing experience; families with a modest or average background having to 'self-manage' the care of their elderly and wealthy families being able to recruit qualified personnel (assuming the latter are available in sufficient numbers, which is far from certain in view of the current situation).

Family solidarities are sometimes at the limits of their scope

Undeniably, family solidarity is on the whole highly requested during ageing. However, several factors or situations may impede families' ability to meet their elderly's needs.

Solidarity facing multiple economic constraints

One of the elements affecting the 'traditional' operation of family solidarity is unemployment amongst the younger generations and their lack of secure employment. The young are indeed remaining the beneficiaries of family solidarity for

longer than previously. One consequence is that individuals of the 'pivot' generation must both support their financially dependent adult offspring (children and/
or grandchildren), whilst at the same time the health of their older ageing relatives
requires increased attention from them plus increased material and/or financial
support. Another major constraint comes from the cost of the goods and health services to which the elderly must increasingly resort as they grow older. Family support, and primarily that of their offspring, thus appears to be essential. The results
of the 2006 ENPA revealed that 42.4% of the elderly reported that all or part of
the cost of the health care they received (including the purchase of medicines) was
borne by their children (Fassi Fihri, 2009). For elderly women, this proportion rose
to 56.7%, compared to 24% for elderly men, revealing their greater dependence on
family solidarity. To illustrate the importance of the cost of health care in relation
to the budget of the elderly and their families, we note that those elderly people
who say they are ill but have not used the health-care system represent a third of
the elderly population who is ill (Fassi Fihri, 2009). Of these, 59.1% reported not
having used the health-care system because of a lack of resources.

Family solidarity in difficultly faced with situations of dependency

In the absence of appropriate care facilities[20] and a lack of access to the assistance
of skilled personnel that can help in the home, families generally have to deal
on their own with dependant elders. In most cases, several family members are
involved in a complementary way to handle a dependency situation. This was the
case, for example, with an 80-year-old man suffering from stroke whose situation
was related by one of his grandchildren (Sajoux and Amar, 2015). Although this
man was used to being very active, he soon found himself unable to make himself
understood when speaking, nor could he walk alone.

> Mentally, he had suffered a shock, he would shout all the time, he would cry
> and swear. [. . .] His wife would wash him and occasionally sh*e was helped by
> her own mother. [. . .] It was hard to bear, it was a sort of psychological harass-
> ment. We couldn't sleep at night, he would shout all the time. Sometimes my
> uncle took over and my grandfather's wife had a few days' rest with her mother.*

This example clearly demonstrates that dependency situations test caregivers'
endurance. In this example, the respite which could benefit the primary caregiver –
the elderly patient's wife – depended entirely on the availability of other family
members to take over. Without outside professional help, the well-being of the
dependent elder cannot always be ensured. Supporting families facing such situations is as important as types of domestic captivity and the risk of caregiver
exhaustion can generate situations of abuse (Polard and Linx, 2014).

When family solidarity is organised, but struggling to cope

Amongst the diseases whose prevalence increases sharply with age are Alzheimer's disease and related diseases. In Morocco, the total number of sufferers (far
from all of them have been diagnosed), could be around 150,000.[21] During our

exploratory investigations to understand how the elderly and their families cope when faced with the onset of neurodegenerative diseases, we realized that 'strategies' based on 'multi-stakeholder and interlocking solidarity' were established within families, in the sense that we defined previously. Even though these diseases affect only a statistically small proportion of the elderly, examination of them also highlights significant deficiencies in society's capacity to meet the specific needs of some of the elderly and to support family caregivers.

Onset and worsening of the disease: towards increased activation of interlocking family solidarity

Mobilisation of the various siblings when confronted with the situation of an elder's acute disease is illustrated by the case of Zineb. The latter, who passed away a few years ago at approximately 80 years of age and had been diagnosed as having Alzheimer's disease three years before her death, had been a widow for 25 years. Zineb had a daughter, the eldest of the siblings, and four sons, two of whom were still unmarried and lived with her in the house built by their late father. Both sons had very modest incomes. Zineb's daughter, having undertaken higher education and working in a profession which occupied a lot of her time, lived in the same town with her husband and two of her children, still students. Zineb's other two sons were both married and had children, one of them being an executive in the civil service in another town and the other living and working in Europe. Zineb received a modest widow's pension of around 800 dirhams. She also benefited from social cover allowing reimbursement of her medical expenses which were initially limited to medication for the treatment of hypertension. With the means at her disposal, and thanks to the occasional support from her offspring, Zineb managed to live normally and coped with the limited expenses her health problems required. But three years before she died, the situation became more complicated with the onset of the first symptoms of Alzheimer's disease. Memory and behavioural disorders intensified; then came a fall, when she was at home alone which, as it caused a fracture, made close monitoring more necessary. One of the two sons living with her then decided to marry by marrying a cousin who was none other than his mother's niece. By marrying a woman who was not working, and deliberately choosing endogamy, this son wanted to both guarantee regular attendance for his sick mother and ensure that his wife would treat her mother-in-law like her own mother.

However, as the disorders related to the disease worsened this, 'solution' quickly showed its limits. The work, both in terms of time and of energy, had become too much for the young wife, who was going to have a baby. They had to find a way to help her and the choice fell on a maternal cousin of the young woman who accepted a fee of 1,000 dirhams per month to help her cousin look after her sick aunt/mother-in-law. The payment of this sum was provided in turn by Zineb's daughter, her executive son and the son working in Europe. This 'arrangement', which remained in force until Zineb's death, seemed to be based on an implicit agreement whereby the sons cohabiting with the mother ensured the moral responsibility for daily management of the disease and did not have to contribute financially to the additional costs it caused; indeed, they had not the means.

Intra-generational solidarity faced with worsening illness

When the elderly find themselves in serious trouble, solidarity can develop between indirect descendants. This type of situation can be illustrated by the case of one neurologist's patient, a 70-year-old single woman, retired from the civil services. She was living alone when the doctor saw her for the first time. She was accompanied by her brother, who was the only family she had left. He was 60 years old, married and father of two children. He had noticed a big change in his sister's behaviour. Usually calm, she was aggressive at times, especially towards her neighbours. This behavioural disorder was actually hiding an already advanced dementia. This doctor then explained what he suspected was the pathology, and warning that the sister would very probably progressively lose her independence. The brother then looked for someone to help his sister in her home and take care of her. After two years of follow-up consultations, over the course of which the patient's neurological condition had remained stable, the day arrived when the patient's brother came to see the doctor alone. The man was now seriously concerned. 'He burst into tears as soon as he walked into my office' [. . .]. 'His sister almost set fire to the building, she was very agitated and he didn't know what to do [. . .] ', the doctor told us. The brother, raised by his sister when he was young, felt a moral obligation to help his sister. He sought a medical solution that would not make him feel he was abandoning his sister. Having no other family, if the woman had not been able to benefit from the support of the brother and his family, with whom she lived, she would have found herself in really dangerous situations which could have led to her being admitted to a psychiatric hospital.

Families faced with serious diseases: no alternative solutions or respite

The scenarios mentioned earlier, although they are specific cases, show that in the absence of alternative solutions the care of the elderly by the family circle can be difficult because of the resources required and the sacrifices engendered. In this respect, family solidarity initially involves one or more of the direct offspring before it has to expand to include all the offspring as the elderly person's state of health deteriorates. This expansion is not always accompanied by uniformity in the forms of support provided by the descendants. The family unit often negotiates a division of labour according to the ability of each one to provide material assistance and/or moral support. Their availability and degree of remoteness from the elderly person's dwelling place, each person's personal and professional constraints and the quality of the offspring and/or their spouse's relationship with the elderly sick person, etc., are all parameters to be integrated into the complex equation for finding a somewhat manageable solution.

The Moroccan family and society have undergone some changes but family solidarity is still undeniably present in Morocco. However, the constraints which they have to face are becoming more complex and tensions can arise over what is socially and morally expected of individuals as regards the provision of support to those elderly who require it and what they are actually able to do. Future demographic changes, which are characterised in particular by a decrease in family size, will make it impossible for multi-stakeholder, interlocking solutions like those observed today to be implemented. Given the ongoing rapid ageing, it is important to ascertain which means and measures are likely to allow these solidarities to be consolidated and relayed in some way as soon as possible.

Notes

1 HCP. (1960–2050). Population par groupes d'âges fonctionnels. Retrieved from http://www.hcp.ma/Population-par-groupes-d-ages-fonctionnels-1960-2050_a681.html

2 HCP. (1960–2050). Projections de la population totale par groupe d'âge et sexe (en milliers et au milieu de l'année). Retrieved from http://www.hcp.ma/Projections-de-la-population-totale-par-groupe-d-age-et-sexe-en-milliers-et-au-milieu-de-l-annee-1960-2050_a676.html

3 For a detailed analysis of the Moroccan demographic transition, the reader is referred to the chapter on Morocco in part one of this book.

4 World Values Survey (WVS), 2010–2014, Morocco.

5 See, for example, Tadmouri et al. (2009).

6 Source: National Multiround Demographic Survey.

7 ENPS-I [National Survey on Family Planning, Fertility and Health of the Population in Morocco] 1987.

8 Source: ENF [National Survey on the Family] 1995

9 It is of the same order of magnitude for men.

10 General Census of the Population and Housing Environment 2014 – Presentation of the first results, Rabat, 13 October 2015. Available on www.hcp.ma.

11 *Etablissements de Soins de Santé de Base* [Basic health-care facilities].

12 Source of data: Office of the High Commissioner for Planning, Directorate of Statistics (National Employment Survey). See also *Le Maroc en chiffres 2015*.

13 The average household size decreased from 5.2 people in 2004 to 4.6 in 2014.

14 The average size of urban households decreased from 4.8 people in 2004 to 4.2 in 2014.

15 The average size of rural households decreased from 6 people in 2004 to 5.3 in 2014.

16 For a detailed approach to differences by gender and residential areas, refer to Azammam (2009).

17 These households are 'vertically descending households' according to the terminology used in the 2006 ENPA.

18 Household type where elderly people and their spouse may live with their elders, offspring and/or other family members (nephews, nieces, cousins, uncles, fathers, father-in-law, grandsons, brothers, sisters, etc.) and/or other unrelated persons.

19 For an overview of key elements of the system of social welfare in old age and health risk cover, see the text on Morocco in appendix 7.1.

20 For the moment, institutional care in Morocco is a method of care exclusively aimed at those elderly most at risk. These Centres for the Elderly (commonly known as 'Dar Al Moussinine' in Arabic, literally 'House of the Elderly') are part of those social welfare institutions which have replaced what used to be called 'charitable homes'. We estimate that the total number of elderly people currently permanently housed in these institutions is around 3,500 people at most. This method of institutional care is the ultimate safety net, relying on national solidarity, and will only intervene when family solidarity completely fails (Amar and Sajoux, 2017).

21 This is the figure indicated to us by members of the Moroccan Alzheimer's Association. Using the prevalence rate adopted by the World Health Organization for the North African-Middle East region (WHO, 2012), the total number of people with dementia could be even higher.

References

Amar, M. and Sajoux, M. (2017). Politiques sociales, vieillesse et vulnérabilité au Maroc. Dispositifs actuels et transformations en cours, in: Golaz, V. and Sajoux, M. (Eds.), *Politiques publiques et vieillesses dans les pays du Sud*. Les Impromptus du LPED.

Azammam, S. (2009). Profil socio-démographique des personnes âgées, in: CERED (Centre d'Etudes et de REcherches Démographiques) (Ed.), *Les personnes âgées au Maroc: profil, santé et rapports sociaux, analyse des résultats de l'Enquête Nationale sur les Personnes Âgées (ENPA 2006)* (pp. 25–58). Rabat: HCP (Haut-Commissariat au Plan).

Bourqia, R. (2010). Valeurs et changement social au Maroc. *Quaderns de la Mediterrània*, (13), 105–115.

CESE (Conseil Economique Social et Environnemental). (2013). *Les soins de santé de base. Vers un accès équitable et généralisé.* Rabat: Conseil Economique Social et Environnemental.

Fassi Fihri, M. (2009). Etat de santé et morbidité chez les personnes âgées au Maroc, in: CERED (Centre d'Etudes et de REcherches Démographiques) (Ed.), *Les personnes âgées au Maroc: profil, santé et rapports sociaux, analyse des résultats de l'Enquête Nationale sur les Personnes Âgées (ENPA 2006)* (pp. 95–134). Rabat: HCP (Haut-Commissariat au Plan).

HCP (Haut-Commissariat au Plan) and Royaume du Maroc. (2008). *Enquête nationale sur les personnes agées au Maroc 2006.* Rabat: HCP (Haut-Commissariat au Plan).

Lecestre-Rollier, B. (2015). Les solidarités familiales au Maroc: permanences et changements. *Mondes en développement*, 3(171), 51–64.

Lfarakh, A. (2012). Fécondité, nuptialité, rupture d'union et remariage: niveaux et tendances. Principaux résultats de l'Enquête Nationale Démographique à Passages Répétés 2009–2010. *Les Cahiers du Plan*, (39), 14–29.

Nowik, L., Azammam, S., Sajoux, M. and Hamzaoui, K. (2012). L'évolution de la cohabitation intergénérationnelle au Maroc: les solidarités privées mises à l'épreuve ? in: *Relations intergénérationnelles, enjeux démographiques* (pp. 853–864). Paris: AIDELF.

Nowik, L. and Lecestre-Rollier, B. (2015). Quand le vieillissement repose sur les familles, in: Nowik, L. and Lecestre-Rollier, B. (Eds.), *Vieillir dans les pays du Sud: les solidarités familiales à l'épreuve du vieillissement* (pp. 19–53). Hommes et sociétés. Paris: Karthala.

Polard, J. and Linx, P. (2014). *Vieillir en huis clos de la surprotection aux abus.* Toulouse: Erès.

Sajoux, M. and Amar, M. (2015). Vieillesse et relations familiales au Maroc. Des solidarités fortes en proie à des cntraintes multiples, in: Nowik, L. and Lecestre-Rollier, B. (Eds.), *Vieillir dans les pays du Sud: les solidarités familiales à l'épreuve du vieillissement* (pp. 187–209). Hommes et sociétés. Paris: Karthala.

Sajoux, M. and Lecestre-Rollier, B. (2015). Inégalités et difficultés sociales dans la vieillesse au Maroc. Mise en évidence des limites des solidarités privées et de besoins croissants en matière de protection sociale, in: Adjamagbo, A. and Antoine, P. (Eds.), *Démographie et politiques sociales.* Ouagadougou. Retrieved from www.erudit.org/livre/aidelf/2010/004169co.pdf

Tadmouri, G. O., Nair, P., Obeid, T., Al Ali, M. T., Al Khaja, N. and Hamamy, H. A. (2009). Consanguinity and reproductive health among Arabs. *Reproductive Health*, 6(17), 9.

WHO (World Health Organization) (Ed.). (2012). *Dementia: a public health priority.* Geneva: WHO.

Appendix 7.1
Survey methodology

The data used in this work are of two types. They are derived from either

- various population and housing censuses conducted in Morocco between 1960 and 2014; or
- large statistical surveys conducted nationally by Morocco's Office of the High Commissioner for Planning (HCP) and in particular by the Centre for Demographic Studies and Research (CERED). The results and analyses from the National Survey of elderly persons conducted in 2006 amongst a sample of 2,500 households involving 3,010 elderly people from all social classes and regions of the country were of particular use.

This work is also based on a content analysis of the qualitative data we collected directly for the project *Vieillir au Maroc, Vieillir au Sénégal: analyse qualitative comparative des relations intergénérationnelles et des formes de soutiens familiaux et institutionnels aux personnes âgées. Identification d'enjeux pour les politiques publiques* (director: Muriel Sajoux). This data is from nearly 50 lengthy interviews conducted in 2011 and 2012, mainly in Meknès, a city located in the northwest of the country, 150 kilometres east of Rabat, the country's capital. These interviews were conducted with men and women over 60 years of age with very varied socio-economic profiles. Local participants, operators from the social or social/medical sector were also interviewed. Additional data was collected in 2013 and 2014 under the INED flagship project *Vieillissement et relations intergénérationnelles au Sud* (directors: Valérie Golaz and Cécile Lefèvre). In late 2015 and early 2016, as part of an exploratory approach intended to clarify the issue of the difficulties encountered by the elderly and their families when faced with neurodegenerative diseases, interviews were conducted with doctors (including neurologists) practising in various cities, members of the 'Maroc Alzheimer' [Moroccan Alzheimer's] association and families dealing with this type of disease.

8 Family mutual support in multigenerational France

Social classes, generations and gender: memberships in question

Thierry Blöss, Isabelle Blöss-Widmer and Michèle Pagès

The ageing of the population undoubtedly constitutes one of the major transformations in our contemporary societies. In France, one of the consequences of an ageing population has been the emergence of a 'multigenerational society'. This does not mean at all that the different generations actually live together or have regular and consistent contact, even if strong personal links may be maintained, as sociological surveys in recent years have shown. The emergence of a multigenerational society in France raises the issue of the functioning of family relations in a context of line of descent lengthening. In real terms, three or even four generations exist alongside one another in a growing number of families. Each of these generations is characterised by its own set of conditions, problems and life paths, which contrasts with the comforting vision of a common family purpose. At present, the family is associated with values that are 'naturally' positive, and the coexistence of the generations is viewed as a guarantee of mutual support. In addition, throughout the conveyed stereotypes on solidarities, what actually singles out individuals in their own ways of concretely living out their family relationships is generally forgotten.

By situating itself within the French context of a changing welfare state, and drawing on new analyses of recent quantitative survey data,[1] this chapter aims to better understand the vitality of family ties. Focusing on the behaviours of family mutual support, it shows on the one hand that the beneficiaries and the donors are clearly distinct, and that some circumstances are more conducive than others to family mutual support throughout the life cycle. On the other hand, it reveals how social factors contribute to strongly clarifying the responsibilities and obligations of the ones and the others. By referring to variables such as belonging to a social class, gender and generation, our purpose is to analyse the intensity of interpersonal relationships within the family structure, by revealing differences in status and social conditions that develop within a kinship and that changes in life cycle have, in some ways, only emphasised and even reinforced.

Ageing population and new generational balance

Numerous scientific studies have addressed the study of family mutual support through the prism of different disciplines (such as sociology, demography, economics, etc.) over the past decades. By making use of the controversial notion of solidarity, they have helped to shed light on the diversity of relationships operating within the family structure. More fundamentally, these studies have emphasised the growing importance of the intergenerational dimension in the study of the contemporary family, so much so that the generational balance has constantly evolved in recent times. Indeed, whilst the ageing of the population means that the number of the elderly has increased faster than the other age groups,[2] this change has also had consequences on the 'balance of power' that exists between generations. The issue of a multigenerational society therefore extends beyond the mere issue of the number of the elderly and it concerns the entire structure and dynamics of the life cycle.

Nevertheless, the transformation of the structure by age eludes any mechanistic interpretation. Although the younger generations tend to be decreasing in number, they constantly attract an ever-increasing attention and support from their parents. As for the most elderly generation, its weight is increasing very markedly, though this cannot necessarily be said to represent an additional burden on their children, as one might be led to believe by the prevailing rhetoric on the dependency of the elderly. However, this new intergenerational balance -or imbalance- is a social factor that must be taken into account in order to understand how each of the generations present will deal with lifestyle changes and will influence the life paths of the other generations.

The advent of the multigenerational society has revealed the crucial existence of an intermediate generation, also termed the 'sandwich' or even 'pivot' generation, as described by Claudine Attias-Donfut (1995). This generation (here defined as those aged 50–64) holds a position in the life cycle that exposes it to more intense family exchanges: as children, members of this generation are indeed increasingly likely to have (very) elderly parents. As parents, they are accordingly confronted with increasing demands for assistance from their children who face difficulties entering the job market and, more generally, in a context of casualisation of the modes of entry into adult life.

It is on this intermediate generation that focuses quite particularly our analysis. Accurately, we aim to better understand the unprecedented dynamics between these generations, and to highlight the specific role it plays as regards financial and material assistance (such as care and support) towards the older generations (aged parents) and the younger ones (adult children). In any event, this role is likely to be reinforced and prolonged over the next few years, as a consequence of the two processes discussed earlier – i.e., the prolongation of both the period of uncertainty for young people and the duration of old age literally 'compels' this intermediate generation to prolong its participation to intergenerational solidarity. The different studies examining this issue have already taken full measure of this process, in the sense that the definitions of this pivot generation have gradually expanded concerning the age bracket so as to straightforwardly acknowledge this established fact.

The emphasis placed on this intermediate generation's behaviours of mutual support is a means of studying how the members of the larger family take action throughout a life cycle that lasts longer and whose different phases have undergone profound changes.[3] Who helps whom, and under what circumstances? In some ways, this formula sums up the argument that follows, and which is based on data processed from the SHARE survey.

Box 8.1 Methodology: using the Share survey ('wave 4')

The Share survey[4] is a European longitudinal (panel) survey conducted every two years since 2004 on the topics of health, ageing and retirement, with samples from households in which one member is aged 50 or over. The original aspect of this European survey is its use of a strictly identical questionnaire, regardless of country, in order to maximise the comparability of the results. The main themes studied ('modules') are, in addition to those allowing a definition of the family and social life of the individual (such as employment, marital status, children, family circle, mutual support, etc.), those concerning the respondent's health (physical and mental health, different forms of consumption, cognitive capacity, health care) as well as money exchanges, housing, property holdings, etc.

Carried out for the first time with 30,816 respondents in 12 European countries (wave 1), specific questions were gradually added into the following waves. In wave 3, these concerned the course of the respondent's life story; in wave 5, in 2013, questions on the use of the Internet and computers were introduced. However, the key addition was in 2009, in wave 4 (16 countries, 58 489 respondents), concerning respondents' social networks. The questions in wave 4 create a deeper understanding of the respondent's social environment, which enables a comparison between the latter and the money transfers and material support given and received.

As for France, the sample for wave 4 consists of 5 615 people born in 1960 or before, and who are thus aged 50 and older (i.e. nearly 23 million people). This representative sample is the largest surveyed by Share in France since its inception (2 793 and 3 038 respondents were surveyed in waves 1 and 2), owing to a most substantial renewal of the panel. The results of the use of wave 4 presented in this chapter deal particularly with transfers of time and money, both given and received, in terms of the 'modules': 'Mutual Support and Services', 'Social Networks', 'Money Transfers' and 'Property Holdings'. Further questions from the section on the 'State of Health' have been used, as well as any others that characterise the respondents in terms of their social background.

	Sample composition (unweighted)		
Men	44.1%	Living with a partner	64.5%
Women	55.9%	Divorced, separated	10.7%
		Unmarried	7.7%
		Widowers/widows	17.1%
50–64	53.2%		
64–75	23.2%	Upper class	17.9%
75 and over	23.6%	Middle class	41.7%
		Working class	40.4%
No degree, CEP, Primary	38.3%		
Brevet, BEPC, CAP, BEP	32.5%	Retired	61.0%
Baccalauréat	9.7%	Still working	26.2%
University graduates	19.6%	Other	12.8%

When the nature of the family mutual support indicates the nature of filiation's links

In considering family mutual support behaviours, two types of 'transactions' can be distinguished: on the one hand, material aid and other favours done, on the other hand, financial support and money loans granted. This well-known distinction is instructive in more ways than one. Through the different surveys, it firstly established that the sum of both types of aid was above all relatively modest, although their contributions were real and effective (Herpin and Déchaux, 2004). One of the first lessons from the Share survey is that more than a quarter of the persons questioned (28.3% of people aged 50 and older) reported having given donations of money,[5] while only 3.6% had received[6] such donations. This means that across France (and Europe), monetary solidarity between the generations concerns a sometimes very small minority of people. These same levels are also found when examining the material favours that people do, or the time they devote to their family circle. From the outset, this allows us to put into perspective the scope commonly ascribed to family solidarity as a potential bulwark against life's difficulties.

The classification of family mutual support between different households also illustrates the 'generational sense' ascribed to these behaviour patterns. Socio-economic surveys have shown that families mainly practice 'solidarity with their descendants' (Masson, 2002). The study of private money transfers[7] clearly shows that in two-thirds of cases, they are made to children and grandchildren (63.9% and 10.8%, respectively). This confirms the idea that this mutual support is provided more evidently when it flows from the older to the younger generations. It is here that belonging to the pivot generation assumes its full importance. This generation has certainly been shown to perform the most money transfers. It is also the pivot generation that embodies most emblematically the direct support parents provide to children, while among older generations, it is conversely support towards grandchildren that is most substantial (Table 8.1).

The chief characteristic of financial support is therefore that it is asymmetric; this means it is not reciprocal and is not reversed over the course of the life cycle. It is more the status in the family that predominates in the practice of financial support, with adult parents playing a central role in the intergenerational dynamics. They are principally donors who mainly support their children. In return, they receive comparatively little from their offspring, and not before reaching old age (Table 8.2).

The central role played by parents in the pivot generation with regards to their children reflects the current organisation of entry into adult life and the requirements that this presents. This phase of the life cycle demands a greater amount of family support (Déchaux, 2007; Barry et al., 1996) and historically reveals the material difficulties that new generations of young people face when leaving the parental home,[8] as well as long afterwards. The 'pivot households' are those who spend the most to support the 18–24 year olds when they leave home. In France, people become eligible for state benefits only after the age of 25[9] if they have not yet secured stable careers. Up to the age of 25 years of age, aid for children who mostly lack professional experience, is, therefore, largely the

Table 8.1 Recipients of financial aid, by age of donor

	50–64 years	*65–74 years*	*75 years and over*	*Total*
To children	71.8%	60.6%	41.5%	63.9%
To grandchildren	3.4%	9.7%	37.4%	10.8%
Other relatives	9.1%	7.1%	6.8%	8.2%
Other than family	15.7%	22.6%	14.3%	17.1%
Total	100.0%	100.0%	100.0%	100.0%
				(N = 979)

Field: People 50 years of age and older, who reported having given €250 or more in the past 12 months. % calculated on weighted numbers.

The table reads as follows: 71.8% of respondents aged 50–64 who state they have given €250 or more, had given this money to their children.

Table 8.2 Origin of financial aid, by age of beneficiary

	50–64 years	*65–74 years*	*75 years and over*	*Total*
From parents	60.1%	21.0%	3.0%	48.4%
From children	19.2%	51.8%	90.5%	31.4%
Other relatives	8.0%	7.5%	0.0%	7.1%
Other than family	12.7%	19.7%	6.5%	13.1%
Total	100.0%	100.0%	100.0%	100.0%
				(N = 136)

Field: People aged 50 and over who reported receiving €250 or more in the past 12 months. % calculated on weighted numbers.

The table reads as follows: 19.2% of respondents aged 50–64 who reported having received €250 or more had obtained this sum from their children.

family's responsibility. However, after the age of 25, this parental support does not stop, and it assists in mitigating the effects of the period of material instability that young households face (Herpin and Déchaux, 2004). This support often constitutes a resource supplement, including in cases when young persons have a paying job that is nonetheless insufficient to guarantee their autonomy. In this sense, the multigenerational society is the site of practices unprecedented in their longevity, in the context of casualisation in the status of young adults. Intermediate generations must intervene for longer periods in the lives of their children, for whom the attainment of independence is delayed, among other effects.

While the prolongation of the support that parents offer to young adults reveals the recent instability of this critical stage of the life cycle, it also reflects the permanence of a moral norm surrounding parental responsibilities that is taking root and updating itself, including within institutions. The French Civil Code,[10] which normally governs such relationships within the family, states that the obligation of parents to address the needs of their offspring does not automatically cease when a child reaches adulthood. Section 371 amended now states that 'parents and children owe each other mutual respect, consideration and solidarity'. This duty of solidarity towards direct descendants, made into a legal obligation, illustrates the increasing requirements society makes on families at a time when the welfare state is being eroded and is more constrained than ever in its supposed role of regulating social inequalities. This duty has come to sturdily influence common sense by presenting itself as a collective cultural value.

The results of data processing of the Share survey show that the financial exchanges between parents and children are organised within an intergenerational system in which each helper is somehow helped by their own parent and what is more within a vertical framework which massively favours descendants. Indeed, the set of financial flows examined shows mainly that the pivot generation, who are mostly helpers to their own children, also benefit from financial support from their own parents, even though, as has already been demonstrated (Barry et al., 1996) and as our results confirm, it is not that frequent (Figure 8.1).

The results of the Share survey nonetheless show that the pivot generation, as descendants, has inherited twice as much as it has itself passed on. In terms of financial support, it is therefore the very identity of the so-called pivot generation which is at stake. This generation is much less able to meet the challenges of a double front, or a double request, than to play the role of a link in an intergenerational chain where direct filiation gives the direction to financial flows. The money relationships do function according to combinations that reveal the predominance of parents-children pairs. This generation of 50–64 year olds is, as such, both the principal beneficiary of financial support from their own parents (Table 8.3), whether in the form of loans, donations or bequests, and it is in turn best positioned to redistribute them to their own children (Appendix 8.1). This generation is in a position where its moral duty of parental support is thus reinforced or encouraged by the benefit it takes from the support it receives (Table 8.3).

The dynamics of the highlighted mutual support behaviours, in particular the strength of links towards descendants, illustrate the relationship between hitherto little studied patrimonial practices and mutual support patterns of behaviour between generations.[11] The main feature of financial transfers between

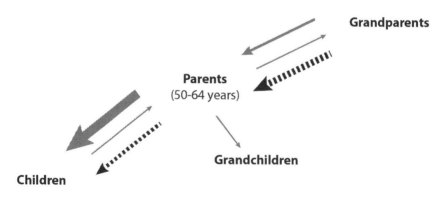

→ Direction and intensity of financial support

·‑‑‑► Direction and intensity of donations and inheritances

Figure 8.1 Gross financial flows between family generations

Table 8.3 Financial aid received, by age of beneficiary

	% Stating having received financial support of €250 or more during the year	*Has already received a gift or inheritance of €5,000 or more*
50–64 years	5.2%	15.0%
65–74 years	2.4%	12.8%
75 and over	1.4%	5.4%
Total	3.6%	12.0%

Field: People 50 years of age and older. % calculated on weighted numbers of people.

The table reads as follows: 15.0% of respondents aged 50–64 stated they had received a gift or inheritance of €5,000 or more.

generations is their transitivity. Parents are favoured in their support towards their descendants by patrimonial transfers they have themselves received, and which they partly restore to their own children. This redistribution process is not unrelated to the more advanced age when one inherits, which is de facto skipping a generation. The pivot generation is here representative of the intermediate generation that both benefits from the legacies of their elderly parents and redistributes their inheritance (Appendix 8.1). These results contribute to qualify the actions of this intermediate generation, by situating them within a generalised exchange that reveals its own inherited social characteristics. In a context of generations which coexist or even overlap, to borrow Martine Segalen's expression (1995), taking into account the financial flows within the family structure not only allows for an improved understanding of the strategic position of each existing generation but also of the role that family solidarities play in social reproduction and of which the hereditary nature of patterns of monetary support is one component.

Accordingly, parenthood constitutes one of the emblematic sites of generational consciousness. But this genealogical responsibility is relative, in that it depends on the resources available to the helping generations. These resources are economic and above all social, if we mean by this the full range of strategic provisions of the helpers but also the positions of those helped. We might introduce our subject in the following way: the more one belongs to the upper classes and the more one helps, the better one finds a satisfactory place in society and the more one is helped.[12]

Mutual financial support and 'social reproduction' of generations

There are barely any scientific papers on family solidarities that do not highlight the family spirit and the intensity of ties between members of an expanding kinship network in its various dimensions. Our point would not break with this tradition if we omitted to mention once more the degree to which practical support in time and money remains relatively modest or infrequent, and also the degree to which these practices are unequally distributed in social terms (Herpin and Déchaux, 2004; Degenne and Lebeaux, 1991). In line with the aforementioned investigations, the results of the Share survey confirm that family support reproduces and accentuates existing social inequalities rather than correcting them. The upper and middle classes are more often represented (33% of the upper classes and 38% of the middle classes) among those who have received financial support. The most educated categories are also those who receive the most support (usually through the social networks they have formed, rather than the family).

The common thread of kinship is often interlaced with a silver strand (Attias-Donfut et al., 2002). This beautiful phrase underlines the importance of financial transfers in relationships between generations. We know that the increase in donations is concentrated among the wealthiest strata of the population and, in 90% of cases, these transfers involve real estate, housing and professional tools (Arrondel and Masson, 1991). This trend shows that in terms of intergenerational transmission, social divides have only perpetuated and even reinforced themselves, leaving inequalities in living standards and social conditions intact. Not to mention that, all things being equal, in cases when parents – regardless of their social background – have an economic good they wish to pass on, surveys show that the resulting transfer is markedly larger among the upper strata of society. Transfers of property means occur at more crucial junctures in the lives of their recipients, as one advances each step up the social ladder, judging by the upper strata of society's greater material resources to make anticipated donations during their lifetime. Intergenerational transmission therefore enters the socially unequal field of the donors' strategic capacities.

We must bear in mind that the family remains the domain in which the most striking and definitive inequalities begin and develop. The dynamics of financial transfers between generations deserve to be considered under a certain number of sociological variables. Since each family generation assists according to its means, the intensity of this support depends primarily on social background (Table 8.4).

Table 8.4 Financial supports given, by donor's educational attainment and social category

	% Stated having given financial aid of €250 or more during the year	*Has already received a gift or inheritance of €5,000 or more*
No diploma, CEP [Certificate of Primary Education], Primary	16.8%	4.9%
Brevet, BEPC, CAP, BEP	25.8%	6.1%
Baccalauréat	32.5%	7.8%
University Graduates	48.0%	17.7%
Working Class	17.7%	5.8%
Middle Class	29.3%	8.5%
Upper Class	49.7%	15.8%
Total	28.3%	8.5%

Field: People of 50 and older. % calculated on weighted numbers.

The table reads as follows: 49.7% of 'upper class' respondents say that they have donated €250 or more during the year, compared to only 17.7% of 'working-class' respondents.

These results, combined with others (Paugam and Zoyem, 1998), illustrate to what extent one's level of education and socio-professional position facilitate the expansion of financial support. The economic status of the caregivers is unquestionably another determining factor. Being in possession of a moveable property[13] thus indicates an increased possibility that one is able provide financial support (Appendix 8.1).

This finding occurs even more in cases when the money paid by households is to their own offspring: 19.4% of parents with this kind of savings say that they have financially supported their children. This is twice as many as those who have no such savings (9.3%).[14] Children and grandchildren are clearly the primary beneficiaries of the financial support provided by older generations. The scope of this support increases when it comes to more important financial donations: almost all donations of €5,000 or more (89.1%) are to children. Consequently, grandchildren represent a more marginal beneficiary group (3.3%). These conditions are a measure of the contribution that financial transfers make to the social reproduction of family lineages. Financial transfers are not the only form of mutual assistance that characterise intergenerational relations. Various other services add real value to the lifestyles of older generations.

Social variations of the favours done. . . to the elderly

Behaviour patterns related to intergenerational transfers studied in the Share survey revealed the importance of time given and enjoyed as a form of support between the different coexisting generations. Confirming the results of the first data collection, wave 4 shows that favours (done and received) are even more prevalent than financial transfers (paid and received), at 42.7% to 31.9%, respectively. As for financial support, it is noteworthy that on the one hand material support is modest, and on the other hand – for all social categories – respondents always state they give more help than they receive: 25.5% of respondents say that they provided[15] help to a third party (whether through personal care, doing shopping and household chores, or carrying out small DIY tasks or gardening), against 17.2% who state they were beneficiaries of such assistance during the 12 last months.[16] This asymmetry of transfers (by age) is consistent with changes in family solidarity during the life cycle. However, this calls for further cross-examination, insofar as the category of those of 50 or more (who gives more than it gets) subsumes a wide variety of socio-economic situations widely dependent on professional status, gender and also age itself. As with financial support, the material support provided shows social variations. It is principally those who are socially and culturally well off who devote the most time to this form of material support. The working class thus do not compensate in terms of material solidarities for the financial assistance that they are unable to afford.

For the vast majority of cases (61%), support is provided to a family member: firstly parents (32%); then children (16%), while siblings (5.6%) and other family members come far behind. This means that in 39% of cases, this support goes to someone outside the family structure. The exchange of services between neighbours or friends is more common in a working-class milieu. This is a form of everyday mutual support which is probably becoming more and more significant (Bonvalet and Ogg, 2005) in the event of difficulties. Although material support is more reciprocal than financial support, it focuses on the parents. This orientation is clearly the consequence of the ageing that sees elderly parents make growing demands on the adult generations within the family lineage (Figure 8.2).

This predominantly upward support is more often observed among the middle and upper classes. This surprising result, to say the least, reinforces the socially unequal nature of family support, which has been discussed earlier in relation to financial transfers. Further examination of mutual support within the family structure also reveals the extent to which women are, so to speak, consigned to the domestic sphere. The persistence of a social model that posits men as the principal providers of financial resources and women as the source of domestic ones is embodied in gender divisions of intergenerational support. In these terms, men are largely characterised by the financial support they provide, while women are largely defined by the domestic support they can offer. The gendered division of domestic roles is manifested throughout the cycle of family life (Blöss, 2016). When it comes to practices of material solidarity between generations, women are, therefore, on the front line: 27.3% of women state that they 'give their time' (Attias-Donfut and Ogg, 2009). This participation is all the more important when considering it amongst the upper social class (37.1%) and amongst the interme-diate generations (36.7%). The generations most inclined to be 'caregivers' are those aged between 50 and 64 (among whom 34.1% reported having provided support). Then, with age, the support provided declines to 21.8% for those aged 65–74, and a mere 11.5% for those over 75.

Thus participation in domestic activities or health care is predominantly wom-en's work (Appendix 8.2). Research on 'informal caregivers' shows that the exchanges that bind family members together are those that are likely to miti-gate life's hazards, especially those related to old age. The role played by women in supporting the a fortiori dependent elderly, which has been stressed many times, and the manner in which domestic health care becomes the responsibil-ity of women constitute a powerful social norm (Clément, 2000). Putting this

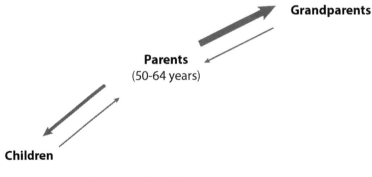

Figure 8.2 Flows of material support (care and domestic help) between family generations

social norm into practice through care for partners, as well as for elderly parents, requires arbitrations in the organization of the everyday life. From this perspective, the family structure is not the only source of help, since official support from public social policies must also be considered.

The prolonging of old age: between private support and public assistance

Women belonging to the pivot generation personify the iconic figure of the 'family caregivers' in relation to the older generations.[17] In return, they are also the main beneficiaries. This shows that, since ageing accentuates gender inequalities (Attias-Donfut, 2000), women more frequently become vulnerable as they age, all the more so when they are without a partner. From this perspective, family ties between caregivers and those receiving care vary by gender, with men principally receiving care from their partners, and women from their children. This is mainly due to differences in life expectancy between men and women and to age differences within couples (HCF, 2011). In the Share survey, 21.2% of women reported receiving material support (compared to 11.9% of men). This proportion rises gradually as one moves up the age scale: 9.7% in the pivot generation (50–64), 22.6% among those aged 65–74 and 39.2% among the most elderly (75 and over). This represents the highest frequency recorded in this survey.

Notwithstanding this finding, living as a couple in later life is certainly a less vulnerable situation than living alone, and one in which the support from children is less likely to be needed. These considerations on the importance of the family background point to the idea that ageing is a greater factor of vulnerability when the elderly live alone. Using the material of the Share survey also shows that domestic favours done to parents become even more important as the latter age. Only 8.4% of the pivot generation reported receiving such support, while this figure rises to 15.8% among those aged 65–74 and 35.8% amongst the most elderly (75 and over) (Appendix 8.2). The frequency with which material support is received also increases with the degree of the health 'handicap', for all age groups. This trend is reinforced by ageing, as the two variables are correlated. The older generation whose deteriorating health is most pronounced, is from this perspective the most affected by the process. While 35.8% of this generation report receiving support from outside the household, regardless of their physical condition, this figure rises to 50.6% for those who report being in poor health (Figure 8.3) and even 53.9% for those who report being severely restricted in their activities (Figure 8.4).

While the need for support increases with age and health problems, it is partly fulfilled by the family environment, friendship networks and the use of professional caregivers. A number of lessons can be drawn from this dividing up. The primary finding is that two-thirds of the support received (63.8%) come from outside the family, if the one provided by social contacts in the broadest sense is added up (including colleagues and neighbours) as well as the one provided by paid, professional third parties (46.5%). Consequently, the family, in the broadest sense, only provides a third of the material support that elderly report receiving.

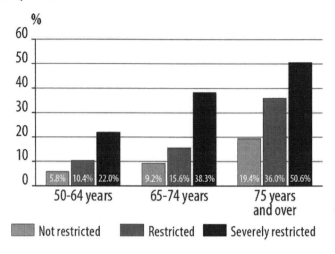

Figure 8.3 Material support received, according to degree of limitation of daily activities and by generation

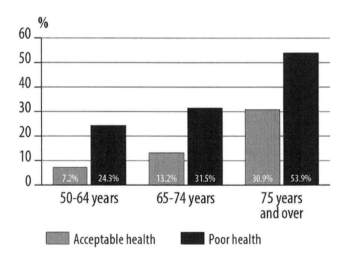

Figure 8.4 Material support received, according to general health status and by generation

This result illustrates the strong tendency in French society for public or institutional solidarity to be embodied, first and foremost, by society's support for the elderly (Chauvel, 2007). This analysis is corroborated by André Masson (2007), who found that at present, as a result of an ageing population and longer life spans, the French who are over 60 receive more (in terms of health and retirement benefits) than all other age classes (in terms of health, education, unemployment and family benefits).

The second lesson that can be drawn is that children are by far (28.2%) the main source of the support that elderly persons can expect from the family circle.

This material support from the offspring is not commensurate with the financial support that parents are able to provide, proving thus that intergenerational exchanges, even when deferred, are only reciprocal to a relative or limited extent. This support from children, although proportionally more modest, is nevertheless decisive when circumstances demand it, especially when the health of the parents starts to fail. However, this assistance is only observed in certain social and family configurations. Those aged 75 and over are in fact no more homogeneous, as a social class, than other age brackets or generations, which means that the assistance they receive cannot be considered in isolation from their social and family status. The use of a professional caregiver (to help with personal hygiene, housework, etc.) is all in all widely practiced among all social classes, precisely because this professional caregiving is partially provided for by public social policies (through social schemes and mutual insurance).

However, working-class people as well as women – and especially widows – differ by the personal care they receive from their children. What is remarkable about middle and upper class people in that field is the fact that they significantly use their social networks (colleagues, friends and neighbours) (Table 8.5).

The table reads as follows: 23.2% of upper class respondents who reported receiving assistance have done so from neighbours, friends or colleagues; this proportion was only 12.6% for working-class respondents.

The final lesson that can be drawn, somewhat surprisingly, is that people living in couples are more likely to receive support from third-party professionals than those living alone, especially widows. In accordance with the trends already put forward in previous surveys (Attias-Donfut and Ogg, 2009), this means that public and private support are not in opposition, but are complementary. For elderly couples, the use of external support is favoured by domestic mutual support, as well as by the greater financial resources these couples possess. For those who have been widowed and who experience greater isolation and economic insecurity as a result, the use of paid external assistance is reduced in favour of informal support from children or relatives. Living as a couple in later life is unquestionably

Table 8.5 Origin of material support received, by social category of the beneficiary

	Working Class	*Middle Class*	*Upper Class*	*Total*[*]
Paid caregiving from a third party	39.4%	54.7%	53.0%	46.6%
Assistance from children	35.5%	13.6%	19.3%	25.7%
Assistance from neighbours, friends and colleagues	12.6%	25.0%	23.2%	18.3%
From other relatives	12.5%	6.7%	4.5%	9.4%
Total	100.0%	100.0%	100.0%	100.0% (N = 294)

Field: People aged 75 and over, who reported receiving material assistance in the last 12 months. % calculated on weighted numbers.

[*] Marginal frequency may vary from one table to another due to failure to reply.

a less vulnerable situation than living alone, and requires less frequently the support from children. The importance of the family context reinforces the idea that ageing is an even greater factor of social vulnerability, as well as social inequality, when experienced by people living alone, particularly women (Appendix 8.2).

Conclusion

Longer life expectancy, and the resulting ageing population in France and throughout Europe, can be considered as an essential 'motor' of changes in the family (Théry, 2007) over the last decades, particularly for intergenerational relations. They provide an analyser of the family's capacities and of the new social responsibilities with which it is confronted, in view of professional and family changes in the life cycle, but also of its own limitations. The coexistence, on paper, of several generations is not necessarily an indication of mutual support, when the ordinary lot of each generation is to address its own problems. In everyday life, the acuteness of these difficulties prevails, more often than can be thought, over behaviour patterns of mutual support, which is a sign that that these patterns do not apply in all circumstances, or in an automatic or unconditional way, in contrast with the widespread belief that such practices are natural and necessary acts. Family mutual support does not work in the same way according to the class, gender or generation of the 'helpers' and the 'helped'.

International comparisons of the results of several waves of the Share survey (Attias-Donfut and Ogg, 2009) show overall rather similar trends to those analysed here, in terms of financial and material support between generations (e.g. limited scope and direction of mutual family support, gender division in caregiving to the elderly). In these comparisons, north/south differences within Europe are relevant when observing the actual cohabitation of generations (especially between parents and young adults). While this is regarded as a de facto form of economic support, it appears to be more common in European countries bordering the Mediterranean than in Northern Europe. This socio-geographical distribution also shows significant differences in material support within the family (particularly in terms of time spent). In this regard, countries in the North appear to be more 'generous' than those of the south (Wolff and Attias-Donfut, 2007), which again contradicts largely stereotypical current representations.

From this point of view, the challenge that French society will face in coming years is less the actual ageing of the population (and its economic effects in terms of the working/nonworking population ratio) than the social conditions in which the new generations of older persons will approach their period of retirement and prolonged old age, which is break from a historical cycle of social progress. The consequences of the transformation of their way of life, as we have shown, will extend far beyond the issue of their own living conditions to include their capacity to engage in mutual support with their offspring. Ultimately, it is the dynamics of intergenerational exchange which is at stake. Future pivot generations, with access to a lower level of material support, will certainly find it more difficult to help their children, if support from their own parents is lacking. All the more so that their own social conditions as helpers won't fail to be affected by the growing insecurity of their status as adult 'helpers'. In this hypothesis of growing social casualisation around the status of adults, widespread intergenerational mutual support (among the young adult generation, the pivot generation and the older generation), will undoubtedly result in a further deepening of social inequalities.

The different results and analyses presented in this chapter emphasise to what extent each generation fundamentally has a relative value which mainly depends on its own social conditions of existence. This position is essentially estimated by the other generations according to the social position of the individuals who constitute it, and thus in accordance with their capacity to exist in relation to others, to act or give mutual support. This is the essential criticism, we believe, that must be made to the notion of the 'multigenerational society' that tends to consensually encompass the various strategic mechanisms and capacities of the stakeholders, disregarding distinctions of class and gender – that is to say, *a minima* disregarding distinctions of the resources they have access to.

Notes

1 This chapter involved the use of data from wave 4 of the Share survey (Survey of Health, Ageing and Retirement in Europe) conducted in 2009. Unless otherwise indicated, all percentages presented in this chapter are calculated from weighted numbers of people.

2 For example, the number of people aged 75 and over has increased 3.5 times in France in more than half a century. In the same period, those aged 50–64 (symbolising adult generations) has multiplied by 1.8, and those aged 18–25 by 1.2.

3 Other than the changes in the means of entry into adult life, characterised by growing and long-standing casualisation for young people, and changes in lifestyle linked to prolonged old age, mention must be made of all the changes that have taken place in the 'adult' life cycle, such as growing conjugal and professional instability.

4 SHARE: Survey of Health, Ageing and Retirement in Europe (50+). Share data collection was primarily funded by the fifth European Community Framework Programme (Project QLK6-CT-2001–00360 on the theme of quality of life). Funds were also provided by the US National Institute on Aging (U01 AG09740–13S2, P01 AG005842, P01 AG08291, P30 AG12815, Y1-AG-4553–01 and OGHA 04–064). In France, additional funding for data collection was provided by CNAV, CNAM, COR, DREES, DARES, the Caisse des Dépôts et Consignations, and the General Commission du Plan. In 2012, the LEDa-LEGOS team at the University of Paris-Dauphine took over management of the SHARE France survey, which had hitherto been run by IRDES [Institute for health economics research and documentation]. Until wave 4, data collection within France was conducted in partnership with INSEE. Since wave 5, the GfK-ISL polling institute has reconvened the panel established by INSEE (http://share.dauphine.fr/fr/equipes-et-partenaires/lequipe-share-france.html). For more information on the Share France and Share Europe surveys, see: http://share.dauphine.fr/fr.html and www.share-project.org/

5 Response to question FT002: 'Please consider the last 12 months. Disregarding occasions on which you shared accommodation or a meal, have you given a donation or provided financial or material support to any person, who may or may not be a member of your household, amounting to €250 or more? ('Donation' here refers to the payment of sums of money, or the payment of expenses, such as medical costs, tuition fees, provision for housing purchase, etc. Loans, and donations to charity, are excluded)'.

6 Response to question FT009: 'Please consider the past twelve months. Disregarding occasions on which you shared accommodation or a meal, have you received a donation or financial or material support from any person who may or may not be a member of your household, equivalent to €250 or more?'

7 Financial support from parents is generally distributed informally, and for various reasons: loans and regular, periodic or occasional donations (especially in case of need).
It also includes, in a more formal and specific way, the giving of intentional donations
(or inheritance between living persons). Lastly, it may take the form of donations 'in
kind' (when the parent provides accommodation or take responsibility for rent, bills or
a loan).

8 See the statistical survey of Catherine Villeneuve-Gokalp (2000, p. 66), showing that a
growing number of young people leave home with the help of their parents, whether by
moving into accommodation that the parents own or pay for, or by receiving a regular
payment from parents to assist with accommodation.

9 However, the introduction, in June 2009, of the RSA (Revenu de solidarité active
[Active Solidarity Payment]) to replace the RMI (Revenu minimum d'insertion [Mini-
mum Social Inclusion Payment), created an opportunity for young French people aged
18–24 years to receive a financial allowance, on condition that they are single parents
or can demonstrate having worked for a given period (amounting to at least two years,
full time, within the three years preceding the date of the application).

10 See Article 371–2 as amended by Act No. 2002–305 of 4 March 2002, on parental
authority.

11 As Jean-Hugues Déchaux (2007) wrote, 'property transfers are transfers without possibility of direct reciprocity', and abide by strict regulations on inheritance tax. As such
they have been separated from the sociological analysis of informal financial exchanges
between households.

12 As shown in the very recent survey by Julie Solard and Rosalinda Coppoletta (2014),
which confirms the results provided a few years earlier by Catherine Villeneuve Gokalp
(2000). It shows that young people from more advantaged backgrounds or with a better
start in the job market are better able to negotiate the fall in living standards associated
with leaving the parental home. This fall is more easily managed when these young
people continue to benefit from intra-family transfers that are often inadequately taken
in account by indicators of living standards. This is particularly true of young people
leaving home to undertake initial training, more than half of whom receive support
from their relatives.

13 Moveable property consists of financial products held by the respondents (life insurance, shares, mutual fund units, home savings scheme, equity savings plan, etc.)

14 Reverse reasoning places equal stress on the importance of the factor of living standards: 67% of respondents reported having moveable property. This proportion rises
to 81% among those who report having provided financial support to their children.

15 Response to question SP008: I would now like to talk about the help you have given
people in your circle. During the last twelve months, have you personally provided personal care or domestic help to a member of your family not living in your household,
or to a friend or neighbour?

16 Response to question SP002: We will now turn to the topic of mutual support. These
questions refer to the favours you do, or the support you receive from people in your
social circle. Consider the last twelve months. Have you received personal care or
domestic help from a member of your family not living in your household, or from a
friend or neighbour?

17 Sixty-two percent 'official' family caregivers – i.e., those whose status is officially
recognised by the government, and who are eligible for remuneration for the personal
care of elderly people receiving the APA (Aide publique pour l'autonomie [Pub-
lic Autonomy Benefit]), are women (Source: DREES – Études et résultats, No. 459,
January 2006).

18 Response to question FT009: Please consider the past twelve months. Disregarding
occasions on which you shared accommodation or a meal, have you received a donation or financial or material support from any person, who may or may not be a member
of your household, equivalent to €250 or more?

19 Response to question FT002: Please consider the last 12 months. Disregarding occasions on which you shared accommodation or a meal, have you given a donation or

provided financial or material support to any person, who may or may not be a member of your household, amounting to €250 or more? ('Donation' here refers to the payment of sums of money, or the payment of expenses, such as medical costs, tuition fees, provision for housing purchase, etc., loans, and donations to charity, are excluded).

20 Response to question SP002: We will now turn to the topic of mutual support. These questions refer to the favours you do, or the support you receive, from people in your social circle. Consider the last twelve months. Have you received personal care or domestic help from a member of your family not living in your household, or from a friend or a neighbour?

21 Response to question SP008: I would now like to talk about the support you have given to people in your social circle. During the last twelve months, have you personally provided personal care or domestic help to a member of your family not living in your household, or to a friend or a neighbour?

References

Arrondel, L. and Masson, A. (1991). Que nous enseignent les enquêtes sur les transferts patrimoniaux en France ? *Économie & prévision*, 100(4), 93–128.

Attias-Donfut, C. (Ed.). (1995). Les solidarités entre générations: vieillesse, familles, État. Paris: Nathan.

Attias-Donfut, C. (2000). Rapports de générations. Transferts intrafamiliaux et dynamique macrosociale. *Revue française de sociologie*, 41(4), 643–684.

Attias-Donfut, C., Lapierre, N. and Segalen, M. (2002). *Le nouvel esprit de famille*. Paris: Odile Jacob.

Attias-Donfut, C. and Ogg, J. (2009). Évolution des transferts intergénérationnels: vers un modèle européen ? *Retraite et société*, 2(58), 11–29.

Barry, C. de, Eneau, D. and Hourriez, J.-M. (1996). Les aides financières entre ménages. *INSEE Première*, (441), 4.

Blöss, T. (2016). Devoirs maternels. Reproduction sociale et politique des inégalités sexuées. *Actes de la recherche en sciences sociales*, 4(214), 46–65.

Bonvalet, C. and Ogg, J. (2005). Réflexions sur les enquêtes européennes sur les solidarités familiales. *Revue française des affaires sociales*, (4), 183–203.

Chauvel, L. (2007). La solidarité générationnelle, bonheur familialiste, passivité publique, in: Paugam, S. (Ed.), *Repenser la solidarité*. Le lien social. Paris: Presses Universitaires de France.

Clément, S. (2000). Le soin familial aux personnes vieillissantes, in: Keller, P.-H. and Pierret, J. (Eds.), *Qu'est-ce que soigner? Le soin, du professionnel à la personne*. Paris: Syros.

Déchaux, J.-H. (2007). Réalités et limites de l'entraide familiale, in: Paugam, S. (Ed.), *Repenser la solidarité*. Le lien social. Paris: Presses Universitaires de France.

Degenne, A. and Lebeaux, M.-O. (1991). L'entraide entre les ménages: un facteur d'inégalité sociale ? *Sociétés contemporaines*, 8(1), 21–42.

HCF (Haut Conseil de la Famille). (2011). La place des familles dans la prise en charge des personnes âgées. Paris: HCF.

Herpin, N. and Déchaux, J.-H. (2004). Entraide familiale, indépendance économique et sociabilité. *Economie et statistique*, 373(1), 3–32.

Masson, A. (2002). Economie des solidarités. Forces et faiblesses des solidarités comme anti-marché, in: Debordeaux, D. and Strobel, P. (Eds.), *Les solidarités familiales en questions: entraide et transmission* (pp. 143–182). Droit et société. Série sociologie. Paris: L.G.D.J.

Masson, A. (2007). Les avatars de l'altruisme parental, in: Paugam, S. (Ed.), *Repenser la solidarité*. Le lien social. Paris: Presses Universitaires de France.

Paugam, S. and Zoyem, J.-P. (1998). Le soutien financier de la famille: une forme essentielle de la solidarité. *Economie et statistique*, 308(1), 187–210.

Segalen, M. (1995). Continuités et discontinuités familiales: approche socio-historique du lien intergénérationnel, in: Attias-Donfut, C. (Ed.), *Les solidarités entre générations: vieillesse, familles, État* (p. 352). Essais & recherches Sciences sociales. Paris: Nathan.

Solard, J. and Coppoletta, R. (2014). La décohabitation, privilège des jeunes qui réussissent ? *Economie et statistique*, (469–470), 61–84.

Théry, I. (2007). Transformations de la famille et 'solidarités familiales', in: Paugam, S. (Ed.), *Repenser la solidarité*. Le lien social. Paris: Presses Universitaires de France.

Villeneuve-Gokalp, C. (2000). Les jeunes partent toujours au même âge de chez leurs parents. *Economie et statistique*, 337(1), 61–80.

Wolff, F.-C. and Attias-Donfut, C. (2007). Les comportements de transferts intergénérationnels en Europe. *Economie et statistique*, 403(1), 117–141.

Appendix 8.1

Explanatory factors relating to financial support: Logit models

	Financial support received[18] (142 involved)		Financial support provided[19] (1016 involved)		Financial support provided (to children) (579 involved)	
Variables introduced in the model	Coefficient	OR	Coefficient	OR	Coefficient	OR
Age of respondent						
50–64	+ 0.81 *	2.3	ns		+ 0.89 ***	2.4
65–74	+ 0.69 *	2.0	ns		+ 0.71 ***	2.0
75 and +	*ref.*	*1*	*ref.*		*ref.*	*1*
Gender of the respondent						
Woman	ns		ns		ns	
Man	*ref.*		*ref.*		*ref.*	
Job category and educational attainment of the respondent						
Upper class with Bac diploma and +	ns		+ 0.43 ***	1.5	ns	
Upper class with lower degree than Bac	ns		ns		ns	
Middle class with Bac diploma and +	*ref.*		*ref.*	*1*	*ref.*	*1*
Middle class with lower degree than Bac	ns		− 0.22 *	0.8	− 0.29 *	0.8
Working class with Bac diploma and +	ns		ns		ns	
Working class with lower degree than Bac	ns		− 0.74 ***	0.5	− 0.64 ***	0.5
Marital status of the respondent						
Married	*ref.*	*1*	*ref.*	*1*	*ref.*	
Divorced/Separated	+ 1.01 ***	2.7	+ 0.35 **	1.4	ns	

(Continued)

	Financial support received[18] *(142 involved)*		*Financial support provided*[19] *(1016 involved)*		*Financial support provided (to children) (579 involved)*	
Single	+ 0.93 **	2.5	ns		ns	
Widowed	+ 0.62 *	1.8	ns		ns	
Pension and Benefits						
Recipient of pension only	− 0.43 *	0.6	ns		ns	
Recipient of additional disability benefit	ns		ns		ns	
Recipient of a survivor's pension	ns		ns		ns	
Recipient of job seeker's benefit	ns		ns		ns	
Other working persons not involved	*ref.*	*1*	*ref.*		*ref.*	
Surviving older relatives						
At least one ascendant (father or mother)	+ 0.65 **	1.9	+ 0.22 *	1.2	ns	
No living parent	*ref.*	*1*	*ref.*	*1*	*ref.*	
Children						
Has had at least one child	+ 0.84 **	2.3	+ 1.04 ***	2.8		
Has never had children	ns		ns			
Non-response	*ref.*	*1*	*ref.*	*1*		
Property the respondent						
Has property	+ 0.61 **	1.8	+ 1.36 ***	3.9	+ 1.13 ***	3.1
Does not have property	*ref.*	*1*	*ref.*	*1*	*ref.*	*1*
Donations and inheritances						
Has already received a donation or inheritance of €5000 or more	+ 0.67 **	1.9	+ 0.64 **	1.9	+ 0.59 ***	1.8
Never	*ref.* Field: 5615 respondents	*1*	*ref.* Field: 5615 respondents	*1*	*ref.* Field: 3792 respondents with children	*1*

Notes: For each explanatory variable introduced, the baseline against which the effects are studied is indicated in italics. The stars indicate the significance of the coefficients: ** significant parameter threshold of 0.001; ** significant to 0.005 threshold; * significant to 0.05 threshold; ns. Not significant O.R.: 'Odds Ratio', a measure of the ratio of risks between a given modality and its reference in the variable. Logit models, unweighted. Reading (Financial support received): for a given modality of an explanatory variable, the coefficient is even higher when respondents in this situation reported having been helped financially, compared to those in the baseline scenario. For example, respondents aged 50–64, all things being equal, are more likely to receive financial support (positive coefficient of + 0.81*) than those aged 75 and over, who here serve as the baseline. Conversely, a negative coefficient indicates that persons presenting the associated modality are less likely to have received financial support than those in the selected reference category. An O.R. of 2.3 for the 50–64 age group means that men in this age group are 2.3 times more likely to receive financial support than the 75 and over age group taken as a baseline (O.R. = 1).

Source: European Share survey, wave 4 (for some variables, pairings are with waves 1 and 2).

Appendix 8.2

The explanatory factors for material support (caregiving, housework): Logit models

	Material support received[20] (714 involved)		Material support provided[21] (1012 involved)	
Variables introduced in the model	Coefficient	OR	Coefficient	OR
Age of respondent				
50–64	− 0.46 ***	0.6	+ 1.19 ***	3.3
65–74	*ref.*	*1*	+ 0.84 ***	2.3
75 and +	+ 0.88 ***	2.4	*ref.*	*1*
Gender of the respondent				
Woman	+ 0.27 **	1.3	+ 0.38 **	1.4
Man	*ref.*	*1*	*ref.*	*1*
Job category and educational attainment of the respondent				
Upper class with Bac diploma and +	ns		ns	
Upper class with lower degree than Bac	ns		ns	
Middle class with Bac diploma and +	*ref.*		*ref.*	*1*
Middle class with lower degree than Bac	ns		ns	
Working class with Bac diploma and +	ns		ns	

	Material support received[20] (714 involved)		Material support provided[21] (1012 involved)	
Working class with lower degree than Bac	ns		− 0.24 **	0.8
Marital status of the respondent				
Married	*ref.*	*1*	*ref.*	*1*
Divorced/ Separated	+ 0.68 ***	1.9	+ 0.35 **	1.4
Single	+ 0.58 ***	1.8	ns	
Widowed	+ 0.98 ***	2.7	ns	
Pension and Benefits				
Recipient of pension only	ns		+ 0.21 *	1.2
Receives a disability benefit	+ 0.94 ***	2.6	ns	
Recipient of a survivor's pension	ns		+ 0.29 *	1.3
Recipient of job seeker's benefit	ns		*ns*	
Other working persons not involved	*ref.*	*1*	*ref.*	*1*
Surviving older relatives				
At least one ascendant (father or mother)	ns		+ 0.45 *	1.6
No living parent	*ref.*		*ref.*	*1*
Children				
Has never had children	ns		ns	
Has had at least one child	*ref.*		*ref.*	
Property the respondent				
Has property	ns		+ 0.39 ***	1.4
Does not have property	*ref.*		*ref.*	*1*

(*Continued*)

	Material support received[20] (714 involved)		Material support provided[21] (1012 involved)	
Donations and inheritances				
Has already received a donation or inheritance of €5000 or more	ns		+ 0.25 *	1.3
Never	*ref.* Field: 4 313 respondents		*ref.* Field: 4 313 respondents	*1*

Notes: For each explanatory variable introduced, the baseline against which the effects are studied is indicated in italics. The stars indicate the significance of the coefficients: *** significant parameter threshold of 0.001; ** significant to 0.005 threshold; * significant to 0.05 threshold; ns. Not significant O.R.: 'Odds Ratio', a measure of the ratio of risks between a given modality and its reference in the variable. Logit models, unweighted. **Reading** (Material support received): for a given modality of an explanatory variable, the coefficient is even higher when the respondent in this situation reported having received material support (caregiving, housework, etc.) compared to those in the baseline scenario. For example, respondents aged 75 and over, all things being equal, have received more material support (positive coefficient of + 0.88 ***) than those aged 65–74, taken here as the baseline. Conversely, a negative coefficient (50–64) reveals that people presenting the associated modality are less likely to have received material support than those in the selected baseline category (65–74). An O.R. of 2.3 for the group aged 75 and over signifies that men of this age group are 2.4 times more likely to receive material support than those aged 65–74 taken as a baseline (O.R=1).

Source: European Share survey, wave 4 (for some variables, pairings are with waves 1 and 2).

Part III

Uncertainties in gender relations in the Mediterranean

Social trajectories and modes
of political regulation

Introduction

Age, gender and social trajectories: the uneven emancipation of women in Mediterranean societies

Thierry Blöss and Elena Ambrosetti

To varying degrees, the various Mediterranean countries are the scene of an increasingly heterogeneous female population, resulting from a socially differentiated emancipation process. With the development of wage societies (Castel, 2013), largely due to the rise in women's professional activity, it is the relationship between the timetable of human reproduction and the timetable of social reproduction which is being called into question. Family responsibilities primarily force women to make a career choice, between a family and a professional life. These decisions reflect the disparities existing at the very heart of women as a group (Blöss, 2001). They also have consequences on the quality of women's professional lives. Finally, they are a discriminating factor in the differentiated ageing of men and women.

One of the major transformations in the lifestyles of Mediterranean societies has undoubtedly been linked with the changing role of women. More educated, more likely to take up employment and better integrated into the labour market, they are now waiting longer to start a family (González, 2006). In general, the increase in women's professional activity has been significant and even sometimes spectacular, all the more so amongst the 25–54 age group (which corresponds to the most active period of the life cycle, beyond school and excluding an early exit from the labour market). This is the case in Spain, where nearly eight out of ten women have, or are seeking, employment. However, as Margaret Maruani and Monique Meron (2013) argue, in activity there is unemployment: in this country, nearly a quarter of the workforce, men and women, are unemployed. This is a measure of how fragile and precarious the reality of women's work is. This is the main, common characteristic to be found in the different national situations, as the recent history of the terms of female employment demonstrates just how different Mediterranean countries' experiences in this domain have been and illustrates how little convergence there is in the matter. Indeed, whilst Spain recorded a very high-speed growth in female activity (including unemployment), countries such as Italy and Greece progressed at a different pace (Maruani and Meron, 2013). Meanwhile, others such as Morocco even registered an often-sustained withdrawal of women from the labour market.[1]

The feminization of employment, with its share of social inequalities within the labour market, has probably contributed to a change in the timetable of private life, especially that of childbirth, as it has affected women's life paths much more than men's. In these circumstances, the postponement of motherhood for personal career reasons cannot help but clash in reality with the 'biological fertility ceiling'. In such case, 'chosen childlessness' can become 'suffered childlessness'. Southern European countries thus display low fertility rates, in some cases far lower than other countries in the industrialized Western world. This situation partly reflects the difficulties women face in combining professional and family responsibilities. In other words, the problem of what is known as 'reconciling family and professional lives' (González, 2006).

Much research has shown that the issue of family and work responsibilities does not affect men in the same way as women. In recent decades, women, and mothers in particular, have increasingly participated in the labour market, without men (and especially fathers) doing the same in the domestic sphere (Lewis, 2009). This means that women who have children or wish to have some have to consider and organize family and working lives both cumulatively (in terms of working hours) and competitively (in terms of career). This is the situation that Marta Dominguez, Maria José Gonzalez and Irène Lapuerta describe in Spain, whilst emphasizing that the most educated women are also those with the fewest children and that mothers have less secure working conditions and fewer career opportunities than other categories of women (see Chapter 10).

The impossible work-family balance

Large differences remain as regards status and functions between men and women in both the private and the professional sphere. And the arrival of a child generally has no consequences other than the reproduction and the justification of this perpetual unbalance (Blöss, 2016). Over the course of recent decades, the gradual replacement of the traditional family, in which only the man was active, by a type of family configuration in which the man and the woman work, as well as the sometimes spectacular increase in single parents, principally due to separation or divorce, acutely raise the question of the division between work and family life (Letablier and Lanquetin, 2005), and prove that co-parenting is seldom at work in practice. Indeed, adjustments between work and family life mainly affect women and their professional careers. Whilst France holds a specific place amongst Mediterranean countries, combining a high female employment rate with one of the highest fertility rates in the European Union, alongside Ireland, this positive observation should be tempered by the fact that fathers still devote significantly less time to family tasks and that the arrival of a child more often disrupts female career trajectories. This remains infrequent for men (DGAFP, 2013).

Beyond the parental sphere, the unbalanced participation in family tasks is echoed in the care provided to ascendants. Indeed, women continue to bear most of the responsibility for care given to the dependent elderly, since they represent the vast majority of family caregivers (spouses, daughters, daughters-in-law, etc.), and do not hesitate, when they have a job, to take time off or adjust their work schedule to make themselves available for this role (DGAFP, 2013). Therefore, with the ageing of the population, the spectrum of family solidarity activities (care, mutual support, etc.) placed on women is broadening and exacerbating the asymmetry of social gender roles. This statement intends to emphasize the extent to which life paths and careers are structured around care activities (for children and for the elderly) that make them possible. Women's assignment to these responsibilities has created fundamental gender differences (Bessin, 2013).

The effects of gendered trajectories on socially differentiated ageing

However, the ageing process is also a social and political construct, informed by types of social division of labour which are persisting or being reproduced between men and women. The evolution of men and women's career trajectories throughout the life cycle, and also of their responsibilities in more unstable families, place men and women in socially different conditions when facing ageing. When it is time to retire, 'the die is cast', and each person is able to assess the more or less favourable conditions under which they will be able to tackle this phase of existence. The social issue at stake here is the consequences women's professional lives have on their living conditions and lifestyles, in particular at the time they retire. The greater insecurity characterizing women's career trajectories, measured in terms of their working hours, levels of remuneration, legal status of their employment, etc. has indeed tangible repercussions, increasing the risk of social insecurity at the end of the life cycle. Studies which measure poverty based on the individual incomes of men and women (Meulders and O'Dorchai, 2013[2]) demonstrated that the inequality between men and women's incomes is characterized by a sharp increase with age, thus illustrating that ageing is the greatest cause of female social vulnerability. Public social policy actions are not neutral in these situations. Every society demonstrates its State's ability to plan and organize social welfare for its elderly, whether this is through more or less developed pension systems or through broader public support for the elderly. In a context of a sustained ageing society, a number of studies emphasize the need for measures aimed at male/female equality in terms of income and retirement pensions, as well as in access to health care, in particular for the elderly (Austen, 2016). In the long term, the decline in fertility, which is the main factor in the ageing of the population, could prove to be an asset for ageing societies: it is indeed possible that one of the consequences of this decrease in the fertility rate might be a greater female participation in the labour market and a greater investment in terms of human capital in favour of the young (Bloom et al., 2015).

The research questions being posed in this part of the work

In this context, the research questions being posed in this part of the work aim to study the content and effects of changes in the relationship between men and women in the Mediterranean, sorting out the factors conducive to greater male/female equality and those characteristic of a reproduction of current asymmetric models. The chapter having Italy as a study framework analyses male/female inequality closely, in the labour market and within the family. The question of reconciling private and professional life and its interaction with demographic variables (including the formation of couples and fertility rates, against a background of an acute ageing of the Italian population) seems a critical issue both for individuals and for public policies. In the Italian labour market, barriers to equality between men and women are doubled by significant regional differences: in Northern Italy, where women work more, there is a greater demand for formal and informal care services for children and the elderly, but public policies are failing to respond appropriately. Hence the local context needs to be taken into account in policymaking, in order to meet the lifestyle-related requirements characterising the various regions of the same country.

Inequalities between men and women in the labour market develop throughout the life cycle. These are very significant for men and women of reproductive age and become less important for both genders on approaching retirement. However, Maria Rita Sebastiani and Maria Herica La Valle note that these inequalities appear to have been eased in the wake of the economic crisis experienced by Italy and its labour market, in particular since 2008 (see Chapter 9). This phenomenon is not the result of a higher female presence in the labour market, but rather of a deterioration in men's working conditions. In the family setting, the division of domestic work remains a strictly female affair. Adele Menniti et al. stress that the dominant norms in the division of gender social roles have a decisive effect on this distribution (see Chapter 9). From this point of view, reducing the difference between the hours which women and men devote to domestic work, as is for example the case in France, does not necessarily involve greater gender equality. It results much more from the progressive and relative liberation of women from such activities. Here too, as in the labour market, these differences in activity are largely influenced by age. They decrease when men and women approach retirement. In this domain also, significant differences between Northern and Southern Italy are emerging: 'Southern women' work less outside the home and receive less help from their spouses with domestic work. More generally, in the North and in the South, a higher level of education and a better income enable women to have a more balanced contractual relationship with their spouse in the family sphere.

The action of public policies designed to reconcile professional and family lives informs us about the less than 'demanding' nature of the Italian State, which at best, is characterized by ideological awareness campaigns promoting the role of the father, as was recently the case in the province of Bologna. A critical examination of the role of social policies is also conducted in the other chapters included in this part, by investigating the different ways work and family life are reconciled in their gendered dimension. The question of reconciling professional and family life has long been considered to pertain exclusively to the private sphere, including in Western countries, with the exception, according to Jane Lewis (2009), of France[3] and Northern European countries, characteristics of a more protective and influential social State. In such case, Mediterranean countries (thus with the exception of France) exemplify societies in which the welfare State intervenes little in this domain. As well as underdeveloped family policies they also have in common a strong dependence on family solidarity which exacerbates male/female inequalities and overexposes women to the principal domestic activities and the care of dependent family members (González, 2006).

In Spain, Marta Dominguez, Maria José Gonzalez and Irène Lapuerta (see Chapter 10) measure to what extent the Spanish Welfare State, which was already little involved in social welfare, faced with the crisis suffered since 2007, has made it an adjustable variable, by implementing a policy of austerity which involved cuts to the family policy budget. In France, political action in the domains of family life and employment has become in some respects a model largely influenced by the objectives promoted by the European Union. Individuals' independence in the division of their professional and family spheres is encouraged, in particular through improved provision of care for young children, designed to promote women's access to employment and thus encourage the two-working-parents family model. However, Valéria Insarauto (see Chapter 12) shows how numerous the many remaining barriers to male/female equality in the distribution of household tasks are. This proves that a gap can exist between the formulations of laws reflecting the State's wish to make parental roles more egalitarian on the one hand and, and on the other, the actual practice, not to mention social mores still deeply imbued with the principle of male domination.

Characterized by a sharp tension between the traditional logic of gender roles and a logic of the gradual equalising of men and women's social roles, Morocco also constitutes an observatory of this gap between the existence of recently established formal and constitutional provisions in favour of male/female equality in the domains of education, employment and of citizenship, and the continuance of largely conservative attitudes. In their chapter, Mohammed Amar and Ilham Dkhissi (see Chapter 11) emphasize the determining protest role of Moroccan civil society, in the form of women's associations, in Morocco's democratic institutionalization process. Here again, changes in the laws are not being immediately followed by significant changes in behaviours. The limits of the effect of legal campaigns are shown when faced with what could be called the unequal strength of socialization patterns which continues to attribute to individuals within a society differentiated and hierarchical destinies, roles, statuses and respect. If social equality between men and women remains a hollow expression, contrary to the unenforced legal injunctions, it is because women's legitimacy in public life still is inferior to that of men and thus primarily confines them to the private sphere.

Notes

1 The activity rate of women in Morocco (aged 15 and above) has remained low in recent years; it even dropped from 28.1% to 25.5%, in the decade 2000–2011. These general statistics conceal profound regional disparities. Rural areas display the highest rates of female activity (36.6%), whilst the drop in urban areas has led to a considerable decline, from 21.3% to 18.1%. The effect of formal qualifications in urban areas should be noted: the rate of professional activity is twice as high amongst women with higher education as those without a school-leaving diploma: 51.3% to 25.5%.

2 In their study, Danièle Meulders and Sil O'Dorchai calculated the 'financial dependency rate' defined as the risk of poverty an individual is exposed to if they have to meet their needs alone from their own income, without the help of others. Thus, by considering each individual separately, regardless of the household to which they belong, and measuring their individual income, this rate is substantially higher than the 'classic at-risk-of-poverty rate', particularly in Mediterranean countries (Spain, Greece and Portugal).

3 As regards its conciliation policy, France is closer to the Northern European countries than to its neighbours in Southern Europe, especially in terms of childcare, even though the French system is less developed than that of Scandinavian countries (Letablier and Lanquetin, 2005).

References

Austen, S. (2016). Gender issues in an ageing society. *Australian Economic Review*, 49(4), 494–502.

Bessin, M. (2013). Temporalités, parcours de vie et travail, in: Maruani, M. (Ed.), *Travail et genre dans le monde: l'état des savoirs* (pp. 107–116). Paris: La Découverte.

Bloom, D. E., Chatterji, S., Kowal, P., Lloyd-Sherlock, P., McKee, M., Rechel, B., et al. (2015). Macroeconomic implications of population ageing and selected policy responses. *The Lancet*, 385(9968), 649–657.

Blöss, T. (Ed.). (2001). *La dialectique des rapports hommes-femmes*. Paris: Presses universitaires de France.

Blöss, T. (2016). Devoirs maternels. Reproduction sociale et politique des inégalités sexuées. *Actes de la recherche en sciences sociales*, 4(214), 46–65.

Castel, R. (2013). La cohésion sociale, in: Castel, R., Chauvel, L., Merllié, D., Neveu, E. and Piketty, T. (Eds.), *Les mutations de la société française* (pp. 99–123). Les grandes questions économiques et sociales. Paris: La Découverte.

DGAFP (Direction générale de l'administration de la fonction publique). (2013). *Pour une meilleure articulation entre vie professionnelle et vie familiale. Identification des bonnes pratiques des secteurs public et privé en France et à l'étranger*. Paris: Ministère de la réforme de l'Etat, de la décentralisation et de la fonction publique.

González, M. J. (2006). Concilier la vie familiale et la vie professionnelle dans les pays de l'Europe du Sud. *Revue française des affaires sociales*, 1(1), 213–241.

Letablier, M.-T. and Lanquetin, M.-T. (2005). *Concilier travail et famille en France: approches socio-juridiques*. Noisy-le-Grand: Centre d'études de l'emploi.

Lewis, J. (Ed.). (2009). *Work-family balance, gender and policy*. Cheltenham; Northampton: Edward Elgar.

Maruani, M. and Meron, M. (2013). Mouvements de l'activité des femmes dans le temps et l'espace, in: Maruani, M. (Ed.), *Travail et genre dans le monde: l'état des savoirs* (pp. 237–257). Paris: La Découverte.

Meulders, D. and O'Dorchai, S. (2013). Précarité et pauvreté: comment mesurer la dépendance financière des femmes, in: Maruani, M. (Ed.), *Travail et genre dans le monde: l'état des savoirs* (pp. 258–268). Paris: La Découverte.

9 The gender gap at home and in the labour market

The case of Italy[1]

Serena Arima, Pietro Demurtas, Alessandra De Rose, Maria Herica La Valle, Adele Menniti and Maria Rita Sebastiani

In this chapter, we focus on gender inequalities both in housework and in labour market in Italy. This choice is not by chance. Italy, in fact, stands out because of the high level of gender inequalities, notwithstanding the notable progresses achieved by women in the field of education and increasing participation in the labour market (Menniti and Demurtas, 2012). Indeed, Italy holds the sixty-nineth position in the 2014 Global Gender Index ranking, far away from most of the Western countries; the female employment rate is still comparative low (equal to 47.6% in 2015), and fertility is persistently below the replacement level (TFR equal to 1.39 in 2013). Not surprisingly, the case of Italy is quoted as an interesting one and it is quite always included into comparative studies on gender imbalance in family work.

The recent recession has worsened the situation of the Italian labour market. From 2004 to 2013 unemployment increased, employment decreased, inactivity remained almost unchanged. Regional data showed significant differences. Here we analyse data concerning the Italian labour market in order to verify whether gender gap occurred, also at a regional level. Therefore, in the second part of the chapter we will analyze data from the Italian Labour Force Surveys (Istat) concerning employment, unemployment and inactivity according to gender and age from 2004 to 2013 (Levine et al., 2013). Moreover, we will analyse data on employment according to occupation, professional position within the ranking of subordinate jobs, number of hours worked and life span of employment contracts for jobs other than self-employed and by region. In order to highlight the effect of the downturn on the gender gap, we compared data from the recession period (2008–2013) with those of the period 2004–2007.

In the first part of the chapter, we will focus on gender inequalities in housework in Italian couples of any age. We will first give a brief review on the previous literature with reference to Italy (Section 1) and illustrate trends in housework in Italy over the years (Section 2). Then, we will recall the main sociological and economic theoretical approaches explaining gender inequality in family work (Section 3). Finally, we propose an original statistical analysis of the most recent Italian Time-Use Survey (2008–09) with the aim of estimating which factors affect the amount of time men and women allocate on management of the house and if they change with age (Section 4). The second part of the chapter focusses on gender gap in the labour market. In Section 5, we discuss the sociological aspects; in the following four sections, we present the main results obtained by studying in-entrance, horizontal and vertical segregation and gender gap in working conditions. A brief discussion will close the chapter.

Studies on gender inequality at home: the case of Italy

Gender specialization in paid and unpaid work in Italy has been demonstrated by practically all the national and comparative literature, mainly based on time-use data. Mencarini and Tanturri (2004) analyzed the time allocation between market work and non-market time of Italian spouses after the birth of a child and conclude that the market time of men increased while their childcare time was almost unaffected. Bloemen et al. (2010) studied how Italian spouses allocate time, distinguishing between three time uses: paid work, childcare and housework. They found that, while there is a persistent role specialization, education and place of residence make some differences: men married to more highly educated women spend more time with their children and those living in the North do more housework and childcare than in other part of Italy. They also found significant differences between weekdays and weekends suggesting some complementarities between husband's and wife's time inputs into the household production on weekends.

An important contribution to evaluate the role of contextual factors in shaping time allocation of men and women on family work along the life cycle can be found in a comparative study of Anxo et al. (2011). They found that Italian women spend more hours in unpaid household activities than men at all stages of the life cycle, particularly when they live in a couple with children. Italian women with children under age 3 spend in unpaid domestic work on average 40 hours a week, much more than their male counterparts. Sweden, instead, presents the lowest gender gap in time allocation.

Recent comparative studies show that in practically all the examined countries gender gaps are reducing over time during the weekdays and especially weekends (Neilson and Stanfors, 2014). Menniti et al. (2015), focusing on a sub-sample of couples, either married or consensual, with employed women aged 20–49 years and with at least one child under 14 years of age, modelled women's and men's time devoted to housework and childcare separately, and also estimated the effects of the same variables on the asymmetry index.[2] Their results show once again that within Italian couples the domestic burden share is heavily biased: time for housework is disproportionately higher for women than for men and that mothers' time on childcare remains as double as that of fathers. This is true even in the case of dual-earner couples. Overall, Italian men are changing their behavior toward a more equal gender division of family work at a slower pace than in other countries. A positive change is observed quite exclusively among the youngest cohorts and among fathers, who are the more and more willing to allocate their time on childcare. Very few progresses, instead, have been achieved in participation of men on housework (ISTAT, 2010). For this reason, in the rest of this work we will concentrate on time devoted to housework and how it is distributed between men and women in the Italian couples.

Housework: still a long way toward equality

This section focuses on changes occurred in the division of domestic labor among Italian couples. Our analysis covers a period of 20 years and uses the first and the last Italian surveys on time use carried out by Istat in 1988/9 and 2008/9 (Box 9.1).

Table 9.1 shows selected statistics summarizing the participation in and time spent on housework by men and women who are partners in couples and differentiate them according to their age, their occupational status and to whether or not they have children living in the family. Statistics refers to the average time spent on housework and the proportion of men and women who are involved in housework activities (in brackets). Housework includes time devoted to preparing meals, washing dishes and setting the table; cleaning and tidying the house; doing the laundry and ironing; house repair, maintenance, and management; and pet care and gardening.

Compared with the survey carried out in 1988/1989, 20 years later the male participation in housework activities increased from 54% to 62%. It has to be noted that fathers do not activate more than those who are childless, showing no sign of reduction of female domestic burden when the family size increases because of the presence of (young) children. This result confirms the evidence already known,[3] highlighting that adult men are increasing the time devoted to housework if childless while, whether fathers, they are more willing to allocate their time to childcare, reducing that allocated on domestic duties (Menniti and Demurtas, 2012).

The amount of time people devote to housework varies throughout the different stages of the life course; for Italian men, it increases with age. In 1988, men aged

---

Box 9.1   Time-use survey

Time-use surveys are an extremely detailed source of information on daily activities, providing a unique tool to measure the time devoted to different tasks. The data set contains a very rich corpus of information on individuals and households' background and socio-economic situation all collected through direct interviews. Respondents filled out a 24-hour diary, for a particular day suggested by the interviewer, in which they recorded their activities, indicating the time spent on each activity by 10-minute time slots. For any time slot, respondents could distinguish between main and secondary activities. Here we only considered the activities classified as the main ones, thus omitting to consider the time that, although dedicated to family care, was spent alongside other activities considered by the respondents themselves to be more important than the care itself. The survey classifies the activities performed by family members in ten main categories. The information considered here is included in the so-called family work and refer to routine housework.

Table 9.1 Time spent on housework among Italian couples. 1988–1989, and 2008–2008. (Duration in hh:mm; percentage of participation in bracket)

	Male		Female	
	1988/1989	*2008/2009*	*1988/1989*	*2008/2009*
Occupational status:				
Employed	0:40 (48%)	0:45 (55%)	4:09 (99%)	3:19 (97%)
Unemployed	1:09 (60%)	1:42 (64%)	6:22 (99%)	5:42 (99%)
Retired	1:45 (67%)	2:02 (76%)	6:13 (77%)	5:29 (97%)
Age:				
< 34 years	0:34 (48%)	0:40 (51%)	4:51 (99%)	3:48 (97%)
35 to 59 years	0:49 (50%)	0:57 (58%)	5:53 (88%)	4:42 (99%)
60 years and over	1:34 (65%)	1:47 (71%)	5:55 (98%)	5:22 (98%)
Living arrangement:				
Couples with children	0:52 (51%)	1:05 (59%)	5:45 (100%)	4:50 (98%)
Childless couples	1:16 (62%)	1:30 (68%)	5:14 (98%)	3:39 (97%)
Total	0:58 (54%)	1:14 (62%)	5:36 (99%)	4:46 (98%)

Source: Author's elaboration on ISTAT data

less than 34 years spent on average 34 minutes a day on household work, compared with 50 minutes for those aged 35–59 years, and more than 1 hour and half for men aged 60 years and over. In 2008, the same pattern could be observed, with elderly men showing the highest level of contribution to household chores. On the female side, more substantial variations can be observed. As expected, Italian working women devote much less time to housework than the not-employed women who allocate to it 5.5 hours per day. Through time, a dramatic decrease in the commitment of women on housework is observed (by one hour on average). The reduction in housework refers to all women, irrespective to their family arrangement. Overall, gender difference in time devoted running the house narrowed over this period. However, this narrowing is not much due to the greater male collaboration but, more notably, because of the female intense reduction of the amount of time spent in these activities.

Figure 9.1 shows the decrease in gender imbalance in housework over time that, however, remains high. It also highlights which phase of the life cycle is characterized by the lowest gender gap.

Figure 9.2 shows the percentage of young, adult and elderly women and men who live in couple and who do housework by hour of the day. Both young and adult women involvement rank highest in the morning hours and peaks again at dinner time. Male participation in housework follows the same timing of that of female gender, but it remains inexorably lower than that of their partners. Comparing with their younger peers, women aged more than 60 years are more engaged in household chores during morning only, while elderly men increase their involvement in the management of the house throughout the day.

On the basis of the aforementioned trends, a simple calculation allows us to estimate how long it will take to achieve gender equity in domestic labor. Assuming that Italians men continue to increase their involvement in domestic work as

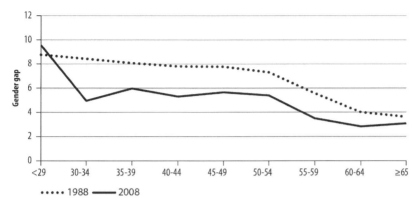

Figure 9.1 Gender gap in time spent on domestic work by age of the partners, 1988 and 2008

Source: author's elaboration on Time use data

they did in the 1998–2008 period (15 minutes), and that the time couples allocate to housework stabilize at the 2008 level, we should wait until the mid of the next century to reach an equal sharing of household tasks among the two genders.

Theoretical approaches on the gender division of housework

In time-use literature, scholars usually apply two main approaches in order to explain inequalities among men and women in housework. The first one is based on a gender-neutral exchange perspective and on the economic principle of the utilitarianism/selfishness of the players involved in the household decisions. The second approach is a gendered oriented perspective that assigns a greater weight to social and cultural influences in shaping gender roles than to individual choices and utilities. The gender-neutral perspective is dominated by three economic models: the human capital theory of household time allocation, the resource-bargaining perspective, and the economic dependency model. The Becker's human capital theory and its 'new household economics' variant argue that the members of a couple allocate their paid and unpaid work in order to maximize the overall utility of the household. Becker (Becker, 1981, 1985) pointed out that male and female preferences on paid/unpaid labor are shaped on their human capital, measured by level of education, wage and previous labor experiences. In this perspective, when one of the partners earns more than the other one, the overall household utility suggests that this partner specializes on paid work, whilst the other partner is expected to spend more time on family activities. Theoretically, this (gender-neutral) mechanism applies symmetrically to both wives and husbands, but in practice, this is not the case, as women often do more housework than their partners, regardless of their occupational status or of their relative income.

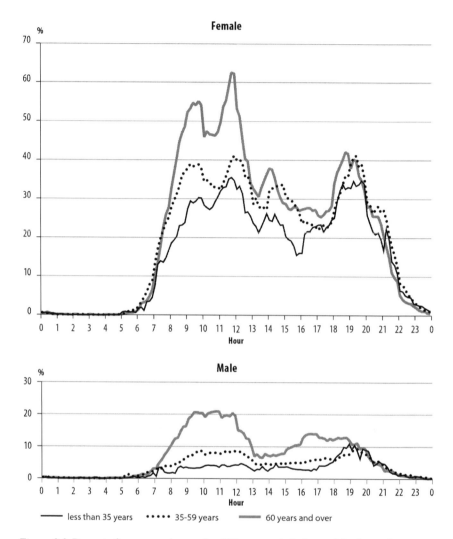

Figure 9.2 Percent of women and men who did housework, by hour of the day and age group

Source: author's elaboration on Time use data

The second economic perspective to explain inequalities within the couple is the resource-bargaining theory. The allocation of time in paid and unpaid work and the income management within the household depend on the power relations within the couple, which, in turn, are influenced by each partner's economic resources. Gender housework distribution is then the outcome of a bargaining process, that – unlike the human capital theory states – is not motivated by the overall household utility. Indeed, this model affirms that partners have potentially conflicting interests (Brines, 1994) and the bargaining is motivated by the self-interest of each partner (Coltrane, 2000). Further, since housework is viewed like a not desirable activity, this model suggests that the partner who has more power will tend to avoid it, whilst the less powerful will do it.

The economic dependent model states that at the beginning of a couple's relationship a contract between partners, even implicitly, establishes that money of the main breadwinner will be exchanged with the housework performed by the dependent partner. Brines (1994) argued that the nature of what breadwinners change with dependents introduces an asymmetry: in fact, housework is by definition without exchange value and – unlike what is brought to the trade by the main breadwinner – is a not portable form of currency. The author also states that a husband or a wife might be considered as dependents only if they rely upon breadwinner for subsistence, whereas they might be considered as independent if capable of supporting themselves after the loss of the breadwinner's contribution. As Todesco (2013) highlights, economic dependence should not be simply seen like an inability to provide for themselves; rather, it implies the risk of losing the lifestyle that is allowed by the access to the main breadwinner income.

The aforementioned three economic perspectives have common features (Coltrane, 2000): they are gender neutral, emphasize choices and give a special prominence to the exchange relations among partners. Due to these similarities, in most time-use studies, these perspectives are lumped into a more comprehensive relative resources hypothesis that considers the division of housekeeping work as the result of a bargaining process between the two partners. The main assumptions of this hypothesis are: a) holding own personal resources grants the individual a certain degree of decision-making power (Mannino and Deutsch, 2007; Hiller, 1984; Blood and Wolfe, 1960) and b) most people consider housework so onerous and tedious that it has to be avoided.[4] In Italy, previous studies partially corroborate the relative resources hypothesis. Menniti and Demurtas (2012) showed that education attainment of men and women has an impact on their own time spent in housework, whereas Dotti Sani (2012) found that highly educated couples share household labor more fairly than those less educated. A recent comparative study highlights that the education gap between partners plays a marginal role in time allocation on housework in countries that are less gender equal, while the relative income matters more (Aassve et al., 2014). A similar result on the most recent time-use data has been found by Menniti et al. (2015).

The second main theoretical approach on gender time-use inequality relies on cultural and sociological perspectives. In his review on time-use studies Coltrane (2000) argues that, given that merely economic hypotheses proved to be insufficient to explain the persistent inequalities in housework, researches on time use need to turn to more gendered oriented theories. Since gender plays a fundamental role even in households in defining an individual's identity and how/where it should be exhibited, men who do not participate in family activities are more likely to justify themselves with reference to their own gender, similarly to what happens to women when they limit their interventions on technical, financial and political issues (Goffman, 1976). Questioning the Goffman's argument, West and Zimmermann pointed out that gender is not simply shown like a play for an audience, but 'done' and continuously 'redone' (West and Zimmerman, 1987, 2009). Moreover, according to these authors gender is not an individual property but a result of situated interactions. Thus the outcomes of domestic division are both materials and symbolic, referring not only to the production of goods and services, but also to the (re)production of gender.[5] In this context, men may feel that they must avoid some tasks to affirm their masculinity and women can perceive an asymmetric distribution of housework as a fair arrangement.

Despite a general agreement, the gender construction perspective is difficult to test without well-structured qualitative studies on daily life and it is often used to account for the 'unexplained residual' differences persisting in housework contribution within couples, net of variables such the labor force participation levels and sex-role attitudes. More often researchers simply refer to a gender ideology hypothesis that posits an inverse relationship between traditional gender attitudes and a fair division of housework (Davis et al., 2007). Rooted in the socialization theory, this perspective states that men and women learn gender roles in childhood, and they successively develop preferences and reproduce behaviors consistent with them. In the literature, it has been confirmed that women with traditional gender roles perform more housework then those holding egalitarian attitudes, whereas men with traditional gender attitudes reduce their contribution (Lachance-Grzela and Bouchard, 2010; Knudsen and Wærness, 2008; Davis et al., 2007). For Italy, the lack of information about gender attitudes never allowed to directly verify this hypothesis. Nevertheless, some authors highlighted an indirect support to gender ideology perspective by means of proxy variables (Menniti et al., 2015; Dotti Sani, 2012) – namely, applying the typical North-South gradient in the geographical distribution of social norms.

Against this background we aim to verify the following: a) in couples where women have a comparative advantage to men in terms of education and economic resources the female burden is reduced and the male involvement increases and b) in couples living in a context where the gender system is less traditional the gender gap in the housework labor narrows. The novelty of our study is in that we simultaneously apply both the economic and cultural perspectives and in that we focus exclusively on housework and not on childcare, which is a less gender-segregated activity even in Italy. For this reason, we did not limit our analysis on reproductive age couples but we include individuals of any age, so that to verify the existence of different behaviors at different stages of the life course.

Explaining gender inequality in housework: an analysis of time-use data

We performed a statistical analysis with the aim of estimating which factors affect the amount of time men and women allocate on management of the house and if they change with age. Our data come from the Italian Time-Use Survey (2008/2009) already introduced in Box 9.1. The overall sample size is of 18,250 households for a total 44,606 individuals. We selected married and unmarried heterosexual couples with partners of any age where both partners filled the diary; the restricted sample includes 10,446 couples. The activities considered here belong to the more general category of 'housework' which includes cooking, dishwashing, laundry, cleaning and house maintenance, gardening and pet care, repairs, purchasing and household management. 'Childcare' is not considered here.

The following individual and couple's characteristics have been included in our analysis:

- Compilation day: weekend and weekday;
- Children: presence (or not) in the family of one or more children;
- Educational gender gap: she > he, she = he, she < he
- Income gender gap: she > he, she = he, she < he
- Age of respondent and his/her partner (in classes)
- Co-habitants: presence or not in the household of relatives or other cohabiting individuals
- Territory: North, Centre, South of Italy
- Place of residence: cities with more or less than 50,000 inhabitants

The main focus of our study is on income difference and its effect on male/female partner time allocation on housework, as well as on territorial division (Figures 9.3 and 9.4).

Figure 9.3 shows the distribution of the time devoted to housework according to the declared income: according to women statements, there is a strong difference when wife's income is smaller than husband's. Instead, according to men declaration, the time spent for housework seems not to be affected by the income gap between the partners. Figure 9.4 shows the geographical distribution of time on housework allocated by men. It is to be noted that the level of (in)equality in Italian family differs when comparing the areas of the country. Regions in North-Centre area are those where men allocate more time on domestic activities; the opposite situation is observed in the South where the amount of time dedicated by men to housework is very low and does not reach one hour a day, both in male

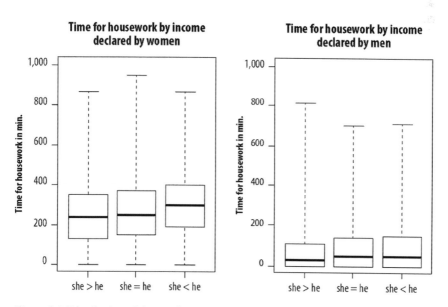

Figure 9.3 Distribution of time on housework by declared income and gender

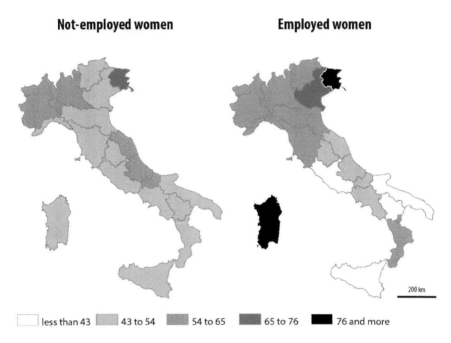

Not-employed women   **Employed women**

less than 43 | 43 to 54 | 54 to 65 | 65 to 76 | 76 and more

Figure 9.4 Distribution of the time spent for housework by men (in minutes) in Italy

Source: author's elaboration

breadwinner and double-earner couples. No remarkable differences have been noted from a similar figure drawn on time devoted to housework by women.

To perform a multivariate analysis, we modelled the time devoted by men and women to the housework separately as a function of several explanatory variables through a hurdle model (see Box 9.2 for details). The main advantage of this model lies in the fact that it allows to distinguish between the effect of a single variable on the probability that an individual does some housework and the effect on the amount of time that he/she devotes to it.

We have applied a hurdle model to time devoted by men and women to the housework using a censored Poisson regression for non-zero counts with the logarithmic transformation as link function. In our context, having non-zero counts means that men or women are involved in domestic activities; positive counts are related to the amount of time devoted to housework. Parameters were estimated using the maximum likelihood approach with Newton-Raphson optimization algorithm.

Results are reported in Table 9.2. The columns headed 'Participation (Zero counts)' show the parameter estimates for the zero outcomes: coefficients should be interpreted as the effect of the explanatory variables on the probability of participating to housework for women and men, respectively, (third and fifth columns). The second and fourth columns show the parameter estimates of the censored regression model: coefficients should be interpreted as the effect of each variable on the amount of time devoted to housework. The coefficients in the columns 3

Box 9.2   Statistical model description

Regression models are not appropriate in this context since the amount of time devoted to housework is equal to zero for 36.3% of the men and 2.2% of the women. This excess weight of extreme values causes biases if the usual linear regression models are used (Verbeek, 2012). In literature, several zero-inflated models have been proposed (see among the others Johnson and Kotz (1969) and Lambert (1992)): in particular, in this context the Tobit model (Menniti et al., 2015; Verbeek, 2012) is widely applied since it allows to easily accommodate the truncated nature of the response variable. The model supposes there is a latent variable that depends linearly on the explanatory variables just as in a linear model. The observed variable is defined to be equal to the latent variable whenever it is above zero and to be zero otherwise. However, one limitation of standard count models is that the zeros and the non-zeros (positives) are assumed to come from the same data-generating process. Indeed, we propose to model these data through a hurdle model (Cameron and Trivedi, 1998) that does not constraint these two processes to be the same. The basic idea is that a Bernoulli probability governs the binary outcome of whether a count variate has a zero or positive realization. If the realization is positive, the hurdle is crossed, and the conditional distribution of the positives is governed by a truncated-at-zero count data model.

---

and 5 show how the independent variables affect the female (male) likelihood to be involved in domestic chores, while the coefficients in the columns 2 and 4 indicate how the variables influence the length of time allocated on household chores.

First of all, let us evaluate whether our findings corroborate the relative resource hypothesis and the gender ideology one. As stated, we included two indicators, which measure the differences between partners in terms of education and income. Outcomes from the model show that in case the partner's income is approximately equal or higher than that of the respondent the latter increases the amount of time spent on domestic chores. This is true both for women than for men. Thus a relative advantage of a woman in terms of income make him increase the amount of time allocated on domestic activities. Interestingly, the 'Zero counts' coefficients associated to this covariate are not significant for men: that is, a weaker condition of the male partners in terms of income does not increase the probability that they contribute to domestic care compared to those who are better off, but, if already participating, they will allocate more time on housework.

The educational gap has a significant effect on the time devoted to home care: as predicted by the relative resources approach, when the women are more educated than men, the latter are more active at home, and women do less housework compared to those who live in couples where partners have the same education. Therefore, results show that in unions where wife is more educated than her husband the share of the domestic burden is more equal than in educationally homogamous couples. Having a higher educational level acts as a resource also for the men: when the male partner is more educated than the woman, he reduces

Table 9.2 Hurdle regression model on time (in minutes) for housework. Women and men

	Female		Male	
	Amount of time allocated on housework (Non-zero counts)	Participation (Zero counts)	Amount of time allocated on housework (Non-zero counts)	Participation (Zero counts)
Intercept	5.406 ***	2.638 ***	4.576 ***	0.657 ***
Income gender gap: partner income > income respondent (ref respondent > partner)	0.150 ***	0.922 **	0.178***	0.153
Income gender gap: respondent = partner (ref respondent > partner)	0.014***	0.471	0.071***	0.162
Educational gender gap: he > she (ref she = he)	-0.017***	0.129	-0.025 ***	0.015
Educational gender gap: she > he (ref she = he)	-0.029 ***	0.258	0.009 ***	0.084
Territory: Center (ref;north)	0.025 ***	-0.217	-0.037 ***	-0.202 **
Territory: South (ref;north)	0.148 ***	0.221	-0.116 ***	-0.422 ***
Place of residence: cities with 50,000 inhabitants and more (ref: cities less than 50,000)	-0.103 ***	-0.046	-0.228 ***	0.018
Day: weekdays (ref: Weekend)	0.015 ***	0.288 *	-0.041 ***	-0.081 ***
Children: yes (ref: no)	0.117 ***	0.633***	0.058 ***	-0.072
Co-habitants: yes (ref: no)	0.048 ***	-0.376*	0.048*	-0.365 ***
Age: she <35 (ref. 35–60)	-0.127***	-0.465	-0.002 ***	-0.167
Age: she >60 (ref. 35–60)	0.077***	-0.423	0.491 °	0.015
Age: he <35 (ref. 35–60)	-0.010***	-0.162	-0.022***	-0.01
Age: he >60 (ref. 35–60)	0.152***	0.243	0.041***	0.230*

Significance level: *** = 0.000 / ** = 0.001 / * = 0.01 / ° = 0.05

the amount of time spent on housework. Surprisingly, in these couples also the woman reduces the amount of time devoted to domestic chores, and this partially challenges the relative resources hypothesis.

In order to verify the gender ideology hypothesis, we included the territorial context as a proxy of culture. Compared to those living in the North, men living in the Central and Southern regions are significantly less involved in domestic labor and, when participating in housework, they spend less time on it. For women, the level of participation does not change from North to South of Italy, but the amount of time spent on housework increases. In Southern Italy the disadvantage of women is wider than elsewhere not only because Southern women are taking up the most of the housework but also because their husbands, as anticipated, are the ones who participate least in running the house. Thus, the North-South gradient is confirmed, with the persistence of a culture that assigns different roles to men and women and delays the transition towards greater gender equity. The other variables' results shed further light on gender differences in family life according to the type of the day. Men participate less and spend less time on domestic activities during weekdays compared with weekend, while the opposite happens for women. These findings indicate the persistence of a gender division of labor between the partners, with men avoiding their involvement in family duties during working days and women specializing in running the house during the days traditionally devoted to paid work. In the weekend, instead, the two partners seem to somewhat sharing the care of own house.

Family composition affects the partner's time allocation on housework as well: 1) the presence of at least one child causes an increase in the amount of time devoted to housework for both parents; only for women also the participation becomes more likely; 2) living in a household with 'others' reduces the likelihood of participation of both partners. It seems that sharing the home with other couples or other non-family members, allows couple to delegate the housework burden to a greater number of cohabiting individuals, such as parents, mothers/fathers in-law, sisters/brothers, friends, or domestic workers. When this is not possible the amount of time on care increases both for men and women. However, the amount of time devoted to housework increases: an interpretation could be that, if the cohabiting person is active and autonomous he/she can help the couple; instead, the presence of an aged or disabled relative results in an extra time-demanding family activity.

Age: the amount of time devoted to household labor is greater among oldest individuals and lower among the youngest ones compared to middle aged, both if the respondents is a woman or a man. The same applies if we consider the partners' age: men and women with a partner aged more than 60 allocate more time on housework. The likelihood to participate in domestic chores, however, does not change among different age classes. It is significantly higher only for the oldest men compared with the youngest or middle aged: that is, men around the age of retirement appear more involved in the household caring activities. It is worth noting that these results have to be read as cohort effects and not in terms of individual aging because of the cross-sectional nature of the survey.

208 Serena Arima et al.

The gender gap in the labour market: an historical and sociological perspective

In the last few decades, many studies have been devoted to gender analyses applied to several social fields. In the literature, the gender gap in the context of the labour market is known as 'employment segregation', distinguishing between 'horizontal segregation' and 'vertical segregation' (Watts, 2005; Bergmann, 1981). 'Horizontal segregation' means the prevalence of women in some economic sectors or occupations considered typically female activities since they are practical or devoted to personal care (social and care services, teaching, administrative services and trade). 'Vertical segregation' indicates the high incidence of women in low and medium positions in the ranking within subordinate jobs and the almost monopoly of the highest positions by men. In addition to horizontal and vertical segregation, other kinds of gender gaps in employment may occur. For instance, with regard to working conditions, those concerning the number of hours worked (full time or part time) and the life span of employment contracts for non-self-employed work (permanent or temporary). Indeed job flexibility is often associated with the female gender. Employment segregation represents disadvantage for employed women compared to employed men. A more general kind of gender gap predates employment segregation and we can define it as 'in-entrance segregation'. It represents the disadvantage of women in terms of their individual ability to integrate into the labour market. In-entrance and employment segregation generate disparities in women's salaries and income levels compared to men's and may cause social exclusion.

During the last few decades, female labour force participation has significantly increased (Mandel and Semyonov, 2006, p. 2; England, 2005). This great result of women's emancipation took place in the twentieth century (Estévez-Abe, 2005) but only accounts for one aspect of the evolution of the labour market's gender dimension in western societies. Although some scholars dealing with this topic and the broad research area of the transformation of women's roles use the word revolution (Andreotti et al., 2013; England, 2010; Esping-Andersen, 2009), they even out the sense of whole radical change by examining other sides of the issue.

According to England (2010), not only has gender revolution currently stalled, but it has also been uneven. By analyzing different indicators, the author stresses the asymmetric modification of the labour market, and suggests some hypotheses on its causes. On one hand, women have had solid economic motivations to occupy positions and perform activities that are typically male-dominated. On the other hand, since modern society still underestimates women's jobs and activities, men have not found any reasons to access them. Moreover, the coexistence of two cultural factors – i.e., equal opportunity individualism and gender essentialism might explain why more women of middle classes origin have moved to male professions and managerial jobs than working-class women have entered blue-collar ones: in spite of the promotion of equal access to education and work, women tend to move to the male-dominated field when they cannot realize upward mobility in their own gender domain.

Esping-Andersen's incomplete revolution (2009) is the starting point of the work realized by Andreotti et al. (2013) about the evolution of women's role in labour force participation across Italian regions. In short, they agree with Esping-Andersen about the idea that in contemporary Europe, gender roles have been deeply modified, above all owing to the increase in female employment, but they do not agree with his statement that all countries involved in this process and that exhibit different speeds,[6] will converge towards the same pattern. In particular, the authors stress the profound difference detectable between the North and the South in terms of female employment rates, which are directly linked to their different family arrangements and public policies; thus, the incomplete revolution is non-linear, plural and divergent (Andreotti et al., 2013, p. 621). Moreover, they argue that the evolution of gender roles can be seen as a result of interacting factors (i.e. the labour market, the public welfare system and informal care arrangements), which produce a deep gap between the North (where it is difficult to realize an integration of work and family roles) and the South (where the female participation and the employment rates are still low), thus leading to a serious social inequality.

By analyzing data from 22 industrialized countries, Mandel and Seymonov (2006) found that progressive welfare states have an ambiguous effect on women's labour force participation and employment inequality by gender: on one hand, they facilitate female labour force participation, but on the other hand discourage women's access to managerial positions. Another suggestion comes from Estévez-Abe (2005). After an overview of theories about occupational sex segregation, the author maintains the limitations of such theories by thoroughly explaining the variations in occupational segregation according to gender across the advanced industrial countries. Thus, she proposes a new skilled-based theory, which goes beyond the classical distinction between skilled and unskilled workers. By making use of two branches of literature – i.e., the feminist works on the welfare state and the varieties of capitalism – she takes into account the comparison of general and specific skills and argues that specific skills are more gender biased than general ones; thus, countries whose national institutions foster firm-specific skills exhibit higher levels of occupational segregation according to gender.

Overall, several explanations seem to co-occur in the context of occupational segregation by gender, which might be seen as a multidimensional concept. As such, it needs to be investigated from several perspectives in order to find multi-level solutions that should vary by country.

Gender gap in-entrance

Employment status comes out as being statistically associated with gender. Women were disadvantaged compared to men, showing a lower employment rate (on average, 34.71% compared to 55.86% for males) and higher unemployment and inactivity rates (on average: for unemployment 9.94% compared to 7.16% for males; for inactivity 61.45% compared to 39.84% for males; see Figure 9.5). The gender gap (calculated by means of the difference: female rate minus male rate) always had the highest values for inactivity and the employment rates. At the regional level (NUTS1), in-entrance segregation was higher in the South (on average, 26.77% for inactivity, −25.1% for employment and 5.34% for unemployment), while the other regions showed similar values (on average, about 19%

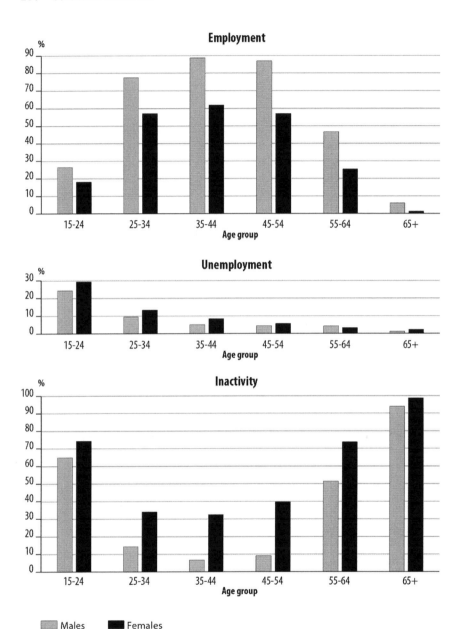

Figure 9.5 Employment, unemployment and inactivity average (percentage) rates according to gender and age in Italy (averages over 2004–2013)

Source: author's elaboration

for inactivity, about –19% for employment and almost 2%–3% for unemployment). Southern women were more disadvantaged than the ones of other areas, because of fewer opportunities for regular paid jobs and because of scarce supply of the welfare state services (collective pre-school childcare services, subsidies and services for care of elderly and disabled people) that instead would help them in conciliating work and family care. These scarcities have penalized especially Southern poorly qualified women belonging to low-income families who, without family arrangements for domestic labour, were frequently discouraged from seeking jobs and took refuge as housewives and in direct family caring roles.

Employment status comes out as being statistically associated with age for both genders. Figure 9.5 shows the values of the employment, unemployment and inactivity (average) rates of the male and female Italian populations according to age over 2004–2013. The curves for males have the same shapes as for females: it is that of a 'U' for inactivity, of an upside-down 'U' for employment and a decreasing curve for unemployment. The inactivity average rate decreased by age up to the class 30–40 and afterwards it increased from the age class 45–54 for both genders, but at different speed degrees. On the male side, it always showed significant decreasing values up to the age class 35–44 (−77.9% between the classes 15–24 and 25–34; −54% between 25–34 and 35–44). For females, the inactivity average rate dropped significantly up to the class 25–34 (−54.1%) and then it reduced very slightly (−4.8% between 25–34 and 35–44). Probably, motherhood contributed mostly to slow down the increase of the feminine activity after the age class 25–34 (in 2004–2013 for Italian women the average age at childbirth took values comprised between 30.79 and 31.49 years). The absolute increase in inactivity between the ages 35–44 and 45–54 was higher for females than for males (+7.12% compared to +2.49%),[7] probably due to the difficulties for women in combining work and family care (children and/or elderly parents), which forced them to leave their jobs. Finally, males covered the final part of the path towards retirement more quickly than females did (for men, the variations in inactivity rate between the ages 45–54 and 55–64 and between 55–64 and 65+ were equal to +464.3% and +83.1%; instead, for women: +86.3% and +33.9%, respectively). Women often have been forced to slow down their way towards retirement, and therefore they tended to retire slightly later than men did (for instance, in 2012, the mean and median retirement age were equal to 57.8 and 58 years for males, and 58.4 and 60 years for females (ISTAT, 2013)). Indeed, feminine working careers were frequently more irregular and discontinuous than masculine ones, also due to the motherhood. Moreover, their contribution periods were often shorter than for men (on average, in 2004–2013 duration of working life was equal to 35.1 years for males and 24.3 for females). Consequently, women often had to continue working until to the compulsory retirement age (32.6% of female retired for this reason), while men often could retire before since they reached the required minimum distribution (53.4% of male retirements).

The employment average rate increased with age until 35–44 and then decreased. As for inactivity, between the ages 35–44 and 45–54 there was a higher variation for women than for men (−4.89% compared to −0.72%), probably due to the same causes already mentioned for inactivity rate. In general, women were disadvantaged at all ages compared to men. Figure 9.6 shows the gender gap in employment status by varying the age, calculated by means of the average rates. For both the employment and inactivity average rates, (their absolute values) the distance between women and men increased with age until 45–54 and then decreased. The curves corresponding to these two rates are practically symmetrical to each other,

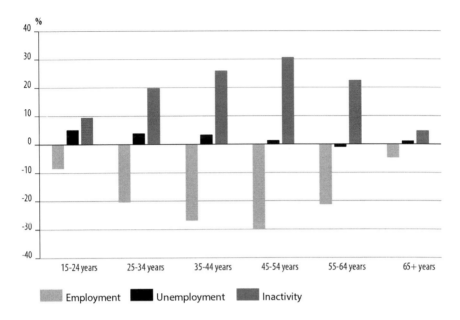

Figure 9.6 Gender gap (female rate minus male rate) in employment, unemployment and inactivity average (percentage) rates according to age in Italy (averages over 2004–2013)

Source: author's elaboration

indicating that the reasons for the gender gap were probably the same. These facts highlight again the fragility of the female condition: in the 15–24 age group, women started with a disadvantage compared to men and the gap increased with age, probably due to their more numerous and demanding tasks in daily life activities. Finally, women were able to equal men only when males have slowed down their working activity in order to retire. The gender gap in unemployment average rates continually decreased with age until 55–64, where instead surprisingly it took a negative value (−0.99%) because of the higher male unemployment rate compared to the female one. In fact, most women aged 55–64 were active only if they had a job, whereas they often became inactive when they lost their jobs. Instead, most men aged 55–64 continued searching for jobs even after they had lost one.

Over time, in-entrance segregation has decreased. Between 2004 and 2013 there was a worsening in the employment status for males (their employment, unemployment and inactivity profiles were tending to become similar to those of females). Simultaneously, there was a slight improvement in both the employment and activity of women. These facts caused a reduction of the gender gap in all areas (NUTS1). For employment, the highest decrease occurred in the South (−25.88%), probably due to the highest decrease in the male employment rates (−15.23%). Analogously, for unemployment, the highest reduction occurred in the South (−67.77%), where the disproportion between the increase in male and female unemployment was higher than elsewhere (+56.63% and +4.65%, respectively). For inactivity, the highest decrease of the gender gap occurred in the North-West (−19.04%), probably due to the highest decline in female inactivity (−4.43%), while the male inactivity rate increased (+3.59%).

All these changes were caused by the recent downturn, which has damaged men more seriously than women. Table 9.3 contains the results of the significance test on the variation in the regional rates (NUTS2) between 2004–2007 and 2008–2013. For men, there was a significant decrease in the employment rates and a significant increase in both the unemployment and inactivity rates, probably because the recession hit heavily the industrial and construction activities, which are traditionally male sectors. For women, there was a significant increase in the employment rates and a significant decrease in the inactivity rates. The increase in the female unemployment rates was less strong than for males; indeed, it resulted statistically significant only at the 5% level but not at the 1%. For all three rates, the reduction of the gender gap was statistically significant.

Over time, in-entrance segregation according to age seemed to be in decline. Table 9.4 shows the variation between 2004 and 2013 of the employment, unemployment and inactivity rates according to age for the Italian male and female populations, and the variation of the gender gap. The gender gap in employment rates has decreased in the youngest ages (due to the increased worsening for men compared to women) and in the adult and older ones too (due to the

Table 9.3 Employment, unemployment and inactivity average (percentage) rates according to gender in the Italian regions (NUTS2): significance test on the variation between 2004–2007 and 2008–2013

		Test	*Value*	*P-value*	*Meaning (significance at the 1 % level)*
Employment	**Male**	Student	8.90	1.67E-08	significant decreasing
	Female	Student	2.91	4.45E-03	significant increasing
	Gender gap	Student	11.54	2.51E-10	significant decreasing
Unemployment	**Male**	Wilcoxon	0.00	9.54E-07	significant increasing
	Female	Wilcoxon	46.00	1.33E-02	non-significant increasing
	Gender gap	Student	4.77	6.67E-05	significant decreasing
Inactivity	**Male**	Student	4.20	2.41E-04	significant increasing
	Female	Student	3.82	5.81E-04	significant decreasing
	Gender gap	Student	9.57	5.31E-09	significant decreasing

Table 9.4 Employment, unemployment and inactivity rates according to gender and age in Italy: percentage variation between 2004 and 2013

		Employment		Unemployment		Inactivity	
		Overall percentage variation	Yearly mean percentage variation	Overall percentage variation	Yearly mean percentage variation	Overall percentage variation	Yearly mean percentage variation
15–24 years	Male	−39.78	−5.48	88.92	7.32	14.04	1.47
	Female	−40.53	−5.61	52.19	4.78	12.14	1.28
	Gender gap	−37.66	−5.12	−63.16	−10.50	−3.10	−0.35
25–34 years	Male	−15.55	−1.86	96.65	7.80	55.89	5.06
	Female	−11.35	−1.33	46.58	4.34	9.54	1.02
	Gender gap	−26.56	−3.37	−39.37	−5.41	−16.56	−1.99
35–44 years	Male	−8.70	−1.01	113.60	8.80	82.49	6.91
	Female	0.42	0.05	39.34	3.75	−8.09	−0.93
	Gender gap	−27.05	−3.44	−33.59	−4.45	−22.95	−2.86
45–54 years	Male	−4.40	−0.50	142.44	10.34	−3.67	−0.41
	Female	11.24	1.19	52.07	4.77	−18.61	−2.26
	Gender gap	−28.72	−3.69	−84.25	−18.56	−23.08	−2.87
55–64 years	Male	25.36	2.54	61.41	5.46	−22.60	−2.81
	Female	68.97	6.00	3.05	0.33	−17.77	−2.15
	Gender gap	−12.54	−1.48	2341.63	42.62	−6.29	−0.72
65 years and over	Male	3.57	0.39	1.56	0.17	−0.23	−0.03
	Female	21.50	2.19	−12.93	−1.53	−0.26	−0.03
	Gender gap	−1.03	−0.12	−38.92	−5.33	−0.95	−0.11

better opportunities for women). Male employment rates reduced in all the age brackets except for 55–64 and 65+ where they increased. Female employment decreased only at the ages 15–24 and 25–34 then instead it increased. In general, employment fell most seriously in the 15–24 age group. Probably, for both genders the rise in employment at the oldest age depends on the recent laws that have extended the age of retirement. The male unemployment rate increased at all ages, especially in 35–44 and 45–54. The female unemployment rate also rose in all the age brackets, apart from age 65+. The increase in unemployment has been more severe for men and consequently the gender gap has decreased. The variation of the gender gap for the 55–64 age group took an exaggerated value since in 2004 the difference between the female and male rates was about zero. The positive sign of this variation means that the gender gap has increased to the disadvantage of men, who at age 55–64 have always had higher unemployment rates than females (except for in 2006). The gender gap in the inactivity rates has also reduced at all ages, especially in 35–44 and 45–54 groups, because of the increased worsening of the male situation and because of the better opportunities for women. The male inactivity rate has increased at all ages until 35–44; then it has decreased. Analogously, the female inactivity rate increased for all ages until 25–34 and then decreased.

Gender gap in occupations

We have collected data on employment according to profession, considering these large groups of occupations (CP2001 classification):

a) 'managers, professionals and technicians' (legislators, senior officials, managers, professionals, technicians, associate professionals);
b) 'white collar' (clerks, service workers, shop and market sales workers);
c) 'blue collar and craft and related trades workers' (skilled agricultural and fishery workers, craft and related trades workers, plant and machine operators and assemblers);
d) 'elementary occupations' (all occupations that do not require any qualifications).

The type of occupation comes out as being statistically associated with gender, also at area level (NUTS1). On average, male employment has been strongly concentrated in the occupations requiring manual and physical skills (the type c: 38.43%) and in the technical and specialized ones (the type a: 33.18%). Female employment has mainly been polarised into the types b and a (39.52% and 38.33%, respectively). With the recession, job quality has worsened slightly especially for men. Compared to 2004–2007, in 2008–2013, employment in the most specialized and technical occupations has decreased. Consequently, employment in the occupations less qualified has increased. The rise of female employment in the 'elementary' type probably reflects the increase of jobs in the care of the elderly sector, due to the aging of the population.

The distributions of (average) employment in Italy over 2004–2013 (Table 9.5) according to gender calculated for each type of occupation, point to the occurrence of horizontal segregation. Indeed, for the occupations requiring intellectual, technical and specialized skills men prevailed numerically (for the types c and a, men were 85% and 56%, respectively). Conversely, the only type of occupation where women have been the most numerous is the b one (57%), where no particular qualifications are required. These distributions were quite stable over time, except for 'elementary occupations', where in 2004–2007 the most numerous were men (52.1%) whereas in 2008–2013 were women (50.1%).

Recently, horizontal segregation appears to have brought a positive consequence for Italian women. Table 9.5 reports the variation between 2004 and 2013 of employment according to type of occupation and gender in Italy. For the 'white collar' occupations, where women were the most numerous, overall employment increased; this rise only occurred for women but not for men. This fact may have contributed to increasing the female employment rate, due to the high incidence of these occupations among females. Conversely, in occupations where men were prevalent (the types a and c), employment decreased for both genders. In the case of the type a, the values of reduction for men and women were very similar. In the case of the type c, women showed a higher decrease than men did; however, the impact on employment rates has been less severe for females, because of the poor incidence of the type c among women compared to the high incidence among men. Probably, the simultaneous occurrence of all these facts has contributed to reducing the gender gap in employment rates.

Gender gap in ranking of subordinate jobs

We only collected data on employment for employees according to professional status (subordinate jobs), considering the following types: a) 'executive', b) 'middle management', c) 'white collar', d) 'blue collar' and e) 'apprentice'. The professional status in the ranking within subordinate jobs comes out as being statistically associated with gender, also at a regional level (NUTS1). On average, for men the most prevalent profiles were 'blue collar' (55.04%) and 'white collar' (32.67%); conversely for women were 'white collar' (54.21%) and 'blue collar' (36.27%). For both genders, the percentages of 'middle management' and 'executives' were quite low (7.33% and 3.56% for men; 6.63% and 1.65% for women), whereas 'apprentices' amounted to about 1% for both males and females. With the downturn, the professional status worsened slightly for both men and women: compared to 2004–2007, in 2008–2013 (Table 9.6), the percentages of high and middle profiles declined whereas that of 'white collar' increased. Moreover, the incidence of both 'blue collar' and 'apprentice' fell.

The situation just described might seem more advantageous for females, since their prevalent professional status is of a higher level than that prevalent for males. In fact, females have clearly been disadvantaged in terms of careers. The distributions of (average) employment according to gender calculated for each type of professional status in Italy over 2004–2013, highlight the occurrence of vertical segregation. The 'executive' and 'middle management' positions were mainly occupied by men (74% and 59%) and this also occurred for the career entry levels (in 'apprentice' and 'blue-collar' men were 59% and 66%). The only

Table 9.5 Employment according to type of occupation and gender in Italy: percentage variation between 2004 and 2013

	Managers, professionals and technicians		White collar		Blue collar and craft and related trades workers		Elementary occupations	
	Overall percentage variation	Yearly mean percentage variation	Overall percentage variation	Yearly mean percentage variation	Overall percentage variation	Yearly mean percentage variation	Overall percentage variation	Yearly mean percentage variation
Male	-1.89	-0.21	-0.29	-0.03	-11.48	-1.35	17.10	1.77
Female	-0.52	-0.06	20.84	2.13	-31.42	-4.10	19.48	2.00
Male and female	-1.30	-0.15	11.50	1.22	-14.86	-1.77	18.25	1.88

Table 9.6 Employment according to professional status (subordinate jobs) and gender in Italy: percentage variation between 2004 and 2013

	Executive		Middle management		White collar		Blue collar		Apprentice	
	Overall percentage variation	Yearly mean percentage variation	Overall percentage variation	Yearly mean percentage variation	Overall percentage variation	Yearly mean percentage variation	Overall percentage variation	Yearly mean percentage variation	Overall percentage variation	Yearly mean percentage variation
Male	-29.21	-3.77	1.11	0.12	3.74	0.41	0.81	0.09	-49.66	-7.34
Female	-8.11	-0.94	10.75	1.14	14.36	1.50	12.15	1.28	-42.31	-5.93
Male and Female	-24.09	-3.02	4.91	0.53	9.59	1.02	4.57	0.50	-46.65	-6.74

profile where females were the most numerous was 'white collar' (56%). This situation represents the well-known 'glass ceiling' (Bollinger and O'Neill, 2008). Compared to men, it was more difficult for women to enter the labour market. Their careers frequently seemed to come to a standstill in intermediate positions and only a few lucky ones have been able to reach the highest profiles. This situation occurred in all areas except for Southern Italy, where in general women were the least numerous at all professional levels. Vertical segregation was stronger in the two Northern areas than elsewhere, showing the highest incidence of men into 'executive' and 'middle management' (about 75% and 59–63%, respectively) and the highest incidence of women into 'white collar' (about 60%).

The recession contributed to rebalancing the distributions of the professional profiles by gender, also due to better chances for women. Table 9.6 reports the variation between 2004 and 2013 of employment according to professional status and gender in Italy. Overall employment in both 'executive' and 'apprentice' profiles, where men were prevalent, decreased but especially for males. In addition, employment slightly increased in all other profiles, and the rise was higher for women.

Gender gap in working conditions: full-time and part-time jobs

Working time comes out as being statistically associated with gender, also at a regional level (NUTS1). Full-time workers were more numerous compared to part time ones for both genders, but the frequency of part-time jobs was much higher for females than for males (28.15% compared to 5.58%). The incidence of part-time jobs was higher for people aged 15–34 than for those aged 35–64[8] (for men: 7.6% compared to 4.2%; for women, 29% compared to 27.6%), reflecting the greatest flexibility of youth jobs. Consequently, the gender gap in working hour was more severe for adults than for the young. During the downturn, the incidence of part-time jobs increased slightly for women (from 26% in 2004–2007 to 29.53% in 2008–2013) and for men too (from 4.77% to 6.14%). The increase in flexibility was higher for young people than for adults and the worsening of the youth jobs was more severe for men than for women (+48.3% compared to +18%).

At the regional level, for females the incidence of part-time jobs took the lowest value in the South (25.71%) and the highest one in the North-East (29.61%), whereas for males the opposite situation was found (4.57% in the North-East and 6.33% in the South). For women, having a part time job might be a good way to conciliate work and family care activities and is therefore a kind of empowerment. Instead, for men having a part time job might be a manifestation of job insecurity. Consequently, the Southern Italian labour market appeared the least empowered and the most precarious compared to the other areas.

The distributions of (average) employment in part-time and full-time jobs according to gender in Italy over 2004–2013 point to the occurrence of segregation in working time. Most part-time jobs were taken by women (77.15%), whereas men were more numerous than women in full-time jobs (66.24%). The analogous distributions calculated separately by age class confirm that the gender gap was more severe for adults than for young people (the percentages of women in part-time jobs were equal to 81% and 74%, respectively). The distributions of part time and full-time jobs according to gender were quite stable over time, except for a slight worsening for men (in part-time jobs men increased from 22.09% in 2004–2007 to 23.27% in 2008–2013; in full-time jobs they reduced from 66.54% to 66.03%). Overall, the South showed the lowest value for the gender gap in part-time jobs (36.25% compared to 54% in the Centre and 61%–65% in the North) and the highest value for the gender gap in full-time jobs (−41.07% compared to about −30% in the other areas). These facts reveal once again the fragility of the Southern Italian labour market. Over time, working conditions have worsened: full-time employment reduced slightly (−7.1% for men and −3.56% for women), whereas part-time employment increased significantly (+60.23% for men and +35.64% for women). For both genders, the incidence of full-time jobs fell and consequently that of part-time ones rose (for men from 4.75% to 7.93%; for women from 24.98% to 31.89%). Although the increase for males was relatively higher than for females, the gap concerning the incidence of part-time jobs increased (from 20.22% to 23.97%), due to the even highest values of incidence for females.

Gender gap in working conditions (non-self-employed employment): permanent or temporary jobs

For non-self-employed jobs, the life span of the employment contract (permanent or temporary) was only slightly affected by gender. Indeed, the percentage of temporary jobs for males was quite close to that for females (11.41% and 14.93%, respectively). With the economic downturn, the situation worsened for men, whereas for women it seemed to be slightly better (the incidence of permanent jobs, for men varied from 89.3% in 2004–2007 to 88.12% in 2008–2013 and for women from 84.77% to 85.25%). This increase for females is probably due to the introduction of new pension laws according to which the retirement age increased for both genders but especially for women. At a regional level, the incidence of temporary jobs showed an increasing trend from North to South for both men and women and so the corresponding gender gap did. This fact marks the highest degree of job insecurity in the South as already described for working time too.

The distributions of (average) non-self-employed employment in permanent and temporary jobs according to gender in Italy over 2004–2013 indicate the occurrence of very slight segregation. Whereas temporary jobs were almost equally distributed between men and women (49.77% and 50.23%), in the permanent job sector males were more numerous than females (57.45% compared to 42.55%). These frequencies were quite stable over time, except for a slight worsening of the male situation (in permanent jobs, men were 58.75% in 2004–2007 and 56.61% in 2008–2013; in temporary jobs, they were 48.72% in 2004–2007 and 50.42% in 2008–2013). At a regional level, the female situation seemed to be much more uncertain in the South than elsewhere. Indeed, in all areas in permanent jobs men were more numerous than women did (about 55% in the Centre-North and 65% in the South). In temporary jobs, females were the most numerous in both the North and Centre (between 52% and 55%) while in the South men prevailed numerically (54.85%). The South showed also the highest absolute values for gender gap in both permanent and temporary jobs (−29.41% and −9.7%).

Over time, jobs have become more unstable due to the recession. Compared to 2004, in 2013 employment in permanent jobs increased slightly (+3.1%) but only due to increasing female employment (+12.17% compared to −3.24% for males), probably due to the aforementioned new pension laws. Employment in temporary jobs increased too (+24.95% for men and +9.25% for women). Overall, the incidence of permanent jobs in employment decreased (from 88.16% to 86.79%) and therefore that of temporary ones increased (from 11.84% to 13.21%). These changes towards more flexible jobs have only affected men: their percentage of permanent jobs fell (from 90.11% to 87.59%) and consequently that of temporary ones rose (from 9.89% to 12.41%). Conversely, for women the incidence of permanent jobs increased slightly (from 85.50% to 85.83%) and that of temporary ones decreased (from 14.5% to 14.17%). Because of all these facts, the gender gap in terms of job insecurity has largely reduced (from 4.61% to 1.76%).

Conclusion

Gender equity in housework and in the labour market is yet to come in Italy. The analysis of the historical trends shows a slight increase in male participation in family work – surely more on childcare than on routinely housework – and a slow narrowing of the differences between men and women as far the amount of time allocated on those activities. Moreover, the observed progresses towards a certain degree of symmetry are due more to changes in (working) women behavior, who reduced their commitment, than to male partners' higher participation. In the Italian labour market, gender distance are reducing and the recession seems to have contributed to the process: the male condition worsened more than the female one, and for some aspects the female condition even seems to have slightly improved. The gender gap in the labour market also reduced in most OECD countries, but Italy had a particularly serious situation also due to the great difference between the South and the other Italian regions.

In the first part of this chapter, using a multivariate analysis on the latest available 2008–2009 Italian Time-Use Survey we tested the relative resource hypothesis and that of the gender ideology. The latter appears completely confirmed by our results: the territorial context influences the allocation of time for housework, with men living in the South of the country very much less active at home than those living in the North, which prove to be the less traditional context in term of gender equity. Instead, the relative resources hypothesis is a bit challenged by our data. Indeed, it is confirmed that the higher the female income the higher her bargaining power and that when women are endowed with a higher education than their partners they obtain more male collaboration at home compared to homogamous couples; however, the comparative advantage of more educated men is not demonstrated by our results.

The main implication of these results is that incentives fostering female employment[9] could have as a side effect an increase in gender equity at home: i.e., any effort aiming at reducing the gender pay gap and promoting the female access to well-paid jobs is likely to have an additive effect in accelerating the gender equality in domestic work. It has also to be noted the different behavior of men and women between weekdays and weekends, with men participating and spending more time during weekends and women more involved during the other days, confirming that the help given by the male partner is neither steady nor generalized.

In conclusions, all these facts show a need for implementing policies – also at local level – and instruments that aim simultaneously to increase overall employment in Italy, to promote female participation into the labour market, to overcome all types of segregation and to ensure Southern women the same social opportunities as the Northern ones.

Notes

1 Authors share the overall argument of the paper and are equally responsible of the results and their interpretation. However, drafting has been handed out as follows: the introduction and Section 'Studies on Gender Inequality at Home: The Case of Italy' by Alessandra De Rose; Section 'Housework: Still a Long Way toward Equality' by Adele Menniti; Section 'Theoretical Approaches on the Gender Division of Housework' by Pietro Demurtas; Section 'Explaining Gender Inequality in Housework: An Analysis of Time-Use Data' by Serena Arima; Section 'The Gender Gap in the Labour Market: An Historical and Sociological Perspective' by Maria Herica La Valle and by Pietro Demurtas; Sections 'Gender Gap In-Entrance', 'Gender Gap in Occupations', 'Gender Gap in Ranking of Subordinate Jobs', 'Gender Gap in Working Conditions: Full-Time and Part-Time Jobs' and 'Gender Gap in Working conditions (Non-self-employed Employment): Permanent to Temporary Jobs' by Maria Rita Sebastiani; Conclusion by Adele Menniti and Maria Rita Sebastiani (for the paragraph concerning the labour).
2 The asymmetry index is computed as the ratio female / (female + male) amount of time devoted housework.
3 According to Istat (2010), the male time allocated to children increases from 25' to 35' (in two earner couples) and from 16' to 32' (in male breadwinner couples).
4 As pointed out by some scholars (Menniti et al., 2015; Bloemen et al., 2010; Pailhé and Solaz, 2008; Mannino and Deutsch, 2007), this may not be the case of childcare, because of the greater emotional investment that characterizes this activity.
5 'What are also frequently produced and reproduced are the dominant and subordinate statuses of the sex categories.' (West and Zimmerman, 1987, p. 144)
6 As noted in Andreotti et al. (2013), Italy is one of the 'laggard' countries detected by Esping-Andersen (2009).
7 Actually, the percentage increase of the inactivity rate between the age class 35–44 and 45–54 was higher for men than for women (+37.6% compared to +21.9%), because the male inactivity rate for the class 35–44 was lower than the female one.
8 Database we used shows distribution of part-time jobs according the two classes of age 15–34 and 35–64. Actually, in the case of women, this rough classification does not allow to observe differences due to the motherhood, since the class 35–64 includes both women in fertile age and women who are not fertile anymore.
9 Notice that the variable occupational status has not been included in the model because of potential multicollinearity due to strong correlation with the variable on income gap.

References

Aassve, A., Fuochi, G. and Mencarini, L. (2014). Desperate housework: relative resources, time availability, economic dependency, and gender ideology across Europe. *Journal of Family Issues*, 35(8), 1000–1022.

Andreotti, A., Mingione, E. and Pratschke, J. (2013). Female employment and the economic crisis. *European Societies*, 15(4), 617–635.

Anxo, D., Mencarini, L., Pailhé, A., Solaz, A., Tanturri, M. L. and Flood, L. (2011). Gender differences in time use over the life course in France, Italy, Sweden, and the US. *Feminist Economics*, 17(3), 159–195.

Becker, G. S. (1981). *A treatise on the family*. Cambridge: Harvard University Press.

Becker, G. S. (1985). Human capital, effort, and the sexual division of labor. *Journal of Labor Economics*, 3(1), 33–58.

Bergmann, B. R. (1981). The economic risks of being a housewife. *The American Economic Review*, 71(2), 81–86.

Bloemen, H. G., Pasqua, S. and Stancanelli, E. G. F. (2010). An empirical analysis of the time allocation of italian couples: are they responsive? *Review of Economics of the Household*, 8(3), 345–369.

Blood, O. and Wolfe, D. M. (1960). *Husband and wives: the dynamics of married living*. Glencoe: Free Press.

Bollinger, L. and O'Neill, C. (2008). *Women in media careers: success despite the odds*. Lanham: University Press of America.

Brines, J. (1994). Economic dependency, gender, and the division of labor at home. *American Journal of Sociology*, 100(3), 652–688.

Cameron, C. and Trivedi, P. (1998). *Regression analysis of count data*. New York: Cambridge University Press.

Coltrane, S. (2000). Research on household labor: modeling and measuring the social embeddedness of routine family work. *Journal of Marriage and Family*, 62(4), 1208–1233.

Davis, S. N., Greenstein, T. N. and Gerteisen Marks, J. P. (2007). Effects of union type on division of household labor: do cohabiting men really perform more housework? *Journal of Family Issues*, 28(9), 1246–1272.

Dotti Sani, G. M. (2012). La divisione del lavoro domestico e delle attività di cura nelle coppie italiane: un'analisi empirica. *Stato e mercato*, (1), 161–194.

England, P. (2005). Gender inequality in labor markets: the role of motherhood and segregation. *Social Politics: International Studies in Gender, State & Society*, 12(2), 264–288.

England, P. (2010). The gender revolution uneven and stalled. *Gender & Society*, 2(24), 149–166.

Esping-Andersen, G. (2009). *The incomplete revolution: adapting to women's new roles*. Cambridge: Polity Press.

Estévez-Abe, M. (2005). Gender bias in skills and social policies: the varieties of capitalism perspective on sex segregation. *Social Politics: International Studies in Gender, State & Society*, 12(2), 180–215.

Goffman, E. (1976). Gender display. *Studies in the Anthropology of Visual Communication*, 3, 69–77.

Hiller, D. V. (1984). Power dependence and division of family work. *Sex Roles*, 10(11–12), 1003–1019.

ISTAT. (2010). *La divisione dei ruoli nelle coppie. Anno 2008–2009*. Roma: Istat.

ISTAT. (2013). *Conclusione dell'attivita' lavorativa e transizione verso la pensione*. Roma: Istat.

Johnson, N. L. and Kotz, S. (1969). *Distributions in statistics: discrete distributions*. Boston: Houghton Mifflin Company.

Knudsen, K. and Wærness, K. (2008). National context and spouses' housework in 34 countries. *European Sociological Review*, 24(1), 97–113.

Lachance-Grzela, M. and Bouchard, G. (2010). Why do women do the lion's share of housework? A decade of research. *Sex Roles*, 63(11–12), 767–780.

Lambert, D. (1992). Zero-inflated poisson regression, with an application to defects in manufacturing. *Technometrics*, 34(1), 1–14.

Levine, D. M., Krehbiel, T. C. and Berenson, M. L. (2013). *Business statistics: a first course*. New York: Pearson.

Mandel, H. and Semyonov, M. (2006). A welfare state paradox: state interventions and women's employment opportunities in 22 countries. *American Journal of Sociology*, 111(6), 1910–1949.

Mannino, C. A. and Deutsch, F. M. (2007). Changing the division of household labor: a negotiated process between partners. *Sex Roles*, 56(5–6), 309–324.

Mencarini, L. and Tanturri, M. L. (2004). Time use, family role-set and childbearing among italian working women. *Genus*, 60(1), 111–137.

Menniti, A. and Demurtas, P. (2012). *Disuguaglianze di genere e attività domestiche*. Roma: Istituto di Ricerche sulla Popolazione.

Menniti, A., Demurtas, P., Arima, S. and Rose, A. D. (2015). Housework and childcare in Italy: a persistent case of gender inequality. *Genus*, 71(1), 79–108.

Neilson, J. and Stanfors, M. (2014). It's about time! gender, parenthood, and household divisions of labor under different welfare regimes. *Journal of Family Issues*, 35(8), 1066–1088.

Pailhé, A. and Solaz, A. (2008). Time with children: do fathers and mothers replace each other when one parent is unemployed? *European Journal of Population*, 24(2), 211–236.

Todesco, L. (2013). *Quello che gli uomini non fanno: il lavoro familiare nelle società contemporanee*. Roma: Carocci editore.

Verbeek, M. (2012). *A guide to modern econometrics*. Hoboken: John Wiley & Sons.

Watts, M. J. (2005). On the conceptualisation and measurement of horizontal and vertical occupational gender segregation. *European Sociological Review*, 21(5), 481–488.

West, C. and Zimmerman, D. H. (1987). Doing gender. *Gender & Society*, 1(2), 125–151.

West, C. and Zimmerman, D. H. (2009). Accounting for doing gender. *Gender & Society*, 23(1), 112–122.

Appendix 9.1

Descriptive statistics of the variables of interest

	Women	*Men*
Time spent on housework	260.44 (sd = 141.88)	102.87 (sd = 104.92)
	Equal to 0 for 2.2% of the sample	Equal to 0 for 36.3% of the sample
Day	63% weekend, 37% weekday	63% weekend, 37% weekday
Children < 13 years old	35% no, 65% yes	
Income gender gap	65.7% she < he,	66.4% she < he,
	7.1% she > he,	6.8% she > he,
	27.2% she = he	26.8% she = he
Educational gender gap	23.0% she < he,	23.0% she < he,
	22.2% she > he,	22.2% she > he,
	54.8% she = he	54.8% she = he
Age	38.5 (sd = 6.25)	42.12 (sd = 7.04)
Territory	North: 45%, Centre: 16.3%, South 38.7%	
Co-habitants	Yes: 6.4%, No: 93.6%	

10 Gender inequalities, paid work and family formation in Spain

Marta Domínguez Folgueras, María José González and Irene Lapuerta

Michel Bozon said that marriage represents 'the conjunction of two parallel social careers, the effect of which is to consolidate the positions acquired or to support the evolutions in progress' (1991). The implicit idea is that women, especially the more educated ones, aspire to having professional and family careers alongside their spouses; in other words, both are equally committed to paid work and childcare. This means, for example, that women might be losing interest in men with traditional gender attitudes, or delaying marital formation until they achieve a similar or better economic status than that of their future partners (Oppenheimer, 1997), since the relative resources of the spouses can influence, among other things, the sexual division of labour (Blau et al., 2014; Lundberg and Pollak, 1993).

Women's strategies to achieve equality, if any, certainly depend on many factors, but are not limited to negotiations within the couple. The institutional context – understood here as social norms regarding family and gender roles, characteristics of the labour market and family policies – is a basic axis in shaping current gender inequalities and those that are generated throughout the life cycle. This three-dimensional perspective, which links the woman's situation with the transformation of social norms regarding the couple, the family and the institutional background, is what inspires this work.

The aim of this chapter is to analyse gender inequalities in the couple, and illustrate how they are linked to broader changes in family life, the labour market and family policy in Spain. The chapter, for instance, describes the rapid incorporation of women into the labour market, even during the period of great economic recession, but calls for caution when interpreting this indicator. Data on employment activity offers a false picture of gender equality in the labour market. Men and women have achieved a very similar presence in the labour market, but more detailed statistics on employment patterns and distribution of unpaid work within the couples portray a very different reality. The presence of children in the home remains a key element that separates the working lives of men and women. The penalisation of working mothers is interpreted in the light of family policies besieged by economic cutbacks that still do not sufficiently solve the problems of work-life balance or ensure gender equality.

The chapter is structured into three main sections. The first section analyses the relationship between fertility, employment and the distribution of unpaid work within the couple. The second section links the outcomes with family policies. The third and final section closes with brief conclusions that include a reflection on gender equality within the current context of economic recession. This study is based primarily on data from the Labour Force Survey (LFS) and the Continuous Sample of Working Lives ('Muestra Continua de Vidas Laborales') for the waves 2005–2012.

Fertility, employment and sexual division of labour

The aim of this section is to show the link between demographic behaviour, employment and the division of unpaid work within the couple. To understand the recent socio-demographic changes in Spain we must initially highlight the incorporation of women into the labour market, one of the most significant advances of the twentieth century, and their gradual entry into the education system. At present, Spanish women from the younger cohorts access higher education at the same level as other European countries, and their educational level is higher than men's: in 2014, 47.5% of women between 25 and 34 years old had studied at university, compared with 36.5% of men of the same age (INE – Spanish National Statistics Institute). Education not only means better preparation for the labour market, but also greater expectations in terms of work and equality in intimate relationships (Oppenheimer, 1997).

An interesting and specific characteristic of the Spanish context is that demographic behaviour, particularly fertility, is very related to the educational level of women. Figure 10.1, based on the latest census data available (2011), shows the average number of children per woman by educational attainment for two different cohorts: those between 25 and 39 years old at the time of the survey and those who were between 45 and 49 years old. The second group has had time to complete their fertility, so the comparison between both cannot be made directly, but serves as a reference to contrast their experience with women who were between 25 and 39 years old and who experienced the expansion of the Spanish education system. The figure clearly shows the inverse relationship between educational attainment and fertility: in both cohorts, a higher level of education means fewer children. For the 25–39 cohort, we observed a lower number of children on average, partly due to declining fertility and partly due to the fact that this cohort has not completed its fertile period.

If the educational attainment of Spanish women is now approaching that of other European countries, the same has also occurred with work. Figure 10.2 shows employment rates per gender and age of men and women in Spain at three points in time: 1995, 2005 and 2015. We can see that while in the case of men the rates are very similar for all ages in the three points observed, in the case of women the changes have been remarkable. In 2015, for women between 25 and 49 years old the employment rate exceeds 80%, whereas it was much lower in 1995. This data shows that the incorporation of women into the labour market has been huge, and not only for the younger age groups. As a result of this incorporation, the traditional family model, in which only the man is active in the labour market, has lost relevance, since the vast majority of men and women are

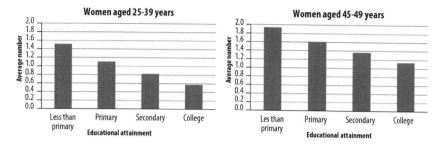

Figure 10.1 Average number of children per woman, by educational attainment and age group: Spain, 2011

Source: Census micro-data, 2011

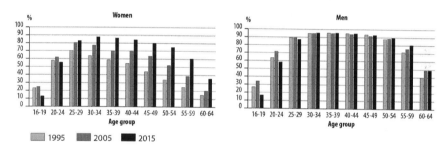

Figure 10.2 Employment rates by sex and age: 1995, 2005 and 2015, Spain

Source: INE database (labour market) for the second quarter of each year

employed, especially in the case of men and women of childbearing age. According to LFS data, the proportion of young adult couples (women between 30 and 45 years old) in which the man was the sole economic provider was 48% in 1999 and 27% in 2014. By contrast, couples in the same age group in which both were employed, the so-called dual-earner couples accounted for 43% in 1999 and rose to 61% in 2007 (González, 2015). Their proportion fell slightly because of the economic crisis and the increase of unemployment rate, but such couples are the prevailing model and on the rise in Spanish society.

However, it is necessary to make some clarifications about the new role of women in Spanish society and, in particular, within the labour market. Despite the massive incorporation of women into paid work, we should stress that this does not occur on an equal footing with men. Unemployment, temporary work and undesirable part-time work affect women more than men, and horizontal and vertical segregation complicates women's employment status (Torns and Recio, 2012). An important difference between the status of men and women in the labour market has to do with the life cycle. As shown in Figure 10.3, employment rates for women are lower when they have children, especially when they have two or more. In contrast, employment rates for men with children are precisely higher in those cases. Thus it seems that the link with the labour market is stronger for women without children, whereas it is reversed for men: participation in the

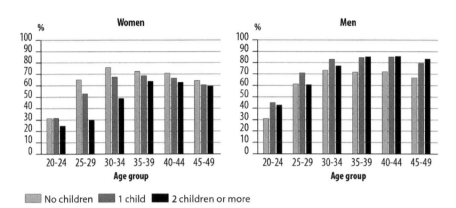

Figure 10.3 Employment rates by sex, age and number of children: 2015, Spain

Source: Labour Force Survey (LFS) micro-data, second quarter

labour market is stronger for those who have children. This data points to the difficulty of achieving a work-family balance and the gender inequality which such difficulty entails: the separation of women from the labour market.

Many people interrupt their careers upon the arrival of children, but these interruptions can assume different forms, such as dropping out of paid work, doing part-time work, part-time parental leave or full-time parental leave for a limited time. In any case, most of these interruptions or adaptations of working hours are done by women (González and Jurado-Guerrero, 2015). In 2015, LFS data shows (Figure 10.4) that among employed men, the vast majority worked full time, with a small percentage working part time, while the percentage of people on parental leave is barely perceptible on the figure. In contrast, for employed women the proportion of part-timers is much more significant, and parental leave is clearly visible on the figure.

Women's employment status is also characterised by unequal wages with regard to men, as shown in Figure 10.5. Women have a stronger presence in the lowest wage scale (41% of women are in that range compared to 19% of men), and a smaller presence in the second and third wage range. The average net salary of women in 2013 was 1,621.60 euros per month, while men earned 2,102.10 euros on average. According to the INE, one of the main reasons for these inequalities in average salary and wage distribution between men and women is that a much greater proportion of women work part time, with temporary contracts and in lower-paid jobs.

These inequalities in the labour market are related to inequalities within couples. As occurs in other countries, unpaid work in the home (domestic and care work) is carried out to a much greater extent by women. Even though in recent years gender inequality in unpaid work has been reduced in industrialised countries where data is available, this reduction has been due specifically to a reduction by women of the time spent on domestic work, rather than to an increase in commitment from men, which has also occurred, but only modestly (Bianchi et al., 2012). Figure 10.6 shows the average time (in minutes) that men and women

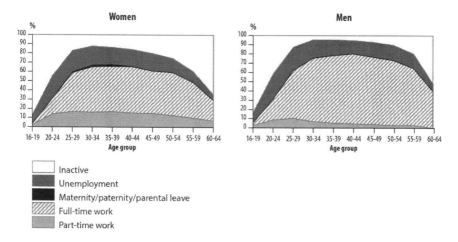

Figure 10.4 Relationship between population and the labour market by sex and age groups: 2015, Spain

Source: Labour Force Survey (LFS) micro-data, second quarter

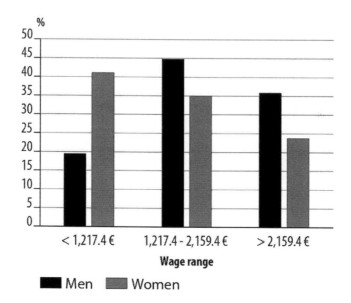

Figure 10.5 Distribution of employees by gender and monthly wage ranges: Spain, 2013

Source: INE (http://www.ine.es/prensa/np874.pdf)

spend on different activities, depending on the number of children. First of all, we see that working time is divided asymmetrically: men always devote more time to paid work than women. Yet this asymmetry also increases with the presence of children: women spend less time on paid work and more time on domestic and care work. Men with children do not spend more time on housework than men

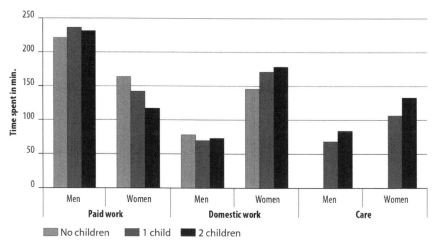

Domestic work includes cooking (food preparation, setting the table, cleaning the table, washing dishes), cleaning the house, washing and looking after clothing, DIY and household shopping

Figure 10.6 Time spent on different tasks (in minutes) per day, by sex and number of children, for people between 25 and 45 years old

Source: Compiled from data from the Time Use Survey 2009–2010 (INE)

without children, but instead devote slightly more time to paid work. Men also devote time to caring, but less so than women.

It is important to note that, along with socialisation and gender roles, one of the factors explaining inequality in unpaid work is economical. Because women have a worse situation in the labour market, they have less bargaining power and their income is less important in the home than their partners' (Blau et al., 2014; Lundberg and Pollak, 1993), which makes them more likely to reduce their labour participation if the family deems it necessary.

We can conclude that in Spain the task of balancing work and family life falls most heavily on women. Despite their high educational attainment and labour market participation, women with children have a weaker link with the labour market. This is related in turn to inequality within households: women usually face a 'second shift' of work and care after their paid work. These inequalities have direct consequences for women in their career and economic prospects, but they also have consequences for family patterns in that they have fewer children and later in life. One would expect that social policies may establish measures that would correct these inequalities in the labour market and their effects on families. However, as we shall see in the next section, these policies have not always been adequate.

Family policy in Spain

In international classifications on family policy, Spain forms part of the Southern European model, characterised by its vision of the family as being primarily responsible for the care and welfare of children and dependent adults (León,

2016). This familialism is also based on a strong intergenerational solidarity, which entails the existence of close ties and shared responsibilities with the extended family. The prominence of the family is also related to the absence of significant public intervention, which is principally reflected in the low levels of public social expenditure on families. In fact, the percentage of gross domestic product for family policies stood at 1.4 in 2012 in Spain, far from the 2.2% average of the OECD countries and 2.7 of the EU-15 (SOCX[1]).

The poor development of Spanish family policy is due to historical reasons. The identification of this area of intervention with the Franco dictatorship, which developed a system of family-related economic benefits in order to strengthen the traditional family model, explains that it was not championed in the transition by political parties or by social organisations as an area of priority action (Valiente, 1996). The overburden of family responsibilities did not become part of the political agenda of successive governments until the end of the 1990s, with the approval of 'Law 39/1999 to promote the work-family life balance of working people' and the first 'Comprehensive Plan for Family Support' (2001–2004) (Campillo, 2014).

As the literature highlights, family policies can support mothers and fathers by providing monetary resources, services and time (Thévenon, 2011). Depending on the greater or lesser role of each of these instruments and their objectives, design and generosity, families will make decisions regarding the number of children, continuity in employment and care arrangements (González, 2015). We also find variations among countries in the levels of family and individual well-being, especially in the case of women and children. Hence the importance of reviewing the configuration and the possible effects of each policy instrument separately.

Monetary resources

In Spain, the cash benefits system is characterised by indirect support playing a greater role than in most countries of the European Union: deductions or tax relief are more important than direct support (León, 2016; Obiol Francés, 2006). These deductions vary depending on the age and number of children, the existence of special family circumstances (e.g. for single-parent families, international adoption, disability) and on the region of residence. They are clearly regressive due to the fact that low-income households, excluded from filing their income tax returns, do not benefit from them. Indirect benefits also favour higher earners as they further reduce their tax burdens (Pazos Morán, 2015).

Specific mention should be given – due to its objectives and format – to the 'deduction for maternity', exclusively aimed at mothers with children under 3 years old and in paid employment. It consists of a tax deduction of 1,200 euros per year, which aims to offset the costs of maternity in the early years of life. It can also be received early in payments of 100 euros per month, which takes the form of non-refundable tax deduction (so-called tax credits in English-speaking literature). This was also the format chosen in the latest tax reform, passed just a few months before the general elections in December 2015, which included three new deductions of the same amount for large families, descendants with disabilities and dependent ascendants who live in the same household.

Meanwhile, direct economic benefits share two features. First of all, none has an universal scope,[2] with the exception of the so-called baby cheque, which was in effect between 2007 and 2010. It consisted of a single payment of 2,500 euros per birth. Secondly, existing benefits are notorious for their limited coverage and low payments (Cantó and Ayala, 2014). This is the case of the dependent child benefit, which recognises an allowance of 291 euros per year per child, conditional on the household having a very low income,[3] or an allowance of a variable amount if the child has a disability, in which case there is no income limit.

The latest research shows that the impact of the Spanish family cash benefits is very limited on reducing child poverty and promoting fertility. They also have contradictory effects on encouraging female employment. For example, Azmat and González (2010) state that the simultaneous implementation in 2013 of the 'deduction for maternity' and the extension of tax deductions for children in the household caused an increase of 5% in the gross fertility rate, but only a 3% increase in the employment rate of women with children under 3 years old. According to these authors, the impact of the employment reform would have been higher in the absence of tax deductions, since these discourage mothers from working.

The opposing effects between the fertility and employment rates of mothers are also evident when assessing the 'baby cheque' benefit. González (2013) shows that, even though the cheque represented an annual increase of 6% in the number of births during the three years it was in place, mothers were less likely to work in the year following the birth. This effect disappeared two years later. As a result, the cheque introduced changes in the time that mothers spent at home and was used for compensating the lack of economic payments from the parental leave system after the fifth month, as we shall explain later. Besides, Cantó and Ayala (2014) show that the economic benefits payment system had no impact on reducing child poverty, which places Spain as the European Union country, along with Bulgaria and Romania, with the highest rates of child poverty.

Services

The second resources available to families are childcare and pre-school services, which constitute the main sources of formal care. From the 1990s and until the 2001–2002 school year, enrolment for children from 3 years of age increased dramatically as a result of the universalisation process of the second cycle of Pre-school Education (children age 3–6), which achieved a coverage of over 95% in subsequent school years, despite being a stage of non-compulsory, although free, education.

This trend contrasts with the much more moderate progress of the enrolment rate in the first cycle of Pre-school Education (children aged under 3 years), which stood at 31.8% in the 2012–2013 school year. The implementation of the 'Educa3 programme' by the socialist government between 2007 and 2012 meant an increase of 75% in public school places, with the consequent expansion of coverage, which grew 12 percentage points in just 6 school years (Felgueroso, 2012). However, these figures hide huge differences depending on the age of the children. In the

2012–2013 school year, the enrolment rate of children under 1 year old was 9.8%, 32.6% for 1-year-olds and 51.8% for 2-year-olds (MECD, 2011).

Access to the first cycle of Pre-school Education is also strongly marked by regional differences: while in the 2012–2013 school year the enrolment rate among 2-year-old children stood at 26.3% in Asturias, in Madrid, it reached 67.4% and in the Basque Country 92.4% (MECD, 2011). However, more worrying still are the biased access detected by the socio-demographic characteristics of the parents. Felgueroso (2012) points out, for example, that in 2009 the average enrolment rate for 1-year-old children whose mothers had a university education was 35 percentage points higher than children with mothers who had studied up to compulsory secondary education. The 30-point gap continued among 2-year-old children and was also visible when analysing variables such as the nationality of the mother or household income. This data calls into question the ability of childcare services to support all families and reduce the intergenerational transfer of inequality, especially among the most disadvantaged groups.

The first possible cause of lower levels of enrolment rates among the most vulnerable children, and in particular those whose mothers have low income prospects in the labour market, is the high price of these services. In 2010, the monthly fee for a public school place ranged from a minimum of 71 euros in Extremadura and a maximum of 221 in Catalonia, with an extra charge of 100 euros per month for the meal service. The average price of public school places in these regions was 128 and 363 euros, respectively (León, 2016). The removal of many public subsidies due to the economic crisis, especially from 2012, has led to a general rise in these costs for families (Escobedo et al., 2014).

The second cause concerns the access requirements for public childcare services established by each region, which award more points when both parents are working, compared with other criteria such as proximity of the school to the child's home or siblings enrolled at the same school. As Felgueroso (2012) stresses, insofar as the parents' jobs are correlated with a higher level of family income, poorer households are not guaranteed a public school place in the event of excess demand. This is a particularly common situation within the Spanish context where the number of public places in the zero- to two-year cycle is limited.[4] Neither are they likely to be able to afford a private place, so their children would not be enrolled and therefore accumulate educational disadvantages from an early age.

Parental leaves

The third and last resource available to families to achieve a work-family life balance is parental leave. This consists of regulating working times so that parents can meet the children's care needs. As reflected in Table 10.1, Spanish legislation provides different types of leave, three of them paid at 100%: 16-week maternity leave, of which the mother has to take 6 weeks following the birth and another 10 can be transferred to the father; 15-day paternity leave (13 in the case of self-employed workers); and breastfeeding leave, which grants one of the two parents two half-hour breaks during the working day or a half-hour reduction in the

Table 10.1 Types and characteristics of parental leaves in Spain. 2015

	Type of leave				
Criteria	Maternity leave	Paternity leave	Breastfeeding leave	Full-time parental leave	Part-time parental leave (reduced working hours)
Entitlement	Individual (mother, 10 weeks transferable to the father)	Individual (father)	Family	Individual	Individual
Eligibility	180 days of tax contributions within the previous 7 years at the start of the leave or 360 days throughout employment history[1]	180 days of tax contributions within the previous 7 years at the start of the leave or 360 days throughout employment history[1]	Salaried employees[2] No contribution requirements		
Duration	16 weeks[3]	15 days (13 for self-employed workers)[3]	1 hour a day, up to 9 months or the equivalent accumulated time	Until the child is 3 years old	Until the child is 12 years old
Wage compensation	100%	100%	100%	None	None
Job protection	Yes	Yes	Yes	1 year	Yes
Social Security Contributions	Yes	Yes	Yes	3 years	2 years

[1] In the case of maternity leave, the eligibility requirement varies according to the age of the mother at the time of giving birth. No minimum contribution period is required if she is under 21 years old, whereas if she is between 21 and 26 years old, 90 days of contributions during the immediately preceding 7 years or 180 days throughout employment history are required.

[2] The right is not granted to self-employed workers.

[3] The duration of both leave periods is higher in cases of multiple births or child with a disability.

Source: own elaboration

normal working day until the child is 9 months old. This leave can also be taken cumulatively, provided that it is stipulated in the collective agreements at company level or agreed with the employer.

Full-time parental leave and part-time parental leave, on the other hand, do not involve wage compensation. The first one enables both parents to interrupt their employment until the child is 3 years old. However, getting the same job back is only guaranteed for the first year. For the rest of the time, return to work is linked to a position with an equivalent category, but not necessarily the same job. Since 2013, Social Security has assumed workers' contribution throughout the entire leave, which was previously limited to a period of 2 years. Finally, part-time parental leave enables employees to reduce their working hours from an eighth to a half to care for the child until he/she is 12 years old. This age limit was also extended in 2013 (previously set at 9 years old). Self-employed workers are not granted the right to breastfeeding leave, full-time or part-time parental leaves.

The Spanish parental leave system is therefore generous in time but barely affordable due to the lack of economic compensations, apart from the first five months after childbirth (Lapuerta, 2012). In fact, numerous studies show that the majority of mothers normally use such accumulated paid leave (maternity and breastfeeding) and add holiday time to take a working break of 4 or 6 months. Only mothers who have a more favourable situation in the labour market – with higher educational attainment, stable employment contracts, full-time employment, greater seniority in the company and positions in companies with high levels of protection (public sector or employees of large companies) – extend this period using parental leave or reduced working hours (Lapuerta, 2012). Fathers, on the other hand, are not often absent for more than a month, adding paternity leave to holidays (Abril et al., 2015; González, 2015). Therefore, the gender bias in the system is evident. In 2014, only 1.8% of fathers took the transferable part of maternity leave and accounted for 6% of full-time leave users that year (MESS, 2015). Less than 1% of men entitled to full-time parental leave and part-time parental leave end up exercising one of these rights (Lapuerta, 2012).

Figure 10.7 shows the take up of full-time and part-time parental leaves for women who had a child in the period 2005–2009 and who were working before they gave birth. It takes into account the use of these policies during the three years that follow the birth of the child.[5]

The figure shows that part-time parental leave is more popular than full-time parental leave. In fact, the full-time parental leave take-up rate decreased slightly among these mothers from 12.1%, in the case of children born in 2005, to 10.2% for those born in 2009. Conversely, reduced working hours have undergone the opposite trend, with an increase in the take-up rates observed, especially for children born since 2007. This pattern may be due to two reasons. Firstly, the establishment in 2007 of a compensation scheme for Social Security payments, equivalent to 100% of the working day,[6] which made this a more attractive resource. Secondly, it is likely that in the context of economic recession, mothers have preferred to maintain links with employment and a part of their wages instead of enduring a period without income. Finally, a small percentage of mothers, approximately 4%, used both forms of leave.

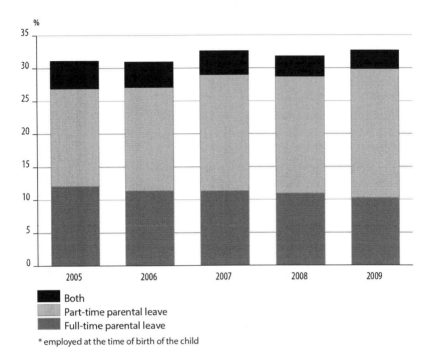

Figure 10.7 Take-up rates of parental leave (full time and part time) among working mothers who had a child between 2005–2009 in the three years after giving birth.
Spain: 2005–2012

Source: CSWL, waves 2005–2012

Conclusion

In this chapter, we have analysed gender inequalities in couples and their link to
the institutional context in Spain. Despite the massive incorporation of women
into the labour market, their situation is still not equal to men's, as illustrated by
the more detailed statistics on employment that we have presented. The division
of tasks in the home remains a predominantly female responsibility. Furthermore,
the presence of children in the family seems to be a key element that separates the
working lives of men and women, and it is the latter who are penalised. The family policies analysed do not foster work-life balance in the majority of households
and there create even antagonistic effects when we consider their main objectives:
increasing the birth rate, reducing child poverty, fostering child development and
welfare, promoting female employment and encouraging gender equality (Thévenon, 2011). The economic and financial crisis, which began in 2007, has only
accentuated these inconsistencies.

The austerity measures implemented since 2010 to contain public spending
have triggered a clear reversal in many areas of social and labour policies, leaving many families neglected precisely in the years of greatest need (González,
2015). The cutbacks in the family policies led to the abolition of the 'baby cheque'

and the freezing of the child benefit in 2011; the discontinuation of the 'Educa3 Programme' in 2012, along with other measures to contain expenditure on education; and the postponement of the extension of paternity leave from 15 days to one month, initially scheduled for 2011. Furthermore, certain incentives intended to promote equal opportunities in the labour market, by means of allowances in employers' contributions to Social Security for women to return to their work after maternity leave, have been abolished.[7] The cutbacks have also affected the cash family benefits offered by regions in Spain. As proof of this, of the total of 34 allowances which existed in 2006 on a regional level to support families with children, only 14 were still in force in 2013, and many of them had undergone changes that greatly limited their generosity and coverage (Di Prieto, 2014).

All these cutbacks in the area of work-life balance and childcare have increased the economic vulnerability of households, due to the difficulties for parents – especially mothers – to continue working after the birth of their children, which in turn jeopardises the welfare of many children (González, 2015). But not only that, they have triggered a trend in the re-privatisation of care, thereby making it difficult to achieve gender equality in couples and encouraging more traditional family models (Gálvez, 2013). Clear examples of this tendency are the measures adopted to extend the period in which working hours can be reduced to take care of children or the increase in the Social Security contributions without providing for wage compensation and without establishing explicit incentives for the involvement of men in the use of parental leaves, as well as the launch of new tax credits to care for ascendants at home. In addition, in a context of high unemployment rates a rapid deterioration of employment conditions, it is becoming increasingly difficult to justify rights related to work-life balance within companies. Therefore, Spain is moving away from the timid initiative of promoting family welfare and gender equality, which began in the late 1990s.

Notes

1 OECD Social Expenditure Database (SOCX), www.oecd.org/social/expenditure.htm
2 Only 6 of the 28 countries in the European Union, including Spain, have no universal benefits (González-Bueno and Bello, 2014).
3 The income limit for each child in 2016 is 11,547 euros per annum, plus 15% for each child after the second born. This limit coincides approximately with the threshold set for the declaration of income tax, which means that most families receiving this benefit will not benefit from tax deductions (Obiol Francés, 2006).
4 Children aged under 3 years enrolled in public schools accounted for 52% of the total in the 2011–2012 school year (González, 2015).
5 It should be remembered that leave can be taken until the child is 3 years old, while reduced working hours can be taken until the child is 12 years old. Consequently, the figure underestimates the influence of reduced working hours.
6 Prior to 2007, the contribution to Social Security decreased in proportion to the reduction in working hours, which had effects on the calculation of future labour rights (for example, pensions or new maternity/paternity leaves).
7 These allowances were extended to companies and self-employed workers and meant that Social Security payments were exempt for four years for female employees, and for one year for female self-employed, as long as they returned to work within two years of the birth of the baby. Currently, these allowances have been linked to the recruitment of new workers who replace mothers during their leave.

References

Abril, P., Amigot, P., Botía-Morillas, C., Domínguez-Folgueras, M., González, M. J., Jurado-Guerrero, T., et al. (2015). Ideales igualitarios y planes tradicionales: análisis de parejas primerizas en España. *Revista Española de Investigaciones Sociológicas*, (150), 3–22.

Azmat, G. and González, L. (2010). Targeting fertility and female participation through the income tax. *Labour Economics*, 17(3), 487–502.

Bianchi, S. M., Sayer, L. C., Milkie, M. A. and Robinson, J. P. (2012). Housework: who did, does or will do it, and how much does it matter? *Social Forces*, 91(1), 55–63.

Blau, F. D., Ferber, M. A. and Winkler, A. E. (2014). *The economics of women, men, and work*. Boston: Pearson.

Bozon, M. (1991). Mariage et mobilité sociale en France. *European Journal of Population*, 7(2), 171–190.

Campillo, I. (2014). Desarrollo y crisis de las políticas de conciliación de la vida laboral y familiar en España (1997–2014). Un marco explicativo. *Investigaciones Feministas*, 5, 207–231.

Cantó, O. and Ayala, L. (2014). *Políticas públicas para reducir la pobreza infantil en España: análisis de impacto*. Madrid: UNICEF Comité Español – Huygens Editorial.

Di Prieto, L. (2014). *La dimensión autonómica de las prestaciones económicas de apoyo a las familias: un análisis del periodo 2000–2014*, Trabajo Fin de Máster, Universidad Pública de Navarra.

Escobedo, A., Meil, G. and Lapuerta, I. (2014). Spain country note, in: Moss, P. (Ed.), *10th international review of leave policies and research 2014* (pp. 277–290). International Network on Leave Policies and Research. Retrieved from www.leavenetwork.org/fileadmin/Leavenetwork/Annual_reviews/2014_annual_review_korr.pdf

Felgueroso, F. (2012). Recortes educativos y responsabilidad fiscal: la escuela infantil. Planeta euskadi. *Nada est Gratis*. Retrieved from http://nadaesgratis.es/felgueroso/recortes-educativos-y-responsabilidad-fiscal-la-escuela-infantil-ii-planeta-euskadi

Gálvez, L. (2013). Una lectura feminista del austericidio. *Revista de Economía Crítica*, 1(15), 80–110.

González, L. (2013). The effect of a universal child benefit on conception, abortions, and early maternal labor supply. *American Economic Journal: Economic Policy*, 5(3), 160–188.

González, M. J. (2015). Padres primerizos en tiempos de crisis, in: González, M. J. and Jurado-Guerrero, T. (Eds.), *Padres y madres corresponsables: una utopía real*. Madrid: Los Libros de la Catarata.

González, M. J. and Jurado-Guerrero, T. (Eds.). (2015). *Padres y madres corresponsables: una utopía real*. Madrid: Los Libros de la Catarata.

González-Bueno, G. and Bello, A. (2014). *La infancia en España 2014. El valor social de los niños: hacia un pacto de estado por la infancia*. Madrid: UNICEF Comité Español.

Lapuerta, I. (2012). *Employment, motherhood and parental leaves in Spain*, Thesis, Universitat Pompeu Fabra.

León, M. (Ed.). (2016). *Empleo y maternidad: obstáculos y desafíos a la conciliación de la vida laboral y familiar*. Madrid: Funcas.

Lundberg, S. and Pollak, R. A. (1993). Separate spheres bargaining and the marriage market. *Journal of Political Economy*, 101(6), 988–1010.

MECD (Ministerio de Educación, Cultura y Deporte). (2011). *Objetivos educativos europeos y españoles: estrategia de educación y formación 2020. Informe español.*

Retrieved   from   www.mecd.gob.es/dctm/ievaluacion/indicadores-educativos/objetivos-et2020-informe-2011.pdf?documentId=0901e72b80faaff5

MESS (Ministerio de Empleo y la Seguridad Social). (2015). *Anuario de estadísticas del mMinisterio de empleo y la seguridad social. Año 2014.* Retrieved from www.empleo.gob.es/es/estadisticas/anuarios/2014/index.htm

Obiol Francés, S. (2006). El sistema de prestaciones por hijo a cargo en España. *Revista Internacional de Sociología,* 64(43), 95–117.

Oppenheimer, V. K. (1997). Women's employment and the gain to marriage: the specialization and trading model. *Annual Review of Sociology,* 23(1), 431–453.

Pazos Morán, M. (2015). *Desiguales por ley: las políticas públicas contra la igualdad de género.* Madrid: Los Libros de la Catarata.

Thévenon, O. (2011). Family policies in OECD countries: a comparative analysis. *Population and Development Review,* 37(1), 57–87.

Torns, T. and Recio, C. (2012). Desigualdades de género en el mercado de trabajo: entre la continuidad y la transformación. *Revista de Economía Crítica,* 14, 178–202.

Valiente, C. (1996). The rejection of authoritarian policy legacies: family policy in Spain (1975–1995). *South European Society and Politics,* 1(1), 95–114.

11 Morocco between women's emancipation and reproduction of gender inequalities

Mohammed Amar and Ilham Dkhissi

Despite the measures taken in favour of women's emancipation for many years, deep disparities between women and men persist in Morocco. The main objective of this chapter is to examine the effects of recent transformations in the Moroccan institutional context, in particular changes in the political system which have resulted in three constitutional reforms over the past 25 years. An examination of the evolution of gender relations shows that social change needs to be 'seen in the perspective of the importance of the discrimination which still affects women's status in Morocco' (Alami M'chichi et al., 2004). This chapter will indeed try to distinguish those elements favouring more equal relationships between men and women from those which help to maintain an asymmetry in gender positions. Is this contradictory evolution the subject of a public debate? How is it reflected in the development and implementation of public policies? Which areas of daily life are affected? These are the main questions which this chapter is attempting to answer.

In 2014, women account for slightly more than half of the Moroccan population (50.3%). They have a higher life expectancy at birth: 75.6 years compared to 73.9 years for men in 2010 (HCP,[1] 2009). The main transformations from this point of view concern the fertility rate which is lower than before: 2.21 children per woman in 2014 compared to 7.2 in 1962 (HCP, RGPH,[2] 2014). Women die less frequency during childbirth than in the past thanks to medical advances in this field (HCP, 2008). Finally, the majority of Moroccan women are marrying at an increasingly late age: 25.8 years of age in 2014 compared to 17.5 in 1962 (HCP, RGPH, 2014). On the basis of these observations, we will focus primarily on the expression of views on gender roles, particularly within the family context, and the changes which may have occurred in these opinions.

The changing views on gender relations

Fairly recently, a public opinion survey among a representative sample confirmed the attachment of the majority of Moroccans to the traditional role models within the family. In the expressed representations,

> family relationships appeared strongly hierarchical, with a strict division of roles. The father is thus represented as the head of the family and, as such, is

responsible for providing for the material needs of household members. The mother is responsible for the smooth running of the home, for carrying out the housework and bringing up the children.

(ADFM, 2004)

Three-quarters of men (77%) considered that a woman's work in the home was more important than what she could accomplish outside it and only 17% believed that it was equally important. The fact remains that 'the financial input of women and their contribution to improving or maintaining living conditions increase their bargaining power with the head of the family'. Thus, an important part of 'the Moroccan population accepts the idea of women's participation in decision-making [. . .] (given that) almost half of respondents (47%) stated that women were not excluded from decision-making'. 'Paid work outside the domestic sphere and the financial independence it gives women are undeniably the drivers of the transformation in gender relations' (ADFM, 2004). However, women's behaviour is still controlled by men. This is due to various factors such as women's ignorance of their rights, their financial dependence on their spouse or, more broadly, to the continuance of discriminatory laws and the still significant stereotypes about women's inferiority. The survey also revealed some willingness to change: indeed, 86% of the population interviewed expressed support for decisions to be taken jointly by men and women. However, more women (92%) than men (79%) advocated this sharing. This survey shows that there is a real willingness to establish partnerships between spouses within the family alongside the maintenance of traditional roles. It is similarly interesting to note that more than a third of respondents considered that working outside the family to meet their needs is also part of a woman's role; only a quarter of respondents considered that men should also carry out household chores (ADFM, 2004).

The National Survey on Values conducted in 2004 also showed that certain traditional values such as obedience to the spouse and towards their ascendants persist, although nowadays they take the form of respect rather than that of a strictly subordinate relationship. The survey also reveals that the standard values are passing through 'a transition phase, which is more or less accepted by Moroccans, and is characterised by the coexistence of the traditional values and the emerging and consolidating new values'. This coexistence, which affects urban and rural environments, leads Moroccans to accept 'the ambivalence of two groups of values, traditional and modern, deploying one or the other depending on their situation without this appearing contradictory to them'. Thus the transformations to the value system in Morocco arise more from a rather complex process of sedimentation than from the result of ruptures and substitution (Comité Directeur, 2006, p. 51 and p. 53).

Another survey conducted a few years after the adoption of the Family Code showed that those interviewed strongly supported the principle of equality in the family (Benradi et al., 2007): 78.62% of women and 62.93% of men, respectively. Yet one of the authors of this work states that 'too often, studies tend to consider that the rule of law is sufficient in itself to ensure that equality becomes a reality' and that 'many obstacles thwart the achievement of equality' (Alami M'chichi, 2007). She adds,

Two different logics are still a source of tension within Moroccan family culture: a logic of the asymmetry of gender positions, specific to a patriarchal system, and a contemporary logic of equality [. . .], logics which, far from being independent of one another, are tangled and intermingled.

(Benradi et al., 2007)

A sociological examination of Moroccan society (see in particular HCP, 1998a) shows more fundamentally that it is still marked by traditional representations which constitute an obstacle to the economic and social integration of women since the gender division of roles mostly assigns women the status of wife, sister, mother, etc. Evidence of this is found in the ways of life. The socialisation of roles within the family usually results in some sort of sexual hierarchy. Indeed, household chores are almost exclusively reserved for women; women and girls are at the service of the rest of the family. This is confirmed by an analysis of Moroccan women's timetables conducted by the HCP. Female temporality is split in two: time spent on professional work and time spent on domestic work. Men spend more of their time in work-related activity (four times more than women on average). This ratio is even higher in urban areas. As for domestic activities, men's contribution is limited to tasks outside the home. According to figures from the HCP, 95% of Moroccan women dedicate five hours a day to domestic chores while 45% of men spend an average of 43 minutes a day on domestic tasks. The classical model of the male 'head of household' and the women 'at home' is clearly seen in the organisation of their timetables (HCP, 2015). As the family is the one institution in which a lack of distinction between natural and social functions is often the rule, the questioning of traditional representations causes tension between personal choices on the one hand and those social norms passed down and instilled by family culture on the other (Locoh and Ouadah-Bedidi, 2014; Benradi et al., 2007; Blöss, 2001). Women and young people's aspirations are often in collision with their elders and men who are the traditional holders of power.

Gender relations in Morocco have also been transformed because of rapid changes in the population growth rate. In one generation, the fertility rate decreased from 7 children per woman in the early '60s to 2.21 in 2014. This decrease is due firstly to the increased age at first marriage and secondly to the increasingly widespread use of contraception (Locoh and Ouadah-Bedidi, 2014; Fargues, 2003). Compared to the 1960s and 1970s, when it was common for men and women to marry at 20 and 15 years of age, respectively, for just over a decade the age of the first union has been around 26 for women and around 31 for men (RGPH, 2004, 2014). This increase in the average age at marriage has shortened the length of a woman's reproductive life which, until the 1980s, was the main factor in explaining the decline in the fertility rate. It was not until the 1990s that medical contraception took over and became the main driver of this decline. The proportion of women using contraception rose from 5% in the late 1970s to 63% in 2003–2004 (Locoh and Ouadah-Bedidi, 2014).

These profound changes are explained by the decline in the mortality of the under 5's on the one hand[3] and by an increase in women's education on the other. The proportion of illiterate women decreased from 96% in 1960 to less than 42% in 2014, with a wide disparity between urban (30.5%) and rural (60.4%) areas.

The percentage of girls aged 7 to 12 years being educated rose to above 94% in 2014 compared to 37% in 1990 (HCP, 2014; Locoh and Ouadah-Bedidi, 2014). Whereas from puberty onwards their world used to be essentially limited to the domestic sphere, widespread education for girls and women's access to the labour market have opened the public sphere to them and changed the matrimonial calendar. Demographic change and the sharp increase in education have led to a significant decrease in descendants and upset traditional patterns of family life. With families now having only two children on average, the foundations of patriarchy are being challenged. Redefining roles within the family is nonetheless proving difficult because it calls into question the long-standing privileges which are legitimated by tradition and religion. The latter is a cultural reference and an identity marker in Morocco, 'it extends to the political social dynamic and sometimes to the ideological mobilisation used to justify and assert a position in [. . .] the debate of ideas' (Comité Directeur, 2006). To understand the meaning of the developments and their contradictory nature, it is also necessary to examine the role of the institutions involved in the debate.

The religious dimension as an issue in the debate on gender relations

In order to understand this issue, the contribution of women's associations to the political, legal and ideological development of Morocco should be noted. Although these organisations have been campaigning since the 1970s,[4] their work noticeably intensified in the political context of the mid-1990s. It was during this period that 12 women's associations sent the prime minister a motion which, amongst its the demands, included the development of a national strategy for the promotion of women in consultation with women's associations, human rights organisations, etc. Amongst other items, the motion demanded the inclusion of a course on women's rights in the teaching of human rights and compliance with Morocco's international commitments, in particular, ratification of the Convention on the Elimination of All Forms of Discrimination against Women. It also demanded the revision of national legislation and its harmonisation with the convention's provisions to establish equality between the sexes (HCP, 1998b).

However, the feminist movement had to change these ideological references and its protest speeches to adapt both to the international context and to the reality within the country. Indeed, while Moroccan activists consider themselves individually as laywomen, in their group stance, they adopt a discourse based on a dual universal and religious framework. They have had to consult religious reference works with the help of experts in Islamic law in order to achieve a legal-religious basis which may 'respond to attempts to use religion against the recognition of women's rights and promotion of their status' (Collectif 95 Maghreb-Egalité, 2003). As rightly pointed out by Benradi et al.,

> in the Muslim cultural sphere, as family rights are based on religious references their development is subject to the readings made by various schools on the precepts of the Koran and the Sunnah.[5] Therefore, the ability of fam-

ily law to consider social change is compromised by the restrictive readings which have dominated the history of family law in the Muslim world and thus women's rights have been limited.

(Benradi et al., 2007)

The 1990s were marked by the initiation of a dynamic change whose main issue was questioning the naturalistic conception of gender relations and the acquisition of new rights by women. However, as the gender equality model is a highly contested concept, and is a relatively recent one, the question of its compatibility with the system of values regulating social relations within Moroccan society is particularly acute. Since then, gender relations have indeed been the subject of a heated debate, revealing a

gap between the constitutional model of equal citizenship [. . .] on the one hand, expressed by public policies which take into consideration the need to improve women's status, and on the other, the patriarchal *logic* [. . .] which limits the scope of these policies.

(Alami M'chichi et al., 2004)

In March 2000, for the first time in Morocco's history, the presentation of a National Action Plan for Integration of Women in Development[6] led to such an intense ideological conflict within society that two major demonstrations were organised: one in Rabat in support of the Plan and one in Casablanca firmly opposing it. Thus, the changing of gender relations is the subject of confrontations between conservatives calling for strict respect for the religious directions and reformers advocating secularisation and a certain freedom of interpretation of religious texts. The reform of the Personal Status Code therefore represented an issue around which Moroccan society was divided into two opposing camps. The deadlock caused by the crystallization of this conflict demonstrated a certain inability of Parliament, political forces and civil organisations to work out a compromise on issues related to gender relations. The religious character of certain provisions of the Personal Status Code required royal arbitration[7] through the establishment of a preparatory commission on the proposals for reform. This commission's mission[8] was the subject of ideological guidance expressing the royal wish 'to consolidate and strengthen the major advances, crowned by the Family Code, which established the rights and obligations on the basis not only of the principle of equality between men and women, but equally and primarily, on that of preserving family cohesion and protecting its authentic national identity'.[9] The king, as Commander of the Faithful, cannot go against directions/ proscriptions clearly stated in the Koran and prophetic tradition. This institutional 'construct' has prevailed whenever it has been necessary to implement reforms from legal provisions governing the status of women and gender relations.

Women's associations have chosen to rely on this dual frame of reference in most of the memoranda submitted to the king for the amendment of the Personal Status Code, by using the opinion of many Muslims legal scholars as a basis for showing that there is no contradiction between their demands and the precepts of Islam. However, given the range of grievances of women's associations and human rights organisations, the king's room for manoeuvre is reduced. Indeed, as Commander of the Faithful, he cannot authorise what is clearly prohibited by the religion. Some progress has, however, been made, such as the decriminalisation of medical abortion. The king received both the ministers of justice and of Islamic affairs and the president of the National Council of Human Rights and gave them a month for reflection and consultation, including with the Council of Ulemas[10] in order to submit proposals to him for amending the articles of the Criminal Code which criminalised abortion. A decriminalisation of medical abortion is thus envisioned, but only in cases of rape or incest followed by pregnancy and congenital defects given that the current legislation does not prohibit abortion when the pregnancy poses a danger to the mother's life.

Women's associations have also played a crucial role in raising awareness of violence against women. In its second report, the National Network of Listening Centres for Women Victims of Violence (RNCEFVV, 2007) revealed that nearly three-quarters (74%) of such violence involved the victims' spouses as the aggressor. Very common, domestic violence takes many forms: legal (43.6%), for example, depriving women of their maintenance allowance after divorce (58.4%), physical (30.4%) and sexual (the main form of which being rape). The report also establishes two profiles: first, that of the victim, a married woman (71.1%), at home (56.2%), with no particular level of education (43.3%) who has filed complaints with the competent authorities (68.2%) and that of the aggressor, a married man (87.9%), aged between 30 and 40 (34.9%), known to the victim (95.4%), illiterate (34.7%) or no education above primary school level.

However, the role of women's associations is not limited to the constitution of demands. They also participate in the production of data on single mothers, for example. In the absence of studies and statistics on this issue, the activity report (quoted by Tarik H. (2010) of the association for children and single mothers (Insaf[11]) shows that for the year 2008, over 54% of single mothers were aged between 31 and 40 and over 20% were aged between 21 and 30. Most of them have no education beyond primary school level and work as domestic help (28%) or are labourers (23%); nearly a quarter of them are unemployed and more than half come from poor neighbourhoods, nearly 16% come from rural and peri-urban areas, nearly 10% from middle-class districts and 6% from slums. The 2007 reform of the Civil Status Code recognised such women's right to declare the birth of their children to the civil state. The children can thus have an identity, civil rights and therefore a better chance of social integration.

Evolution of public policies and the legal framework governing gender relations

The growing importance granted to women's issues by successive governments since the 1990s is displayed by the way ministerial departments in charge of these issues were designated. This went from a situation where these policies were managed by a Ministry of Employment and Social Affairs in 1997 to management of these policies by the State Secretariat for Social Welfare and Children with the arrival of the government for change in 1998. For around ten years, between the 2002 parliamentary elections and those of 2012, the Secretary of State was elevated to the Ministry of Social, Family and Solidarity Development. Since the appointment of the current government, the term 'women' has appeared for the first time in the designation of the Ministry of Solidarity, Women, Family and Social Development.

The late 1990s were characterised by the implementation of public policies towards women. This process started in 1997 with the preparation of a draft national strategy by the Ministry of Employment and Social Affairs whose objectives was related to legal protection, education and training, health protection, participation in decision-making power and the mass media. This project never came to fruition because it was not converted into programmes and actions in the context of the various departments' public policies (HCP, 1998b). Women were treated as subjects and not as stakeholders of development. It was not until 2004 that the Ministry of Social, Family and Solidarity Development launched an action plan for the fight against violence to women with the establishment of a national listening centre, reception centres and units within the police services, police stations, courts and hospital units. Two years later, a national strategy for gender equality was implemented to integrate the gender approach into plans and action programmes of the sector and into development projects. The National Charter to improve the image of women in the media was developed in the same year to promote a culture of equality and the fight against stereotypes.

From 2008, two five-year plans have followed one another: that of 2008–2012, aimed, amongst other things, at ensuring equity and equality between the sexes, strengthening women's legal status and their full participation in development, and that of 2012–2016, called the 'government plan for equality', which provides measures aimed at implementing constitutional provisions relating to equality between men and women.[12] This latest plan takes its references from Islam, the Constitution, Morocco's commitment to achieve the Millennium Goals for Development, and international conventions, particularly that of the Convention on the Elimination of All Forms of Discrimination Against Women (CEDAW).

In terms of women's human rights, the debates seen in Morocco since the early 2000s have led to a number of reforms. In 2003, a new labour code came into force. It includes the obligation to protect working women against all forms of discrimination and prohibits 'a consideration of gender [. . .], marital status or family responsibilities as acceptable justifications for disciplinary actions or dismissal' (Royaume du Maroc, 2013b). On 10 October 2004,[13] a new Family Code was adopted. It introduced a number of changes, such as joint responsibility of the spouses for the family, the removal of guardianship for the marriage of young adult women (aged 18), the right to divorce without the need for evidence or a witness, a guaranteed home for the children of divorce, etc. This code has set the reciprocal rights and obligations of spouses on an equal footing by submitting 'polygamy or the various forms of marriage dissolution to strict conditions and the control of the judges, establishing egalitarian provisions and creating guarantee mechanisms' (Benradi et al., 2007). Nonetheless, some discrimination persists. On the one hand, it can be pointed that mothers can only become the legal guardians of minor children in the event of the death or legal incapacity of the father and on the other; one can also point to the delay permitted in recognising marriages which were not subject to a contract, which is used as a means to circumvent the law on child marriage and polygamy. Indeed, in spite of Article 16 of the Family Code, which stipulates that the contract is the only proof of marriage, the transitional period of five years provided by this code for the legalisation of traditional marriages has undergone several extensions, including the latest dated December 2015. This allows the retrospective recognition of polygamous and/or child marriages. For the latter, statistics from the Ministry of Justice show that the number of child marriages almost doubled over ten years, from 18,341 in 2004 to 35,152 in 2013, 7% and 12% of marriages, respectively. It should be noted that according to the same source, 99.8% of requests concern girls of which 96.3% are aged between 16 and 17 (ADFM, 2015).

The Nationality Code was reformed in 2007 to enable Moroccan women to transmit their nationality to children born of foreign fathers. Section 6 of the Code stipulates that: 'a child born of a Moroccan father or a Moroccan mother is Moroccan' while in the former text, nationality could only be transferred through the father. In 2008, on the occasion of the sixtieth anniversary of the Universal Declaration of Human Rights, the Moroccan government lifted the restrictions on the CEDAW. Although this agreement had been ratified with restrictions since June 1993, the draft bill relating to the Optional Protocol of CEDAW on male-female equality was not adopted in parliament until July 7, 2015.[14]

In a context of political tensions caused by the Arab Spring, Moroccan citizens adopted a new Constitution by a referendum organised on 1st July 2011. In Article 19 this stipulates that 'men and women shall enjoy equal, civil, political, economic, social, cultural and environmental rights and freedoms' and that 'the Moroccan State is working to achieve parity between men and women'. Article 31 of this Constitution specifies that 'the State, public institutions and local authorities are working to mobilise all means available to facilitate equal access of male and female citizens to conditions allowing them to enjoy their rights'. The provisions of the new constitution give primacy to the treaties and conventions ratified by Morocco over national legislation.

Furthermore, a draft reform of the Penal Code, introduced in April 2015, provides for the repeal of 40 articles, the addition of 187 and the amendment of 576 giving better legal protection for women through sanctions imposed on spouses failing to meet marital obligations or squandering funds to evade child support. The Family Support Fund, set up in 2010, makes 'grants to impoverished divorced mothers and children who are due child support following the dissolution of the marriage contract' to counter this kind of situation, which is detrimental to women (Royaume du Maroc, 2013b). What have been the results of the implementation of this set of measures so far? It is appropriate at this point to examine the effects of these measures on the situation of contemporary Moroccan women and the relations binding the two sexes.

The role of gender relations in the transformations of lifestyles

Education, health, employment and access to decision-making posts, including political representation, are areas where women's emancipation issues have proven to be most significant and have sometimes given rise to considerable variations between the country's regions. In education, despite the continued growth in the percentage of women being educated in recent years, women's illiteracy rate (41.9%) remains higher than that of men (22.1%) (RGPH, 2014). This difference is even more pronounced in rural areas (60.4% for women and 35.2% for men). It is explained by the remoteness of schools in relation to housing in rural areas, by the priority sometimes given to boys' education to the detriment of that of girls amongst siblings when resources are insufficient, and by the persistence of attitudes more rooted in tradition in the countryside where girls, generally married at an early age, are expected to be supported by their husbands, etc. Although the law has made education compulsory for children up to the age of 15, and though the proportion of children aged between 7 and 15 who work has been cut by three-quarters, from nearly 9.7% in 1999 to 2.5% in 2011,[15] the law remains partially unimplemented given that in 2012, 92,000 children aged between 7 and 15 were working, 92.4% of whom were from rural areas (ADFM, 2015). The spread of women's education in the future could affect gender relations. In urban areas, women are nearly as educated as the men of their generation and since education is a factor in authority, the overtaking of fathers and husbands by wives and daughters might very well challenge the patriarchal order (Fargues, 2003).

If we examine women's health indicators, the mortality rate of mothers after childbirth has decreased by 66%, from 332 in 1992 to 112/100,000 live births in 2010. However, there are significant disparities in Morocco between urban and rural areas since the rate was twice as high in the countryside (148/100,000) as in the towns (73/100,000). Rural women have the most difficulty in obtaining skilled attendance during childbirth, since only 55% of rural women benefit from such assistance compared to 92.1% in towns (ADFM, 2015).[16] As for the conditions of access to the labour market, low participation of women in economic activity is recorded. Indeed, HCP figures show that the proportion of active workers amongst women of working age was only 24.7% in 2012. This proportion was 28.1% in 2000 – i.e. a drop of 3.4 points. In 2012, the proportion of women reaching working age (15 and over) increased by 25.7% compared to 2000. Of these women, only 32.9% were graduates at any levels (HCP, 2013). According RGPH in 2014, the female participation rate[17] (14.7%) was very low compared to men (54.1%). The women's unemployment rate in 2014 was 28.3%, compared to 12.2% for men. This discrimination between the sexes is much greater in rural than in urban areas since rural women suffer from unemployment three times more than men (23.5% and 8%, respectively) whilst in urban areas the women's unemployment rate (29.5%) is nearly twice as high as that of men (15%) (RGPH, 2014). It should be noted that the women's unemployment rate increased between 2004 and 2014, from 25.5% to 28.3%, whilst that of men decreased (from 13.7% to 12.2%) during the same period.

Even though we can legitimately question the reliability of statistics on female employment,[18] the weakness and the drop in women's participation rates and the increase in unemployment rate can be explained by the fact that some working women choose to stop working and devote themselves to family life; others have this imposed on them by husbands who believe that women should not continue to work after marriage and/or childbirth (Locoh and Ouadah-Bedidi, 2014). A recent study[19] shows that family constraints prevent 53.5% of women entering the labour market. It also states that 100,000 working women left the job market when they married. The results of a survey conducted as part of this study indicate that 33.2% of these women were prevented from working by their husbands, compared to 12.5% by fathers, and that 30.3% of the women were unemployed because they could not find a job which allowed them to reconcile their work with their family commitments. This study also shows that while 93% of women with only primary school education were unemployed, this proportion was 37% for women who had gone on to higher education.

Another study conducted by the Office of the High Commissioner for Planning also establishes that upward rather than downward social mobility is most often in favour of the urban environment and men. The study reveals that the promotion of men is clearly favoured by social norms. Inequalities in access to school and employment are major obstacles to promoting women's status. Although exercising an occupation allows women to contribute to household expenses and gain some independence, these benefits are counteracted by the fact that they have the dual responsibility of an occupation and domestic work. They also often suffer discrimination both in the hierarchical positions they occupy and in terms of pay.[20] In 2012, whilst women represented 41.9% of senior staff, only 24.2% had management roles and out of 140 appointments to senior positions in public administration, only 16 women were appointed (ADFM, 2015). Moreover, the male-female gap in terms of salary increased from 47.2% in 1983 to 52.4% in 2002 (Alami M'chichi et al., 2004).

The principle of gender equality should be distinguished from egalitarian practice; women's access to the labour market is often accompanied by the appearance of new forms of discrimination since, for these women, the public sphere and the workplace become in their turn places of relations of 'male domination in the jobs hierarchy, in the allocation of social roles and in the misogynist culture' (Alami M'chichi et al., 2004). Blöss (2001) confirms this when he states,

> The widespread access of women to the labour market cannot be [. . .] interpreted as an indicator of their emancipation from their domestic roles, for reasons related to both the inertia of the labour market, the existing power relationships in the domestic sphere itself and the weighting of class membership in occupational/family activity interactions.

Finally, through the establishment of a quota system, 35 women were able to enter parliament in the 2002 parliamentary elections (representing 10.8% of the seats instead of 0.66% before 2002). The participation rate of women in municipal councils rose from 0.56% in 2003 to 12% in 2009 and to 44.4% in 2015.[21] During the 2011 parliamentary elections, women's representation in the House of Representatives was able to increase to 17% (67 seats of 395) thanks to the establishment of national women's lists. This representation was still further improved in the last parliamentary elections in 2016 given that 20.5% of parliamentarians are now women. Finally,

> to ensure representation of women in management bodies, Article 26 of the Organic Law on Political Parties (29–11 Act of 22 October 2011) stipulates that all political parties must work towards having one-third of the participants in proceedings at national and regional levels being women, in order to gradually achieve parity between men and women.

Conclusion

This chapter has highlighted the changes experienced by Morocco from the point of view of women's legal status since the establishment of the constitutional reforms of the 1990s, of the Personal Status Code in 2004 and particularly since the adoption of the 2011 constitution. This country has been experiencing a process of opening up politically for two decades which has, amongst other things, allowed the debate on the issue of gender relations to be triggered. The idea of gender equality is still the subject of discussion in the current values system in Moroccan society; the model produced has only been included in these discussions recently, in a partial fashion, and is highly contested. The situation is actually characterised by a gap between an egalitarian citizenship model, clearly stipulated by the constitutional provisions, and a reality strongly marked by a patriarchal logic which runs against the introduction of public policies to improve the status of women.

The frame of reference for the values governing social relations between Moroccan citizens is in a transitional phase characterised by the coexistence of traditional values, which are subject to change, and 'modern' values which are gradually being introduced. This coexistence leads to ambivalence in the behaviour of individuals as regards the transformations in gender relations. On such a sensitive societal subject, even if there is some difficulty in reconciling the ideas from opposing political and ideological trends, the changing attitudes and the possibility of reaching a compromise on issues related to religion allow us to glimpse the potential for women's emancipation. This chapter shows that although government action is essential for establishing and implementing the political, legal, economic and social basis governing fair and equitable gender relations, the fact remains that it was the arbitration of the king, as head of State and Commander of the Faithful, which was crucial in leading to reforms in this area. Although the efforts of the authorities to improve the economic and social situation of women are not without effect, we have equally underlined the central role of the feminist movement in raising public awareness, in producing data on taboo issues and in enacting laws which give women greater legal protection against abuse and discrimination.

Notes

1 Office of the High Commissioner for Planning.
2 General Census of the Population and the Housing Environment
3 There was a 60% decrease between 1990 and 2011. Source: WHO, January 2014. www.who.int/features/2014/morocco-maternal-health/fr/
4 See in particular Benadada and El Bouhsini (coords) (2014).
5 Prophetic tradition.
6 This plan, asserting the idea that women's rights are universal, was presented by Mohammed Essaadi, a member of the Party of Progress and Socialism serving as Secretary of State for Social Protection and Children in the so-called government of 'consensual change' appointed by King Hassan II nearly 16 months before he died.
7 In Morocco, the king, through the Constitution, has the roles of head of state and 'Commander of the Faithful': *'Amir Al Mouminine'*.
8 This commission includes figures from all political and ideological leanings, others with no political affiliation and Muslim legal scholars known for their moderation.
9 The king's speech, on 30 July 2005 in the newspaper 'Le Matin du Sahara' of July 31, 2005.

10 Legal scholars or Islamic theologians.
11 Insaf is the name of a non-profit and state-approved association founded in 1999 that develops actions in favour of material support and legal protection to single mothers and their children as well as girls under eighteen.
12 These provisions are aimed in particular at: the empowerment of women and the fight against the precariousness of their situation, particularly in terms of illiteracy, poverty, discrimination and violence; the promotion of the culture of respect for the rights, freedoms and dignity of women; the encouragement of women's participation in political parties and civil society organisations as well as the promotion of equal opportunities between the sexes on the labour market (Royaume du Maroc, 2013a, pp. 4–17).
13 It has since become National Women's Day.
14 See the newspaper *L'économiste* of Thursday, July 9, 2015.
15 Unless otherwise indicated, the figures in this section are from the Report of the Kingdom of Morocco (2014, pp. 15–50).
16 This is explained by the remoteness and/or lack of access to health facilities in rural areas, by the absence or inadequacy of medical care during pregnancy, which is often due to the lack of qualified medical personnel and lack of ambulances, and by the practice of home birth.
17 According to the HCP, the participation rate shows the proportion of working people in the total population. It is calculated by comparing the number of active workers with that of the whole population (www.hcp.ma/Activite_r87.html).
18 It is questionable whether rural women's activities such as trips to water sources, the time spent collecting wood for heating and cooking and some income generating activities such as farmyard and craftwork are actually taken into account by these statistics.
19 Study by the Japanese agency for international cooperation on representations on Moroccan women's work quoted by the newspaper Assabah (meaning morning in Arabic) no. 4747 of July 22, 2015, in an article entitled 'Fathers and husbands responsible for women's unemployment'.
20 In 2008, 64.8% of females were in vulnerable employment.
21 Moroccan Ministry of the Interior, www.maroc.ma/fr/actualites/election-des-conseils-communaux-2015-6673-sieges-pour-les-femmes.

References

ADFM (Association Démocratique des Femmes du Maroc). (2004). *L'égalité entre les hommes et les femmes point de vue de la population marocaine*. Rabat: General Consulting.

ADFM (Association Démocratique des Femmes du Maroc) (Ed.). (2015). *Situation des femmes au Maroc 20 ans après Beijing. Etat des lieux et recommandations*. Rabat: Imprimerie El Maarif Al Jadida.

Alami M'chichi, H. (2007). Changement social et perceptions du nouveau code de la famille, in: Benradi, M., Alami M'chichi, H., Ounnir, A., Mouaqit, M., Boukaïssi, F. Z. and Zeidguy, R. (Eds.), *Le code de la famille. Perceptions et pratique judiciaire* (pp. 27–88). Fès: Friedrich Ebert Stiftung-ImprimElite.

Alami M'chichi, H., Benradi, M., Chaker, A., Mouaqit, M., Saadi, M. S. and Yaakoubd, A.-I. (2004). *Féminin – masculin: la marche vers l'égalité au Maroc 1993–2003*. Fès: Friedrich-Ebert-Stiftung.

Benadada, A. and El Bouhsini, L. (Eds.). (2014). *Le mouvement des droits humains des femmes au Maroc: approche historique et archivistique*. Rabat: Publications du Conseil national des Droits de l'Homme et la Faculté des Lettres et des Sciences humaines de Rabat-Agdal.

Benradi, M., Alami M'chichi, H., Ounnir, A., Mouaqit, M., Boukaïssi, F. Z. and Zeidguy, R. (2007). *Le code de la famille. Perceptions et pratique judiciaire*. Fès: Friedrich Ebert Stiftung-ImprimElite.

Blöss, T. (Ed.). (2001). *La dialectique des rapports hommes-femmes*. Paris: Presses universitaires de France.

Collectif 95 Maghreb-Egalité. (2003). *Autoportrait d'un mouvement: les femmes pour l'égalité au Maghreb*. Rabat: Imprimerie El Maarif Al Jadida.

Comité Directeur. (2006). *50 ans de développement humain et perspectives 2025. Le Maroc possible. Une offre de débat pour une ambition collective*. Casablanca: Editions Maghrébines.

Fargues, P. (2003). La femme dans les pays arabes: vers une remise en cause du système patriarcal ? *Population et Sociétés*, (4), 387.

HCP (Haut-Commissariat au Plan). (1998a). *Situation socio-économique et défis démographiques au Maroc*. Rabat: HCP (Haut-Commissariat au Plan).

HCP (Haut-Commissariat au Plan). (1998b). *Genre et développement: aspects socio-démographiques et culturels de la différenciation sexuelle*. Rabat: CERED (Centre d'Etudes et de REcherches Démographiques).

HCP (Haut-Commissariat au Plan). (2008). *La femme marocaine en chiffres, tendances d'évolution des caractéristiques démographiques et socioprofessionnelles*. Rabat: HCP (Haut-Commissariat au Plan).

HCP (Haut-Commissariat au Plan). (2009). *Enquête Nationale sur la Prévalence de la Violence à l'égard des Femmes au Maroc*. Rabat: HCP (Haut-Commissariat au Plan).

HCP (Haut-Commissariat au Plan). (2013). *Femmes marocaines et marché du travail: caractéristiques et évolution*. Rabat: HCP (Haut-Commissariat au Plan).

HCP (Haut-Commissariat au Plan). (2014). *Premiers résultats de l'enquête Nationale sur l'emploi du Temps au Maroc 2011/ 2012*. Rabat: HCP (Haut-Commissariat au Plan).

HCP (Haut-Commissariat au Plan). (2015). *Recensement Général de La Population et de l'Habitat 2014: présentation des principaux résultats*. Rabat: HCP (Haut-Commissariat au Plan).

Locoh, T. and Ouadah-Bedidi, Z. (2014). *Familles et rapports de genre au Maghreb, évolutions ou révolutions*. Paris: Institut National d'Etudes Démographiques.

RNCEFVV (Réseau National des Centres d'Ecoute des Femmes Victimes de Violences). (2007). *Les violences fondées sur le genre au Maroc. Deuxième rapport. Analyse des plaintes enregistrées par les centres d'écoute et d'assistance juridique des femmes victimes de violence*. Rabat: RNCEFVV.

Royaume du Maroc. (2013a). *Participation du Royaume du Maroc lors de sa participation aux travaux de la 57ème session de la Commission sur la situation de la femme à New York*. Power Point. Rabat: Royaume du Maroc.

Royaume du Maroc. (2013b). *Population et développement au Maroc. Vingt ans après la Conférence du Caire de 1994*. Rabat: Royaume du Maroc.

Royaume du Maroc. (2014). *L'évaluation du Plan d'action de Pékin + 20*. Rabat: Royaume du Maroc.

Tarik, H. (Ed.). (2010). *Rapport sur les politiques publiques dédiées au social au Maroc. Situation sociale 2009–2010*. Rabat: Réseau Marocain des Politiques Publiques.

12 Work-life balance through the lens of the dynamics of individualisation in France

Valeria Insarauto

In Europe today, social policies affecting family life and employment represent one of the most active areas of reform (Daly, 2011). For European institutions, a balance between family life and professional career is an important response to the social, economic and demographic challenges faced by Europe (Silvera, 2010; Le Bihan-Youinou and Martin, 2008). The concerns of European decision makers in this regard seem to be influenced by macroeconomic imperatives and focused by the high priority given to promoting the professional sphere. This is linked to more general objectives around increasing female employment rates (Silvera, 2010; Nicole-Drancourt, 2009; Lewis and Giullari, 2005). From this perspective, the European Community's policy approach strongly advocates a family model comprising dual-earner couples in order to increase the economic independence and individual autonomy of each partner, especially that of women (Letablier, 2009). Developing childcare services is often presented as a leading solution to achieve this goal. The possibility of children being cared for outside the family would allow women the choice of full participation in the labour market and the achievement of the same level of independence and autonomy as men.

This policy vision is partly simplistic and does not reflect the complexity of the issue. It neglects a key aspect: balancing professional work and family responsibilities is still 'women's work', and being able to entrust children to care outside the home does not necessarily help to change the asymmetrical division of men and women's roles (Stefan-Makay, 2009; Le Bihan-Youinou and Martin, 2008; Lewis and Giullari, 2005). Family arrangements for sharing domestic responsibilities should therefore not be neglected by these policies aiming to increase individual autonomy. Such is the central topic on which this chapter is based. Its aim is to demonstrate, by analysing survey data (Box 12.1), that the institutional desire to spread the two-working-parent model of the family should be compared with the social reality of the inequalities between the sexes. These still largely underlie behaviours when it comes to the work-life balance, as well as the policies implemented in this field.

Studying the role of public policies in implementing family arrangements is explained by the specific situation of the French national framework which aims to promote independence and individual autonomy amongst individuals. This specificity allows the contradictions embodied by such an objective to be highlighted. France is indeed a country where the family model is generally one in which both partners work. Childcare services are widely developed through

---

Box 12.1   Field of analysis and data processing

This work is based on analysing data from European survey EU-SILC (EU Statistics on Income and Living Conditions) which aims to produce statistics on both these areas. First carried out in 2004 and coordinated by Eurostat, it is conducted annually using data provided by EU member states and follows on the survey from the European Community Household Panel undertaken between 1994 and 2001. This data allows us to obtain detailed information regarding models for work-life balance and recourse to childcare services thanks to the use of both the individual panel and the household panel, with the additional possibility of reconstructing partner relationships. We used the longitudinal version and conducted a 'cross-sectional' analysis by comparing two waves of the survey; that of 2005 and that of 2011.

Firstly, we conducted an analysis based on the descriptive statistics at an individual level. This field comprised every individual, man or woman, aged 25 to 49. Our sample included 7996 individuals in 2005 (4176 women and 3820 men) and 8376 in 2011 (4314 women and 4062 men). All the results were calculated on the basis of the individual weights provided by the longitudinal version of the survey. We then conducted an analysis based on the descriptive statistics for couples. This field comprised heterosexual couples of individuals aged 25 to 49. Our sample included 2082 couples in 2005 and 2175 couples in 2011. All the results were calculated on the basis of household weights provided by the longitudinal version of the survey. The characteristics of the sample for both individuals and couples are presented in Appendixes 12.1 and 12.2.

---

significant public investment in the childcare sector (Ortalda, 2010; Boyer, 1999). However, the sharing of domestic and family tasks between the sexes remains uneven and the burden of balancing work and home life continues to fall mainly on women (Pailhé and Solaz, 2006, 2010).

Social changes in the areas of work and the family: what are the policy responses and for what kind of balance?

Sociological surveys of the past two decades have shown how the 'male breadwinner' family model, under which it was generally the man's role to earn the money whilst the woman's was to care for family members, has significantly reduced in Western societies. This change is primarily the consequence of women's entry into the labour market en masse together with a large-scale process of the transformation of family structures. The structure, role and composition of the family as a social institution have changed, as can be seen through the dynamics of family formation and the changing participation in the labour market of its various members. On the whole, all these transformations have led to changes in ideas about relationships between the sexes as well as about the contribution that women and men should make to family and social life (Lewis and Giullari, 2005).

One of the hypotheses developed to explain these changes establishes the existence of a powerful 'individualisation' movement in society. This term signifies that the personal choices made by individuals and their desire for autonomy tend to become the values to be advocated and promoted in society. In this process, each individual is supposed to be the author of their own story, forge their own path and make their own choices, at all times (Le Bihan-Youinou and Martin, 2008; Anxo and Boulin, 2006; Naegele et al., 2003). The creation of individual life paths would thus be a result of personal preferences and would be less subject to family ties and structures. In this process still, men and women would somehow be on equal terms in attaining their goals.

Public policies on work and the family seem to rely increasingly on this hypothesis (Daly, 2011). The approach to balancing work and family life advocated by the European Union's policies is representative of this trend. In this approach, all adults are expected to participate fully in the labour market in order to guarantee their own individual autonomy. At the same time, they can choose to temporarily reduce their professional commitments at various times in their lives if they need to balance their work and private lives (Lewis et al., 2009; Annesley, 2007; Lewis and Giullari, 2005). In this context, the development of childcare services for young children is seen as a key element; by facilitating access to full employment for both women and men, it will solve the dilemmas arising from balancing work and the home (Lewis and Giullari, 2005). The family model which emerges from this approach is called the 'working adult model'.

In this model, there are no notable differences in the choices available to the sexes as regards the balance between the professional and the family sphere (Lewis and Giullari, 2005). The main reason for this is that this model sees the family simply a backdrop to the forging of its members' individual life paths; its specific role as an unequal playing field where power and duties are unequally distributed between men and women being completely obscured (Daly, 2011). However, in the current social situation, the issue of balance remains mainly a consideration for women, including in France, where children's services are well developed (Nicole-Drancourt, 2009; Daune-Richard, 2001). The bulk of domestic and family responsibilities still fall to women as a result of the traditional norms which continue to dominate the family sphere. In addition, women's contributions to family income remain generally below those of men, who are maintaining their role as the main income providers within households (Letablier, 2009). In reality, despite recent advances in emancipation, women still mostly find themselves a long way from achieving the individual autonomy sought by the working adult model. How, therefore, should we interpret changes in the distribution of social gender roles and what credence should be given to the explanatory 'working adult' model?

The work-life balance in France: what choices do individuals have?

Traditionally, French family policy as regards the work-life balance has been characterised by a dual dynamics seeking both to encourage women to work and to support maternity (Daune-Richard, 2005; Fagnani and Letablier, 2005;

Hantrais, 2004). Public support for balance has thus often taken the form of additional systems set up to help mothers look after their children, especially through a wide range of childcare options.[1] From the 1990s onwards, the rhetoric of 'free choice' began to feature in political discourse surrounding the work-life balance. It started to target both parents with the objective to allow them to choose, and alter over time, how they managed their working lives and their parental responsibilities. A sharp increase in childcare options and their diversification supported this rhetoric, especially with the development of measures encouraging individual childcare plans (Boyer, 1999). Gradually, the goal became to allow parents to obtain a personalised service based on their own preferences (Martin, 2010). In other words, government bodies emphasised the importance of parental 'free choice', believing that no childcare method should be imposed, especially if this was outside the family (Séraphin, 2013).

This 'free choice' rhetoric featured heavily in the creation of the Early Childhood Benefits,[2] which is one of the most recent reforms in family policy in France and a key measure in helping parents balance work and family life.[3] The purpose of this measure, strongly focused around parental preferences, is to encourage a public and family context in which each person can have the actual and moral chance of making their own choices when it comes to achieving balance (Letablier and Lanquetin, 2005). Specifically, parents should be able to make their own choices in a range of areas: who should look after the children (parents themselves rather than someone outside the family sphere), the type of service they prefer (individual or collective) and the financial cost they are able to bear. The notion of 'free choice' also accepts that childcare may be provided by one of the parents if they prefer to look after the child themselves (thereby temporarily stopping or reducing their working hours) (Adema and Thévenon, 2008).

The ways in which the 'free choice' rhetoric is characterised seem to be inspired by the individualisation hypothesis around which the EU policies on the work-life balance are also based, especially through promotion of the 'working adult model' described earlier. Nevertheless, this rhetoric does not just represent a political will to give priority to individual preferences. It also encompasses other contradictions in terms of equality between men and women. Although on the one hand public support for parental choice as regards the work-life balance (especially as regards childcare) is seen as fundamental for achieving greater equality, on the other hand, by emphasising the importance given to parental choice, the 'free choice' rhetoric reinforces a certain traditionalism in the highly unequal division of family responsibilities between women and men. Indeed, it is well known that the task of looking after the family home usually falls to women, who adapt their professional lives to be able to meet their parental responsibilities, whilst men are much less affected by this kind of problem (Pailhé and Solaz, 2006, 2009). Thus, given the way in which family life is currently organised, the idea that taking care of children is principally the woman's role only gains ground from the promotion of 'free choice'. In other words, social representations according to which parental responsibility is almost exclusively the role of women are not being questioned. Instead, they are reinforced by a policy approach which is not addressing the constraints which determine men's and women's choices when it comes to the work-life balance. Through the ideology of individualisation, this policy approach tends to discourage new models of more equal relationships between the sexes being explored. It risks strengthening the existing asymmetry between women and men. This is confirmed by analyses showing that nearly all the recipients of Prestation d'Accueil du Jeune Enfant (PAJE) are women (Joseph et al., 2012; Nicolas, 2010), especially those demonstrating that fathers spend little time alone with their children and are involved in a much more limited range of parental tasks (Villaume and Legendre, 2014; Boyer and Céroux, 2010).

The approach taken by French social policies is thus characterised by a certain level of ambivalence. In giving significant importance to individual choices (through reference to an ideology of individualisation), it increases the influence of family structures around these same choices, thereby helping to perpetuate a certain traditional division of labour between the sexes. The following empirical analysis will allow us to consider how this is reflected in the work-life balance practices of men and women, as both individuals and couples.

A 'freely chosen' but gender-unequal work-life balance

How do practices of work-life balance differ between men and women depending on different family forms and the childcare options chosen? Our main hypothesis is that these practices are strongly determined by these elements but in different ways, depending on their gender. Our intention is to demonstrate how the reality of the work-life balance is still a long way from the aims of independence and individual autonomy promoted by those policies inspired by the individualisation hypothesis. We will therefore first analyse the practices of balance for individuals of both sexes and secondly, for (heterosexual) couples. In this way, we will be able to highlight both the different roles of men and women as regards the work-life balance as well as the constraints imposed upon them within the family sphere which make the possibility of independence and individual autonomy in this area different for the two sexes.

Three types of work-life balance can be defined. Each type involves a different level of independence and individual autonomy. The first kind of balance will be called 'traditional': there is zero participation in the professional sphere and the person is not employed, leading to zero independence and zero individual autonomy (when analysis is done on couples it is assumed that it is the woman who is not working). The second kind of balance will be called 'modified': the person plays some part in the professional sphere by being employed for less than 30 hours per week, leading to some level of independence and individual autonomy (when analysis is done on couples it is assumed that it is the woman who finds herself in this position). The third kind of balance will be called '*parallel*': this involves full participation in the professional sphere by being employed for more than 30 hours per week, leading to great independence and individual autonomy (when analysis is done on couples both partners are in this position).

In France, the majority of men and women are fully occupied in the professional sphere (Figure 12.1).

Only a minority work part time or do not work. These are mainly women, thereby confirming that practices of the work-life balance still differ between

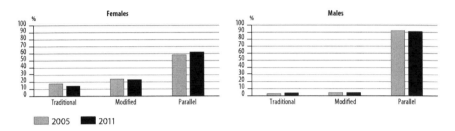

Figure 12.1 Type of balance, by gender and year (in %)

Source: EU-SILC survey (secondary analysis)

the sexes. During the period studied – between 2005 and 2011 – these practices changed slightly: the type of balance we have called 'traditional' decreased
amongst women in favour of a greater recourse to the 'parallel' kind, whilst the
opposite occurred amongst men. Can these changes be seen as a sign of a trend
towards less differentiated practices of the work-life balance between the two
sexes?

Bearing in mind the diversity of family forms, it can be seen that being in a
couple and the presence of dependent children both make a contribution to the
differences in the balance achieved by the sexes (Figure 12.2).

These two elements have a strong influence on women. They also have the most
significant impact on the 'traditional' and 'modified' types of balance. For men,
exactly the opposite can be seen: the 'parallel' type is more common amongst
those who live in a couple, with or without children, as well as for single-parent
fathers, whilst other types are more common when they are not in a couple. It can
be inferred that men living in a couple remain the main income providers and that
the household's financial independence depends on them. In contrast, women in
couples and with dependent children are still the main care providers in the family sphere. However, a change seems to be emerging during the period studied:
between 2005 and 2011, we see an increase in the 'parallel' balance type – i.e., of
'full' commitment in professional and family lives – in women with children who
are part of a couple.

Could it be that easier access to childcare, particularly outside the family circle,
could serve to explain this new trend? To answer this question, we will examine
the use of childcare services – firstly all types of services combined, then differentiating between formal and informal services[4] (Figure 12.3).

The method undertaken involves examining whether the ability to have a child
cared for is a factor likely to make practices of the work-life balance more equal, not
only between women and men but also between women with and without children
by cancelling out what is known as the 'motherhood penalty' – i.e., the handicap
experienced simply by having children. In other words, do women without children and women who are mothers find themselves in equal situations as regards
the work-life balance thanks to the latter being able to have recourse to childcare
services? This question is particularly interesting given that in France, despite the
extension of childcare types outside the family, care provided by the family, mainly

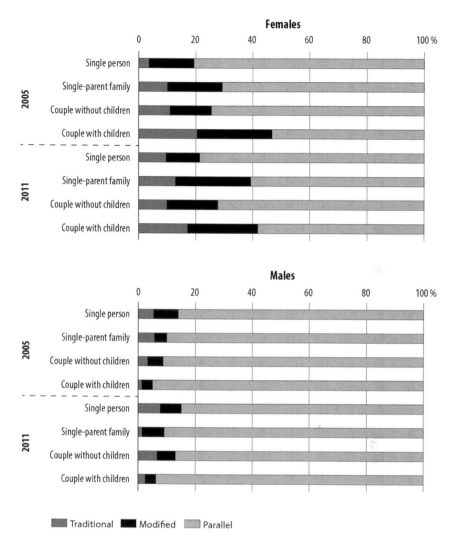

Figure 12.2 Types of balance according to family forms, by gender and year (in %)

Source: EU-SILC survey (secondary analysis)

by mothers, remains predominant (Crepin and Boyer, 2015; Villaume and Legendre, 2014; Fraisse et al., 2009).[5] At first glance, the answer seems to be rather negative. The 'parallel' type of balance is more often seen amongst women who do not have recourse to childcare solutions. In comparison, women who use these services feature more heavily in other types of balance categories which involve less investment in the professional sphere. For men, the situation is reversed which illustrates that having recourse to childcare is of little importance to them.

We cannot therefore say for certain that childcare taking place outside the family has made women equal amongst themselves as regards the work-life balance,

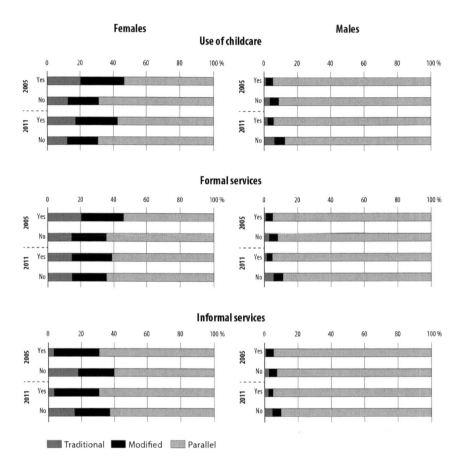

Figure 12.3 Types of balance according to use and childcare type, by gender and year (in %)

Source: EU-SILC survey (secondary analysis)

and even less so when it comes to equality with men. Nevertheless, during the last period (between 2005 and 2011) an increase in the proportion of the 'parallel' model was noted amongst women who do have recourse to childcare services. However, it appears that this development varies according to the type of service used (formal or informal). It is also clear that recourse to informal childcare services is associated with a higher proportion of women who have concomitant or 'parallel' commitments as regards professional work and the private sphere. This trend demonstrates that childcare work cannot be outsourced *ad infinitum* and that being able to entrust childcare to someone in their informal network (family members, friends, neighbours) is often a deciding factor (Villaume and Legendre, 2014).

The trends seen for individuals are also reflected in couples. The latter also show the highest incidence of 'parallel' work-life balance: in more than half of couples, men and women have full-time commitments in the professional sphere in parallel with their family lives (Figure 12.4).

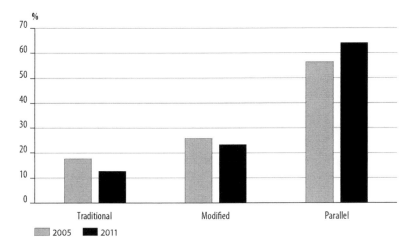

Figure 12.4 Types of balance of couples, by year (in %)
Source: EU-SILC survey (secondary analysis)

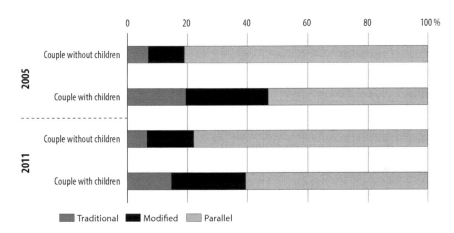

Figure 12.5 Types of balance of couples according to family form, by year (in %)
Source: EU-SILC survey (secondary analysis)

This type of balance increases over the period in question, whilst a significant decrease in the 'traditional' model, which kept women out of the professional sphere, is also seen. This trend might suggest that we are seeing an already well developed dynamics of individualisation and autonomy. However, upon closer analysis of the conditions in which this trend emerges, the picture is a great deal more nuanced. In reality, the 'parallel' type of balance occurs more frequently amongst couples without children (Figure 12.5) and in couples who have recourse to informal childcare services (Figure 12.6). This trend increases between 2005 and 2011, even though over the same period we also see a rise in this type of balance in couples who use formal childcare services. Conversely, the 'traditional'

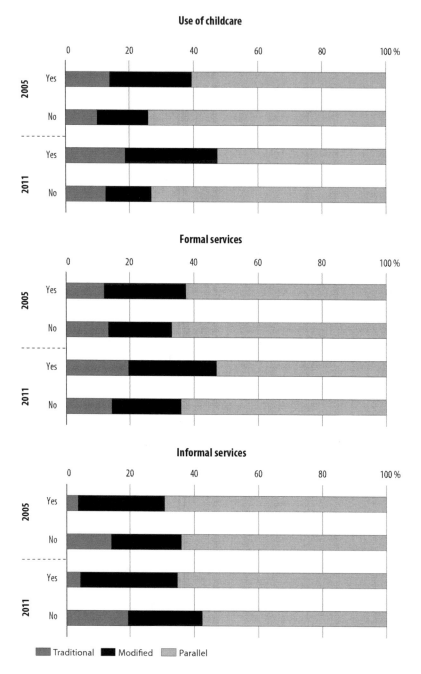

Figure 12.6 Types of balance of couples according to childcare use and type, by year (in %)

Source: EU-SILC survey (secondary analysis)

model is more common amongst couples with children and with those who do not have recourse to informal childcare services.

Undeniably, parenthood remains a factor which penalizes women and perpetuates a highly gender-based division of roles in the household, especially as regards the work-life balance. As such, it would seem that the use of formal childcare services is not enough to change this trend. Here, too, it can be seen that being able to rely on informal support within the family network means neither partner has to sacrifice their participation in the labour market in the name of the said balance. However, only a minority of couples have recourse to this kind of informal support.

Conclusion

The aim of this chapter was to study the ways in which issues around the work-life balance clash with the dynamics of individualisation which characterise current French society to such an extent that they influence the approaches taken by public policies in this area. This is also true for EU policies which advocate the 'working adult' model strongly inspired by the individualisation thesis and the resulting notions of autonomy and independence. This thesis, in its very formulation, obscures the persistent inequalities which still characterise the positions of men and women both in the professional and in the family sphere. The model is based on the idea that developing paid childcare services will be enough to correct these imbalances and make individualisation equally possible for both the sexes. However, the arguments developed in this chapter demonstrate that developing childcare services is not enough to counteract the gender-based differentiation which still characterises the roles of men and women when it comes to the work-life balance.

Our analysis shows that practices of the work-life balance in France remain widely shaped by gender-based dynamics as regards individuals as well as couples. The possibility of childcare is a factor of little importance to men whilst it has a positive effect on women, by allowing them greater access to the labour market. However, it is the possibility of relying on an informal network of family support which makes all the difference, since the available formal services are not a sufficient condition. Specifically, the ability to obtain childcare from formal services does not encourage female autonomy in any decisive way and does not solve the problem of inequality in practices of the work-life balance. Conversely, the importance of informal services shows to what extent the family circle still represents much more than a backdrop in the forging of individuals' own life paths. It may therefore be assumed that as full participation in the labour market is synonymous with individualisation and autonomy for both men and women, within the framework of the 'working adult' model, the fact that support from the family circle affects the work-life balance of women more is a clear contradiction of this very idea of autonomy. These findings confirm that individualisation, as conceived within the framework of the working adult model, does not develop in the same way for men and women. Instead, it still relies heavily on a context of the traditional gender-based division of labour. In this sense, the 'free choice' of both parents as regards childcare seems above all to reinforce a dynamics where men and women remain tied to their conventional roles, as main income provider and family caregiver, respectively.

Would developing formal childcare services be an effective way to encourage models of work-life balance which are more equal between men and women? Our analysis shows that the ability to have a child cared for outside the home through formal childcare services is a necessary condition, but is not enough. Nevertheless, in order to answer this question in-depth, other factors deserve to be taken into account, such as social differentiation when it comes to recourse to childcare, the availability and accessibility of formal childcare services (number of places available, cost and hours) and finally, the range of options available. In this chapter, we have tended to focus on discussing assumptions on which work-life balance polices are based, under the influence of European policies measures. Specifically, after analysing the situation in France, our main argument is that the ideology of individualisation and the ways in which it translates into policies promoting parental 'free choice' in families, are not consistent with pursuing a family model which encourages both individual autonomy and equality between the sexes. This is particularly the case because these policies do not really question the individualisation hypothesis and the resulting family model in relation to the reality of gender issues at the heart of actual practices of the work-life balance. This contradiction is probably linked to the fact that in the very wording of the working adult model, the assumptions made by the principle of individualisation remain gender-based. Therefore, in a context of childcare increasingly taking place outside the family through formal services, there remains the risk of a 'double reinforcement' (Nicole-Drancourt, 2009; Vielle, 2002), reinforcing both the role of women as principal caregivers and the role of men as the main income providers; in other words, a reinforcement of the sexual division of labour.

Notes

1 As regards childcare measures in France, these can be separated into formal and informal services. Formal paid services are all those services offered by the market, the state and the community which can be either individual or collective. Individual childcare principally means childminders (a qualified person who welcomes a variable number of children into their own home for all or part of the day with several families paying a single childminder) and in-home care (a qualified person who goes to the child's home to take care of them; in this case, just one family pays for the service). The collective childcare par excellence is the nursery, which can be municipal, community or family-run (children are looked after in a group by a qualified person). Informal services are usually free and refer to care provided by a family member, whether this be grandparents, other members of the family circle or friends.

2 Prestation d'Accueil du Jeune Enfant (PAJE) [Early Childhood Benefits].

3 The PAJE was introduced in 2004 through a reform to family benefits. It is comprised of the following elements: a fixed sum at birth, a basic (means-tested) monthly allowance for children under three and a 'freedom of choice supplement' which depends on the childcare option selected by parents. Parents can choose to employ someone to look after their child. If they do so, they will receive the 'free choice of childcare' supplement. They can also decide whether one or the other will fully or partially give up work to care for the child. If so, they will receive the 'freedom of choice supplement' (replaced in January 2015 by 'shared child rearing benefit') which is calculated according to the time worked. If work is done on a part-time basis, both supplements can be combined, whilst the 'freedom of choice supplement' is generally not available to parents who entrust their children to a nursery.

4 In the EU-SILC survey, information regarding the use of childcare services is available for children aged up to 12. In our analysis, we have excluded primary school, as it is compulsory for all children.

5 Apart from the parents, the childcare options used most frequently in France, especially for children under 3, are childminder (individual formal service), nursery (collective formal service), grandparents or another family member (informal service). Children aged 3 to 5 are in school for most of the day and are looked after by their parents at other times (Villaume and Legendre, 2014).

References

Adema, W. and Thévenon, O. (2008). Les politiques de conciliation du travail et de la vie familiale en France au regard des pays de l'OCDE. *Recherches et Prévisions*, 93(1), 51–72.

Annesley, C. (2007). Lisbon and social Europe: towards a european 'adult worker model' Welfare System. *Journal of European Social Policy*, 17(3), 195–205.

Anxo, D. and Boulin, J.-Y. (2006). The organisation of time over the life course: european trends. *European Societies*, 8(2), 319–341.

Boyer, D. (1999). Normes et politique familiale: la question du libre choix du mode de garde. *Recherches et Prévisions*, 57(1), 75–84.

Boyer, D. and Céroux, B. (2010). Les limites des politiques publiques de soutien à la paternité. *Travail, genre et sociétés*, 2(24), 47–62.

Crepin, A. and Boyer, D. (2015). Baromètre d'accueil du jeune enfant 2015. *L'e-ssentiel, CNAF*, (160), 4.

Daly, M. (2011). What adult worker model? A critical look at recent social policy reform in Europe from a gender and family perspective. *Social Politics: International Studies in Gender, State & Society*, 18(1), 1–23.

Daune-Richard, A. M. (2001). Hommes et femmes devant le travail et l'emploi, in: Blöss, T. (Ed.), *La dialectique des rapports hommes-femmes*. Sociologie d'aujourd'hui. Paris: Presses universitaires de France.

Daune-Richard, A. M. (2005). Women's work between family and welfare state: part-time work and childcare in France and Sweden, in: Pfau-Effinger, B. and Geissler, B. (Eds.), *Care and social integration in european societies*. Bristol: Policy Press.

Fagnani, J. and Letablier, M. T. (2005). Social rights and care responsibility in the french Welfare State, in: Pfau-Effinger, B. and Geissler, B. (Eds.), *Care and social integration in european societies*. Bristol: Policy Press.

Fraisse, L., Trancart, D., Sabatinello, S. and Boggi, O. (2009). Déterminants des solutions de garde des parents: une comparaison France-Italie, in: Nicole-Drancourt, C. (Ed.), *Conciliation travail-famille: attention travaux*. Logiques sociales. Paris: L'Harmattan.

Hantrais, L. (2004). *Family policy matters: responding to family change in Europe*. Bristol: Policy Press.

Joseph, O., Pailhé, A., Recotillet, I. and Solaz, A. (2012). Faut-il tourner la PAJE ? L'impact de la Prestation d'Accueil du Jeune Enfant sur le parcours professionnel des mères. *Formation emploi. Revue française de sciences sociales*, 2(118), 103–123.

Le Bihan-Youinou, B. and Martin, C. (2008). *Concilier vie familiale et vie professionnelle en Europe*. Rennes: Presses de l'École des hautes études en santé publique.

Letablier, M. (2009). Travail et parentalité: des régimes de conciliation variables en Europe, in: Nicole-Drancourt, C. (Ed.), *Conciliation travail-famille: attention travaux*. Logiques sociales. Paris: L'Harmattan.

Letablier, M.-T. and Lanquetin, M.-T. (2005). *Concilier travail et famille en France: approches socio-juridiques*. Noisy-le-Grand: Centre d'études de l'emploi.

Lewis, J. and Giullari, S. (2005). The adult worker model family, gender equality and care: the search for new policy principles and the possibilities and problems of a capabilities approach. *Economy and Society*, 34(1), 76–104.

Lewis, J., Martin, C. and Ostner, I. (2009). Patterns of development in work/family balance policies for parents in France, Germany, the Netherlands and the UK during the 2000s, in: Lewis, J. (Ed.), *Work-family balance, gender and policy*. Cheltenham; Northampton: Edward Elgar.

Martin, C. (2010). Concilier vie familiale et vie professionnelle: un objectif européen dans le modèle français des politiques de la famille ? *Informations sociales*, 1(157), 114–123.

Naegele, G., Barkholdt, C., Vroom, B. de, Goul Andersen, J. and Krämer, K. (Eds.). (2003). *A new organisation of time over working life*. Luxembourg: Office for Official Publications of the European Communities.

Nicolas, M. (2010). Interrompre ou réduire son activité à la naissance d'un enfant, et bénéficier du CLCA de la PAJE. *L'e-ssentiel*, *CNAF*, (97), 4.

Nicole-Drancourt, C. (Ed.). (2009). *Conciliation travail-famille: attention travaux*. Paris: L'Harmattan.

Ortalda, L. (2010). La diversité des modes d'accueil des jeunes enfants. *Informations sociales*, 4(160), 92–95.

Pailhé, A. and Solaz, A. (2006). Vie professionnelle et naissance: la charge de la conciliation repose essentiellement sur les femmes. *Population et Sociétés*, (426), 4.

Pailhé, A. and Solaz, A. (2009). Les ajustements professionnels des couples autour des naissances: une affaire de femmes ? in: Pailhé, A. and Solaz, A. (Eds.), *Entre famille et travail: des arrangements de couple aux pratiques des employeurs*. Recherches. Paris: La Découverte.

Pailhé, A. and Solaz, A. (2010). Concilier, organiser, renoncer: quel genre d'arrangements ? *Travail, genre et sociétés*, 2(24), 29–46.

Séraphin, G. (2013). *Comprendre la politique familiale*. Paris: Dunod.

Silvera, R. (2010). Temps professionnels et familiaux en Europe: de nouvelles configurations. *Travail, genre et sociétés*, 2(24), 63–88.

Stefan-Makay, S. (2009). Qui garde les jeunes enfants quand la mère travaille ? in: Pailhé, A. and Solaz, A. (Eds.), *Entre famille et travail: des arrangements de couple aux pratiques des employeurs*. Recherches. Paris: La Découverte.

Vielle, P. (2002). *Les femmes et le Droit*. Bruxelles: Presses des Facultés universitaires de Saint Louis.

Villaume, S. and Legendre, E. (2014). Modes de garde et d'accueil des jeunes enfants en 2013. *Etudes et résultats*, Drees. Retrieved from http://drees.solidarites-sante.gouv.fr/etudes-et-statistiques/publications/etudes-et-resultats/article/modes-de-garde-et-d-accueil-des-jeunes-enfants-en-2013.

Appendix 12.1

Sample composition (%),
individuals (aged 25 to 49)

Variable	2005	2001
family configuration		
family type		
single person	9.42	9.76
single-parent family	5.76	5.59
couple without children	19.33	22.46
couple with children	65.49	62.19
childcare services		
used		
no	49.31	49.50
yes	50.69	50.50
formal services		
no	68.36	68.99
yes	31.64	31.01
informal services		
no	89.82	90.84
yes	10.18	9.16
family characteristics		
in a legal union		
no	20.85	23.26
yes	79.15	76.74
number of children (> 18 years)		
0	34.09	36.23
1	24.24	23.44
2	28.99	28.07
3 or more	12.68	12.26
age of youngest child		
no children	34.09	36.23
under 3	22.92	21.88
3 to 5	9.00	7.68
6 to 17	33.98	34.20
individual characteristics		
age		
young adult (25–34)	34.60	34.05
adult (35–49)	65.40	65.95

(*Continued*)

Appendix 12.1 (Continued)

Variable	2005	2001
education level		
low	21.68	13.06
intermediate	47.62	47.97
high	30.69	38.97
income below poverty line		
no	78.39	82.86
yes	21.61	17.14

Source: EU-SILC survey

Appendix 12.2

Sample composition (%), couples

Variable	2005	2011
family configuration		
family type		
couple without children	18.30	20.69
couple with children	81.70	79.31
childcare service		
used		
no	26.85	27.36
yes	73.15	72.64
formal services		
no	49.90	50.30
yes	50.10	49.00
informal services		
no	84.20	85.61
yes	15.80	14.39
family characteristics		
in a legal union		
no	31.60	40.41
yes	68.40	59.59
number of children (> 18 years)		
0	18.35	20.69
1	23.63	23.40
2	41.26	40.23
3 or more	16.75	15.68
age of youngest child		
no children	18.35	20.69
under 3	38.14	36.23
3 to 5	13.78	12.23
6 to 17	29.73	30.85
individual characteristics		
age		
homogamy	78.24	81.20
woman younger	17.72	16.05
woman older	4.03	2.76

(*Continued*)

Appendix 12.2 (Continued)

Variable	2005	2011
education level		
educational homogamy	67.58	72.69
man more educated	19.66	18.98
woman more educated	12.75	8.33
household income below the poverty line		
no	91.02	90.34
yes	8.98	9.66

Source: EU-SILC survey

Index

For Product Safety Concerns and Information please contact our EU
representative GPSR@taylorandfrancis.com Taylor & Francis Verlag GmbH,
Kaufingerstraße 24, 80331 München, Germany

Printed and bound by CPI Group (UK) Ltd, Croydon, CR0 4YY

12/05/2025

01867895-0001